D1147425

Contents

Acknowledgements

There is now available a growing number of texts on housing economics and policy. The purpose of this book is to provide a more detailed criticism of housing market theory and policy than is generally given in such volumes.

The content and tone of this volume has been greatly influenced by numerous individuals. Alisdair Cruickshank first stimulated my interest in the area, Gordon Cameron sustained me with his continued enthusiasm, Tom Wilson taught me to be sceptical and critical, and Laurence Hunter indicated, at an early stage, potentially fruitful areas of research. Colin Jones has always provided helpful comments and further insights. David Pearce played a critical role in transforming random thoughts into the initial proposal for this book. But my greatest academic debt lies, in this field, to two other individuals. Gavin Wood has helped me formulate hypotheses and models over the last three years and helped me to develop a sharper focus on specific issues, and has collaborated closely in the writing of Chapter 5 of this book. At the same time Bill Grigsby has not only encouraged me in my work but has also broadened my vision of housing studies, both geographically and topically.

Although this book is critical of the overall conduct of government policy for housing in Britain this attack is directed at the policy system rather than individuals within it. In this respect, contact with the Scottish Office, the Northern Ireland Housing Executive and the Department of Environment has always proved to be interesting and informative.

Finally, the production of this manuscript would have been impossible but for the secretarial and organisational skills of Janette Schofield and May Gunn and the careful checking of Denis Malone.

Glasgow University
August 1980

1 The developments of microeconomic models of the housing market

Housing economics

Progress in economic science is seldom smooth or balanced. There may be advance or retreat along a particular intellectual frontier and there may be an interaction of deductive modelling and empirical investigation. Microeconomic theory has, since the 1950s, reflected such a confused and patchy state of development. Whilst the neoclassical general equilibrium framework has come to form the core of microeconomic thought, theories of individual decision taking agents have advanced in different ways. In the theory of the firm, simple market structure based models of the firm have come to be supplemented by a series of paradigms for analysing firm behaviour (Loasby 1972). For instance realism in management motivation or realism of behavioural process have come to be central concerns of the theory of the firm. The theory of the consumer has, however, not even paid such lip service to behavioural processes. Rather, there has been a concern to formulate deductively the properties of utility or preference functions which will generate unique single valued and downward sloping demand curves. Consumer theory has paid scant attention to the nature of commodities, consumers or markets (Maclennan and Williams 1980).

The proliferation of sub-specialisms within applied economics such as interests in agricultural or labour markets or the problems of cities, regions or developing countries, and perhaps now housing markets, has reflected the need to embody more reasonable structural assumptions in modelling particular phenomena. Such intra-disciplinary fragmentation of applied economics reflects an emphasis on creating 'general understanding' rather than pursuing 'general equilibrium' as a principal objective of economists' effort. This may, in the short term, seem a very limited view of economics as a discipline. But in the long term a general microeconomic theory may only emerge from a synthesis of the major characteristics of critical markets which have been examined in detail. At the present time the very specific assumptions of general equilibrium theory may preclude applied economists from investigating the operational features of major markets. Presently, therefore, two kinds of questions may be asked by economists examining particular phenomena. First, accepting general neoclassical assumptions regarding consumers, producers and markets, there is a concern to establish what can be deduced from existing models. Second, and this may constitute a required shift of paradigm, the applied economist may be attempting to ascertain how consumers and producers behave in a particular market. This is a very partial view of economics as a discipline, but perhaps it is essential if economics is still to be pedagogic, deductive and relevant. If distinctive markets or phenomena emerge as being important and characteristically different from and more complex than simple economic models, then a new applied area of economics with a common set of policy interests, reasonable assumptions, analytical and econometric technique and specialised literature is likely to emerge.

The application of economic analysis to the housing system may now have reached this stage (Maclennan 1979c). There has been a longstanding interest in the economic aspects of housing markets, particularly in the United States. Continuing from the earlier contributions of land economists the 1950s was a period of some detailed investigations of how housing markets actually worked and the emphasis was empirical and policy oriented (Fisher and Winnick 1951; Grebler 1952; Grigsby 1963). However, since the 1960s this interesting line of development was de-emphasised as urban economists began to apply neoclassical economic models to issues of residential and urban structures (Alonso 1964; Muth 1969; Evans 1973; MacDonald 1979). The access-space trade-off model, or as it became grandiosely known (Richardson 1977) 'the' New Urban Economics, dominates conceptual and applied analysis until the present time. In essence this line of development has, it shall be maintained below, suppressed the investigation of potentially important characteristics of housing markets but, at the same time, has generated useful theoretical and applied insights. Thus, the first section of this book is intended to indicate the strengths and weaknesses of received housing market models and to develop a broader framework of questions regarding how housing markets may be analysed. In this way 'Housing Economics' may be developed.

In this first chapter models of the spatial structure of urban housing markets are examined. In Chapter 2 more detailed attempts to examine housing preferences and demand are assessed. In Chapter 3 a broader microeconomic framework for investigating consumer behaviour in the housing market is proposed. In Chapters 4 and 5, respectively, the microeconomics of the supply of housing and housing finance are examined.

Housing in old and new urban economics

Economists have long been aware that there were apparently systematic patterns of housing and land uses within and around urban centres (Steuart 1769; Von Thunen 1875; Schumpeter 1954). Initially attention was focused on the pattern of agricultural land uses around cities and subsequently the geography of intra-urban land uses merited attention from economists experiencing the first phases of major urban industrial development (Hurd 1903). However, the housing or residential structure of the city was not considered an important research issue in economics or land economy. For instance Hurd believed that:

> The basis of residence values is social and not economic – although the land goes to the highest bidder – the rich selecting the locations which please them, those of moderate means living as nearby as possible, and so on down the scale of wealth (Romanos 1976: 38).

Admittedly within the classical tradition of political economy and in the more informal early stages of neoclassical economics the treatment of housing issues was subjected to standard and more radical economic analysis. However, prior to the 1920s there was no discernible area of research and analysis which could be labelled urban economics, land economy or housing economics.

Intellectual and policy pressures were soon to emerge which did generate the sub-discipline now known as urban economics, and within this development a model of the residential structure of the city has always been important. Surprisingly it was not in the European economies (where the planning of cities and housing was already well underway) that urban economics and land economy developed, but rather it was in the rapidly expanding and *laissez faire* context of North American cities that the modern origins of the present subject can be found. These two major strands were:

1. The large-scale inductive and then deductive studies concerning the social or ecological structure of cities undertaken in Chicago (Park 1925; Robson 1969; Timms 1971).
2. The development of land economy as a discipline to describe and explain the economic operation of housing and land markets (Ratcliff 1949).

The sociological origins of residential location models

The contribution of the Chicago school of social ecologists to modern urban studies in economics and geography should not be underestimated, though the detailed structure of the major early models is now somewhat discredited. The contribution of Burgess, Park and

MacKenzie contained two important elements (Park 1925). First, they argued that cities did have a systematic residential structure and that this structure and its evolution over time could be explained in terms of two major processes – 'competition' and 'invasion with succession'.

Although presented as a sociological model the 'competition' process, which was presented as being the essential 'metabolism' of the city, was described in informal economic terms. The underlying belief of the social ecologists was that existing land values, for which they provided no explanatory mechanism, were the principal factor determining the pattern of residential and non-residential land uses. Urban land values were believed to influence urban residential location and structure because individuals located themselves in such a way as to minimise the combined 'frictional' costs of overcoming 'inaccessibility', namely, land values plus transport costs. Residential differentiation then emerges as a consequence of variations in the rental values of land. Since rents were assumed to fall consistently to compensate for inaccessible locations, a systematic housing structure emerges around the centre of the simple city with each successive ring zone reflecting the presence of a generally higher income group. Around the dominant single central zone of the Central Business District (C.B.D.), which is assumed to contain the bulk of employment opportunities, there are successive rings:

1. The zone of transition contains poor and rundown older property which had either been or was about to be penetrated by the expansion of the C.B.D.
2. The second residential zone was that of working-class homes, with workers required to live close to their locations of work.
3. The zone of high-class residences.
4. The zone of new developments and newly incorporated satellites.

As is indicated in the discussion of the contemporary access-space model, this Ricardian based model of rent is seriously under-specified and the preferences of higher income units for larger or higher quality units are not formally developed in the model. Indeed, given the economic assumptions of this early model it may be possible to reverse the social structure of the rings observed.

Thus the Chicago school not only implied the existence of a well-defined urban social structure but maintained that structure was spatial, manifested via the competitive workings of the housing and land market. This was, however, accomplished without any real attempt to articulate and conceptualise the underlying demand and supply determinants in the housing system.

In the preoccupation with structure the underlying behavioural relationships were oversimplified. This provided one source of criticism for the early opponents of the Chicago school and Firey maintained that individuals and communities did not always move out anomically and easily as income grew or new low income groups invaded (Firey 1947). Rather households became attached by the forces of sentiment and symbolism to existing neighbourhoods. Empirical analysis tended to suggest that well-defined zones did not exist – rather social gradients could be observed, and that concentric rings were generally disturbed by the existence of geographic disturbances or, more importantly, the existence of several commercial or industrial zones within a given city. It is worth noting with hindsight, however, that the expensive and systematic studies of urban residential structure conducted using factor analysis or social area analysis since the 1960s have tended, in general, to confirm the existence of an underlying ring structure (Berry and Horton 1970). Further, it should be stressed that the ecologists did not assume that the rent bidding process took place on a uniform plane but rather that the 'competitive' process was enacted within the received structure of existing dwellings. This important point, as is illustrated below on p 21, is often omitted in economic models of residential structure.

It is perhaps true that the social ecologists of Chicago provided only an informal and incomplete model of the competitive process. Further, they stuck somewhat rigidly to the pure zonal models and they may have been rather influenced by their own empirical context, namely the relatively uniform Chicago of pre-1920, with its dominant urban core and rapid population growth based on the successive influx of different ethnic groups. However, aside from their own residual contribution, the ecologists did stimulate a series of sustained constructive criticisms from land economists.

The response of land economy

The relationship between land values and land uses postulated by land economists ran directly counter to the propositions of the ecological model. The land economists argued that land uses determined land values and not *vice versa*. The modern economists, commonly acquainted with both the supply and demand blades of the Marshallian scissors, will realise that this was a theoretically false debate. For instance, if ecologists were concerned with individual or small group residential changes at a point in time (which was not always the case) then it may seem legitimate to take the rent or land value function as given. That is, short-run supply is fixed and demand determines price. Alternatively land economists or realtors concerned with relatively elastic long-term and large-scale changes in urban structure could well be expected to stress the significance of demand structures.

The early responses of land economists to the ecological school reflected a desire to provide an explicit economic model of the housing and land structures in the city. For instance Haig (1926) transferred the Thunian model of agricultural location to the city with minor modifications. Haig stressed the complementarity of land rent and transport costs. He argued that as the costs of overcoming the frictions of space, namely the direct and indirect costs of travel, rise away from the centre of the city then site rents will fall as individuals prefer accessible to inaccessible locations. Whilst maintaining that households locate to minimise transport costs or 'frictional costs', it should be apparent that in fact the model implies constant travel plus rent costs. It is not at all clear how individuals are therefore allocated to particular locations unless it is argued that richer households can sustain higher transport costs more readily. The theory is essentially indeterminate and unsatisfactory as it fails to consider household lot size and, violating the ecological tradition, it postulates instantaneous development on an isotropic plane.

Following Haig, both Ratcliff and Hoyt (Ratcliff 1949; Hoyt 1939) made telling and still important contributions to the theory of residential location. Ratcliff stressed, in the 1940s, that the city was not dominated by a single employment and commercial centre but rather that a series of internal and peripheral subcentres could be discerned which fragmented the initial ring structure. Further, he noted that households had a variety of social and economic activities which were conducted away from the central city. Thus the notion of a unitary urban housing market with its associated annular spatial structures was consistently under attack. It was already clear that a complex 'mosaic of urban worlds' (Timms 1971) rather than simple rings made up the social, spatial and housing structure of cities. Hoyt also criticised the ecological model on its simple structural assumptions. His model is discussed in the second section of this chapter as it essentially relies on a dynamic process to produce spatial form.

The access-space relationship

During the 1950s land economists and the newly emerging discipline of urban economics continued to criticise and examine the 'rent' and 'travel costs' trade-off model, and a major theoretical advance was first noted, then made explicit. This was the notion that house or plot size was an important determinant of household satisfaction. Further, given that travel to work costs rise with distance from the centre of a city, simple neoclassical models of residential location revealed that land prices would fall, whilst travel costs rose. Thus, for a given level of income there was a trade-off in the household's choice between more access and less space or *vice versa* (Alonso 1964). Variations in income level or access-space preferences across social or economic groups could then produce a ring structure by an explicit economic process (unlike the Haig model).

The access-space trade-off model initiated by Alonso and then extensively extended by Muth, Romanos, Evans *et al.*, has become a central model not only of urban housing market analysis but also of theoretical or new urban economics. Therefore a detailed exposition of the access-space model (its assumptions, technical relations, theorems and empirical tests) is presented since the model represents the real starting point for an analysis of local urban housing markets. The model is currently the dominant paradigm of urban economic research and it is thus important to show its uses, merits and demerits and to develop the model for applied purposes. A variety of specifications of the model have now been developed which embody minor rather than major differences. In this chapter extensive reference is made to the work of Evans, for two reasons. First, because it is developed and tested within a British context and second, and more importantly, the model contains a relatively more satisfactory and simpler treatment of the value of travel time than is generally found in these models.

The access-space trade-off model

The characteristics of the residential structures deduced from the access-space location model are highly dependent upon the detailed assumptions made in the model building process. It is important therefore to outline the nature and apparent purpose of the assumptions and such an elaboration may then allow us an assessment of the relevance of criticisms of the access-space model. The access-space model is not a simple hypothesis but has become a paradigm for urban economic research. Ultimately a rejection of this basis for local housing market research will be made; this rejection is not based on internal inconsistency but on the grounds of its inability to tackle important questions regarding housing markets.

The assumptions of the model
The assumed spatial structure. It is assumed that the urban area is initially a flat, undeveloped and featureless plain. On the plain a central business and employment centre emerges and all residents in the city work in the central location. Around the central business district the transport system extends in a uniform fashion with equal distances in any direction away from the city being equally accessible. It is also usually assumed that the average speed of travel rises with distance travelled in a regular fashion so that accessibility can be systematically discussed and its effects analysed in terms of both distance and time. These simplifying assumptions ensure that the only unique character-

istic of a point in the urban area is its location vis-à-vis the centre and that the systematic structure of space results in a simple geography of the economic (locational) consequences of the existence of space.

Behavioural assumptions. The second set of assumptions relates to the behavioural processes and objective functions of the economic agents who supply and demand housing and locations within the city. The producers of residential spaces, locations and densities, are assumed to be profit maximising firms operating within a decentralised or perfectly competitive structure of space provision. The underlying ownership of land is also assumed to be dispersed and the land market perfectly competitive. The economic behaviour of households is also cast in a competitive neoclassical context with the consumer being viewed as a utility maximising price taker. The assumption of fully informed maximising economic agents combined with competitive market structures allows the model to be developed along formal deductive lines and precisely determined equilibrium solutions to be derived.

The utility function ascribed to the household may be more or less complex but here a simple function is assumed for ease of presentation. The general assumptions underlying the specification of household preferences and constraints is that housing is a complex commodity or stock which is combined with other inputs, including household time, to generate a flow of housing services. This formulation (MacDonald 1979) follows propositions on household consumption devised by Becker (1965) and Lancaster (1966). MacDonald (1979) proposes a general formulation of the access-space model where the utility function of the household is

$$U = U(A, Q, N, C, H) \qquad [1]$$

where A is a composite vector of non-housing goods, Q is a vector of housing and locational services associated with a dwelling and N, C and H are vectors of leisure, commuting and work time respectively.

It is then postulated that the output of housing services Q, is generated from a linear homogenous household production function. For the housing service, Q_i

$$Q_i = Q_i(Z, E') \qquad [2]$$

where Z is the vector of m housing and locational attributes and E' is a vector of household time inputs.

This household utility functional is maximised subject to the constraints of time and income. The income constraint is

$$Y = \Sigma W_j h_j + G = A + \overset{m}{\Sigma} P_{L_{(K)}} Z_{(K)} + \Sigma t_{j_{(K)}} \qquad [3]$$

that is, income is the sum of labour rewards for all members of the household (W_jh_j) and non-labour income G. Expenditure is the sum of non-housing expenditures A, the sum of expenditure on the composite of housing assets at a distance, K, from the city centre, and the sum of commuting costs for all members of the household at location K. The time constraint is presented as

$$E_j = \Sigma E_{ij} + N_j + C_j + H_j \qquad [4]$$

where N, C and H are as defined above, and E_{ij} is the time input by the jth individual to the ith characteristic. MacDonald then concurs that in order to make this model empirically manageable limitations on the number of elements in Q, the vector of housing services and in Z, the vector of housing attribute inputs, have to be made. For pedagogic simplicity a less general but simpler manipulation of the access-space model devised by Evans (1973) is presented below. But the general formulation presented by MacDonald should be borne in mind as it is used below to refute some of the more naïve criticisms of the access-space model.

In the Evans' model the utility function for the household is relatively simple and takes the general form of

$$U = U(q, t, w, a_i) \qquad [5]$$

where q is the number of space units consumed by the household; t the time spent travelling from home to C.B.D. workplace; w is the number of hours worked, and a_i ($i = 1, 2, \ldots, n$) are other household activities.

Closer examination of this function implies that the model treats a house as an extremely simple good, with each address providing a location, or travel time to the centre of the city, and a quantity of space units. It is also implicitly assumed that the activities, a_i, must take place either at the workplace, in travelling, or at the residence site. Otherwise if this were not the case then the model has to (and can) be appropriately altered to contain distance/travel functions defining a series of travel times from home to the activity site (MacDonald 1979). The simple household utility function is then maximised subject to two constraints. First there is a resources or budget constraint of the form

$$rw = qP_{(t)} + C_{(t)} + \Sigma r_i a_i, \qquad [6]$$

where r is the wage rate,

    $P_{(t)}$ the financial cost of travel and

    r_i the cost per hour of each a_i.

It is fundamental to the model that the price of a unit of space, P, and the financial cost of travel, C, are a function of travel time ($P_{(t)}$, $C_{(t)}$) or alternatively distance from the centre of the city ($P_{(K)}$, $C_{(K)}$).

Second, spatial separation between home and workplace implies that time, which has an economic opportunity cost to the traveller, has to be

9

spent in movement. This is reflected not only by the inclusion of travel time, (t), as a negative argument in the utility function, but also in the existence of a constraining time budget.

$$\bar{T} = w + t + \Sigma a_i \qquad [7]$$

where a_i is the time spent pursuing the ith activity, and T is total time available within the chosen period. This economic statement of the residential location problem can be used to show how the spatial structure of the city and its associated movement system will produce a regular pattern of land values and residential supply prices which are brought into equilibrium with a set of spatially defined price offers for different locations and lot sizes by consumers. The analysis is undertaken with the assumption that all supply and demand side changes or transactions are achieved instantaneously; that is, the urban system is always assumed to be in equilibrium and there are no adjustment problems experienced.

Consumer utility maximisation and bid-price functions. The constrained maximisation problem stated above is then solved to provide a statement of the equilibrium location and travel time choice for the household; from these first-order conditions the shape and properties of the consumers bid-rent function can be deduced. That is, a relationship between location, travel time and optimum rent payments for housing services can be derived. Again, following the terminology of Evans, the first order conditions are

$$\frac{\partial u}{\partial q} = \lambda \cdot P_{(t)} \qquad [8]$$

$$\frac{\partial u}{\partial t} = \mu + \lambda \left(q \cdot \frac{\partial P}{\partial t} + \frac{\partial C}{\partial t} \right) \qquad [9]$$

$$\frac{\partial u}{\partial \omega} = \mu - \lambda r \qquad [10]$$

$$\frac{\partial u}{\partial i} = \mu + \lambda r_i, (i = 1, 2 ..., n) \qquad [11]$$

where μ and λ are respectively the Lagrangean multipliers on the time and income constraints (interpreted as the marginal utility of time and income). These conditions for consumer utility maximisation define the conditions for an optimum choice of housing space consumption [8], which suggests that the volume of space consumed will vary with the rent-time (or distance) function. Condition [9] defines the optimum location of the household. Evans then presents a helpful transformation of the marginal conditions. Expression [9] is divided by equation [10] and the terms rearranged so that

$$q \cdot \frac{\partial P}{\partial t} + \frac{\partial c}{\partial t} = - \left[\frac{\frac{\partial u}{\partial t} - \mu}{\frac{\partial u}{\partial \omega} - \mu} \right] r \qquad [12]$$

Let,
$$\frac{dV}{dt} = \frac{\frac{\partial u}{\partial t} - \mu}{\frac{\partial u}{\partial \omega} - \mu}$$

Then a further marginal condition (obtained by dividing [9] by [10]) is that

$$q \cdot \frac{dP}{dt} = - \frac{dc}{dt} + r \frac{dV}{dt} \qquad [13]$$

This condition states that location or travel time is chosen so that total rent savings through further travel, $(q \cdot \frac{dP}{dt})$, are just equal to the increased travel costs which are the sum of direct and indirect effects.

Evans then argues, plausibly, that it is possible, using some empirically and logically reasonable assumptions, to deduce the sign of $\frac{dP}{dt}$, the bid-rent slope, from condition [13]. The wage rate, r, will generally be positive, empirical evidence suggests that for the indirect travel costs, $0 < \frac{dV}{dt} < 0.3$, (that is $\frac{dV}{dt}$ is small and positive), whilst direct travel costs, $\frac{dc}{dt}$, reflecting the frictions of space, will also have a positive value. Similarly only positive quantities of space units, q, can be consumed. Thus $\frac{dP}{dt}$ must have a negative sign. That is, rents per space unit will fall with increased travel time away from the city centre. The same argument can be translated from time to distance dimensions, since $P_{(t)} = P [K_{(t)}]$, that is rent paid per space unit is a function of travel time, but distance travelled is also a function of travel time. This may be stated as

$$\frac{dP}{dt} = \frac{dP}{dK} \cdot \frac{dK}{dt} \qquad [14]$$

It is an obvious truism that $\frac{dK}{dt} > 0$, therefore if $\frac{dP}{dt} < 0$, it follows that $\frac{dP}{dK}$ will be < 0. That is, rents paid will fall with distance away from the city centre.

This theorem regarding the slope of the rent function is derived directly from the first-order conditions for consumer utility maximisation. However, a second theorem regarding the shape of the rent function of consumer bids can be derived from the second-order conditions. (The proof is relatively simple and omitted from this section.) It is sufficient to note that for the first-order conditions to define a stable equilibrium, the net sum of rent savings and increased travel costs from a *non*-marginal relocation must be negative, otherwise the household would relocate away from the city. Therefore, it is required that rents fall at a decreasing rate away from the C.B.D. Evans states this result very clearly:

> If the direct cost of travel increases at a decreasing rate, the speed of travel increases at an increasing rate (with respect to distance travelled) and the imputed value of travel time (per hour) does not vary with increases in time spent travelling, then the rent per space unit will necessarily decline with distance from the central city at a diminishing rate per mile (Evans 1973: 44).

Evans is careful to demonstrate, on the basis of primarily London related evidence, that the relationships between time, distance and speed of travel assumed in the model are reasonably rooted in empirical reality. (See also MacDonald's similar exercise for Chicago (MacDonald 1979).)

The bid-price curves of the household
The optimising condition [12] indicates how the optimum level of rent payments varies with distance and travel time and yields the optimum location once the equilibrium price is established. This requires that we can identify a schedule or family of schedules of rent payments which the household is prepared to make at different locations as well as a rent curve of supply offers at different locations. In this section the concept of the bid-price schedule, which has formed the core of urban economic models since the work of Alonso was first published (Alonso 1964), is analysed.

Assume that a household is initially constrained to locate at the centre of the city and that the central price of housing services is already determined. Accepting these constraints the consumer maximises utility, say at U_2 in Fig. 1.1. Now let the consumer be moved away from the central city location. What rent will the consumer pay at each of these locations and still maintain the same level of satisfaction or real income? That is, starting from the indifference level U_2 it is required to establish a line of indifference between different locations or travel time zones and this locus is derived and maintained by rent changes. The optimising condition stated in [13] implied that the necessary reduction in rent to compensate for increased travel time was just equal to the sum of direct and indirect travel costs. Restating [9] in terms of distance rather than time, then

$$q \cdot \frac{dP}{dK} + \frac{dc}{dK} + r \cdot \frac{dV}{dK} = 0$$

which rearranges to

$$\frac{dP}{dK} = - \left(\frac{\dfrac{dc}{dK} + r \cdot \dfrac{dV}{dK}}{q} \right) \qquad [15]$$

where $\frac{dP}{dK}$ is the slope of the rent gradient or bid-rent function. The shape of the function can also be deduced from [15]. The marginal direct costs of travel with respect to distance ($\frac{dc}{dK}$) generally falls as distance increases. Further, speed of journey tends to increase with distance and hence the marginal valuation of time per mile travelled also falls with increasing distance (that is $r \cdot \frac{dV}{dK}$). On the other hand, substitution effects generally ensure that q increases with distance. As a result, if distance away from the centre increases, then the numerator of expression [15] will fall, whilst the denominator rises. This implies that $\frac{dP}{dK}$ falls with distance from the C.B.D. That is, the bid-rent/price curve flattens away from the city centre along the schedule $R_2 R_2$.

It is then a simple matter to derive a family of such bid-rent curves. If the household is now constrained to locate adjacent to the centre at a level of rents R_3 which exceeds R_2, the initial central rent, then a new higher bid-rent function which represents a lower level of household satisfaction can be derived (see Fig. 1.1). Similarly a further lower rent level R_1 may be suggested at the centre (with $R_1 < R_2 < R_3$) which in turn generates a lower bid-rent function $R_1 R_1$ which represents a level of household satisfaction greater than that associated with $R_2 R_2$ and $R_3 R_3$. Unlike conventional indifference curves, lower bid-rent curves are associated with higher levels of satisfaction or real income. From [15] it is also possible to describe the likely shape of successive bid-price/rent functions. For lower central rents or prices the quantity of housing services consumed, q, is likely to be greater (due to substitution effects) at any given distance away from the centre. *Ceteris paribus*, the increased numerator in [15] implies that lower bid-rent functions have flatter slopes at any given distance away from the city centre.

Condition [15] is important because it can already be seen that variations in the value of any of the expressions within the equation across different demand groups will generate different families of bid-rent functions. For instance, if two groups have different parameters

13

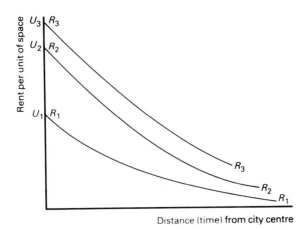

Fig. 1.1 Bid-rent schedules

regarding space units in their utility function, then space lovers (with a consistently higher value for q) will tend to have flatter functions than space neglecters. Similarly differential access to transport technology or differences in the wage rate r will generate differences in sub-group bid-rent functions, as shown in Fig. 14. However, before outlining the model of resulting differences in location patterns the supply of properties over space must be considered.

The rent gradient arising from supply decisions
Evans then continues to develop a parallel model of the supply of housing space units and how density of developments and land values will vary within the urban economy. The simpler model which he presents can be built up in a series of steps.

Assume that there is initially a profit maximising developer facing a given ground rent (or land price) and a given price for housing space units. For simplification it is assumed, at least initially, that density of development will not influence consumers' willingness to pay for such a site. Evans argues, on the basis of relatively scant empirical evidence, that the total costs of development increase, but at a decreasing rate with rising density. In graphical terms (Fig 1.2) the developer will choose a density of development at which marginal costs, MC, are equal to marginal revenue, MR, in this instance at d_1 and profit level π_1. The solution d_1, π_1 is, of course, one of supernormal developers' profits. In this case, it is assumed by Evans, that the landowner can recontract on ground rent and supernormal profits are removed for developers not by reducing price per square unit but by allowing the ground rent to increase and shift up the average cost curve, AC, until the position π_0, d is obtained. If the land market was perfectly competitive, however, new land placed on the market with new developments would reduce developers' initial supernormal profits.

The simple relationship between land rents and developers' costs and profits is then used by Evans to indicate that, because higher rent offers are made nearer the central city, both density of development and land value gradients will decline, and at decreasing rates, away from the central city. The mathematical proofs for the density and land value relationships are presented in Evans (1973: 53 and 57−58 respectively). For a more detailed and formal exposition of the supply side of the access-space model see also Muth (1969) and MacDonald (1979) and Chapter 4.

Equilibrium in the model

Individual equilibrium. In the previous sections spatially defined housing choice schedules for both the suppliers and demanders of location and housing services have been outlined. By integrating the conclusions regarding bid-rent/price functions (the demand side of the model) and rent gradients (the supply side) a description of equilibrium can be obtained. This can be done in three stages, by outlining equilibrium for the representative household, then more than one representative household and, finally, for the market as a whole.

For households the equilibrium location and level of housing services is easily obtained by overlapping the household bid-rent functions on the downward sloping rent gradient, bearing in mind that the household is a price taker and does not influence the shape or position of the rent gradient. In Fig. 1.3, the equilibrium position is at K^e; for at that location the rent gradient, RR, is just tangent to the lowest possible

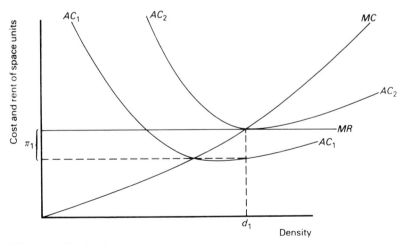

Fig. 1.2 The developers' decision

bid-rent function, BR_2. That is, the constrained maximum level of household satisfaction or real income is incurred at K^e. Given the rent gradient, RR, bid-rent curves lying below BR_2 are not attainable. If the consumer were to locate at any point around K^e then, given the different convexities of the rent gradient and the bid-rent functions, this would imply that the household will be moving to an inferior level of satisfaction. That is, there will be a corner solution at some less preferred satisfaction level on a higher bid-rent function such as BR_1. At the location K^e, the household is just prepared to meet the offer price of the supplier of housing services.

Different groups or individuals
Multiple equilibria. The equilibrium locations of more than one group or household can also be similarly demonstrated using Fig. 1.4. Different households or groups may vary in the level of their budget constraints, perceived valuation of travel time, and in the detailed parameters of their utility functions. For instance, for a given income level some groups may prefer large volumes of housing space whereas others may desire access to the central city. The sociologists' distinction between 'urbanism' (orientation to the activities and attractions of the city, particularly its centrally located cultural artefacts) and 'familism' (stress is placed on activities centred on and located in the family home) may be translated into economic models as an underlying difference in the elements and parameters of the household utility function.

Referring back to p. 13 and the discussion of the slope of the bid-rent function it is apparent that different groups will have families of bid-

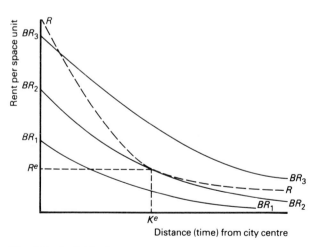

Fig. 1.3 Individual access-space equilibrium

rent curves which show substantial variations in slope and shape across the sub-groups. Consider the optimum location criterion,

$$\frac{dP}{dK} = -\left[\frac{\dfrac{dc}{dK} + r \cdot \dfrac{dV}{dK}}{q}\right] \qquad [15]$$

A 'space'-loving group, such as families with an orientation towards 'familism' as a life style, will generally have a higher level of space units, q, for any income level. As a result, their bid-rent functions will generally be flatter than for 'space'-neutral groups. Similarly, groups with high marginal direct travel costs, and low incomes, are likely to have steeply sloped bid-rent functions. This is also the case with respect to indirect costs of travel with the qualification that such costs also rise with wage rates. The relationship between income and location is discussed further below.

However, at this point it is worth noting that the equilibrium structure of locations by group will depend on the slope of the bid-rent functions. Figure 1.4 indicates the general principle that households or groups with steeper bid-rent functions have optimum locations nearer the centre of the city whereas groups with flatter bid-rent functions tend to have a more suburban location. In this instance let the bid-rent curves $L_1 \ldots L_3$ represent space 'lovers' and those $A_1 \ldots A_3$ reflect space 'averters'. Given R, the lovers will locate at d_L and the averters will be more centrally located at d_A. This result holds and is independent of the economic factors which actually cause households to have differently sloped functions.

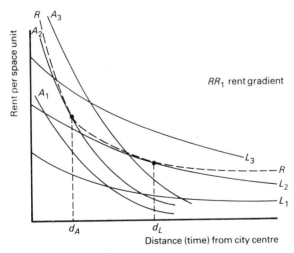

Fig. 1.4 Multiple equilibria in the access-space model

Income and location.   Since there is frequently an implicit assumption that location and income are directly correlated, with an apparently paradoxical arrangement of poor people living close to the centre and richer households living in the suburbs, it is perhaps germane to indicate, following Evans, that such a clear cut pattern does not emerge from the access-space trade-off model.

The argument is easily developed in relation to a change in income level, for a given household, as this abstracts from initial differences in utility function, access to transport, etc. *Ceteris paribus*, assume that a household at a location such as K^e (Fig. 1.3) incurs an increase in income due to an increase in the rate of pay, r. Two changes then occur. First, depending on the income elasticity of the demand for housing space, q will increase from the level q^e and thus a new flatter set of bid-rent curves will emerge. These curves will become flatter the larger the rise of income and the greater the income elasticity of the demand for space. The greater the flattening of the bid-rent surface, the further the household will move outwards and down the rent gradient to a new equilibrium location. If this was the only consequence of an increase in income then an unambiguous relationship, *ceteris paribus*, between location and income could be expected. However, closer examination of the condition for an optimum location indicated in equation [15] shows that increases in income derived from the rate of pay also enter into the numerator of the fraction by increasing the marginal value of travel time. This suggests that higher paid households will have a higher opportunity cost of travel time and therefore seek an equilibrium location on steeper bid-rent functions nearer the central city. Thus increasing income generates two opposing locational pulls, with the new location depending on the relative strength of the two forces.

The resolution of the problem depends on the empirical parameters in a particular context; however, it is from the above clearly possible to have mixed high and low income groups in the central city, middle income groups in the inner suburbs and wealthier groups in the outer suburbs.

In concluding this summary of the technical details of the simple access-space trade-off model, it is now pertinent to turn to the equilibrium of the market as a whole. The above models have pertained to circumstances where the underlying rent and bid-rent functions are independent of each other, that is the rent gradient has been assumed to be given and fixed.

Market equilibrium in the access-space model.   If it is assumed that all households have a similar bid-rent function market equilibrium may be attained as follows. Say the equilibrium bid-rent and rent gradient coincide, as they must (Evans 1973: 81) along *DD* in Fig. 1.5. But suppose that the rent gradient *RR* actually pertains. Households lying nearer the city centre than distance $0B$ can, with RR pertaining, increase satisfaction by moving to lower bid-rent functions at distances beyond B. As a result rents will fall between 0 and B and rise between B and R. This process will continue until RR is dragged down to DD, at distances less than B, and shifted upwards beyond B, until RR and DD are coincidental.

Where more than one group of bid-rent functions exist, then the equilibrium rent gradient will consist of a series of segments such as AB and BC (see Fig. 1.6). If there was a rise in demand for the centre-loving group, through say population change, then the segment AB would be shifted upwards and a new rent gradient $A'B'C$ would be formed. But, in turn, the space lovers displaced outwards by the shift of AB to $A'B'$ will raise rent levels beyond location R', so that BC will be shifted to $B'C'$. In this way equilibrium will be restored, rent levels and densities will rise and the city will expand at the margin.

The access-space model: an evaluation

The simplified presentation here of the access-space model scarcely does credit to the formalised and sophisticated theorising involved in the development of the access-space framework. The model represents both the great strengths and inherent practical weaknesses of relying on a highly deductive approach. When the single model outlined above is articulated in a testable form then a whole series of testable propositions have been generated. Empirical tests in the United States and Britain of residential spatial structure (Berry and Horton 1970; Robson 1969), urban population densities (Mills 1972; White 1977; Evans 1973), the relationship between income and location (Diamond 1980;

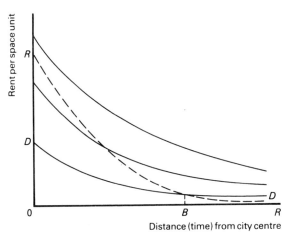

Fig. 1.5 Moves to equilibrium in the access-space model

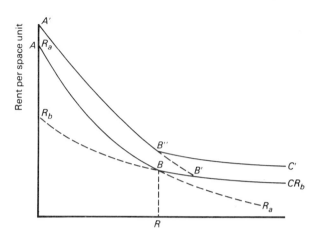

Distance (time) from city centre

Fig. 1.6 Shifts in demand and the bid-rent function

Evans 1973; Ball and Kirwan 1977), and the shape of land value gradients (Evans 1973; Davidson 1970) all tend to suggest that patterns in reality conform to the theoretical predictions of the model. There are a whole series of smaller-scale tests of the model which require further investigation. For instance, what are the effects of changing transport technology, or of rising energy prices? If inflation in housing markets raises non-labour market wealth is outward movement encouraged?

But it is perhaps fair to suggest, following Quigley (1978) that most of the evidence cited above only provides a weak and indirect test of the model. For there is a whole series of influences on urban housing markets which has a pattern of incidence broadly correlated with distance from the centre of a city. Racial structures, neighbourhood quality, vintage of the housing stock and accessibility to peripheral employment are all highly collinear with distance from the central city. Indeed there have been experiments (Harrison and Kain 1974; Maclennan 1979a) which have been conducted with assumptions running counter to the access-space model, which have produced apparently similar results. Thus, the approach of positive economics, as propounded by Friedman and apparently defended by Muth in the specific instance of the access-space model (Muth, 1976: 245) is least convincing when there are a series of highly collinear but different possible processes to explain a particular outcome. In such instances it is always valid to ask, which of the competing theories makes the most plausible assumptions.

In relation to the long-run spatial economic structure of an urban housing market there is no real competing theory to the access-space model. But when the access-space model comes to be used as a central theoretical framework for examining issues of short-run market phenomena such as housing demand (Kirwan and Ball 1977; Straszheim 1975) then it is of more questionable use as a research paradigm. Thus, in evaluating the criticisms of the access-space model a sense of purpose and a sense of balance are both required. The major criticisms relate to:

1. Assumptions about the commodity housing.
2. Assumptions about the spatial structure of activities in the cities.
3. Assumptions about optimising behaviour and the existence of disequilibrium.

The housing commodity. If is often asserted that the access-space model oversimplifies the nature of the housing commodity by discussing only space units and work-home locations. But the general statement of MacDonald's formulation of the access-space model implies that this criticism is not well placed. Indeed MacDonald has cited a list of the standard assumptions of the macroeconomic access-space model and has referred to a series of theoretical or experimental studies to relax simplistic assumptions (MacDonald 1979: 102). But there are two qualifications to this strong argument in defence of the access-space model. The first is, that there are attributes of housing which are important and which only have real significance in housing markets in disequilibrium – for instance the asset and capital gain aspects of owned housing. Second, as soon as complex housing attributes and household activity patterns are asserted to exist – and there still has to be some basis for such assertions – then the capacity of the model to make simple predictions about the use of time and space which can be readily tested becomes exceptionally limited.

The structure of space. The ability of the access-space model to generate simple aggregative spatial structures of housing phenomena is not only compromised by adding commodity complexity. It is also recognised that the central workplace-suburban residence trade-off, which underlies the macro-spatial structures generated by the model, are no longer dominant concerns in urban economies with substantially decentralised employment centres (Romanos 1976).

The introduction of commodity and activity complexity, along with dispersed employment nodes, has lead some authors to stress that the access-space trade-off model is primarily relevant in relation to individuals and their locations. That is, the trade-off is applied to a complex set of household activities which are dispersed over different points in an urban area. This approach (Kirwan and Ball 1977; Straszheim 1975; Nelson 1972; MacDonald 1979) seems logically sound. But, whilst the access-space model may be deemed theoretically suitable for examining

21

group behaviour in long-run equilibrium it is not at all apparent that it is suitable for investigating individual behaviour or choices in the short term.

The behaviour of individuals and markets. The most unsatisfactory assumptions of the access-space model in relation to applied economic analyses are those related to the information and decision taking properties of housing producers and consumers and the assumption of instantaneous equilibrium. Housing theorists and, in particular housing policy analysts, must be relatively concerned about the realism of behavioural assumptions and prior conceptions of markets. In subsequent chapters, particularly Chapters 2 and 3, it is argued that the urban housing market may be segmented and subject to different degrees of disequilibrium and that information constraints on housing market behaviour require consumer search and adjustment processes which are, of course, assumed non-existent in the access-space model.

Before turning to the individualistic applications and extensions of the access-space model and considering alternative housing choice models a review of the second major housing market model 'the filtering model' is presented here.

Succession and filtering

Whilst the access-space model has represented the main concern of economists involved in equilibrium modelling of the urban housing system, economists have frequently utilised 'filtering models' as a framework for applied studies. These filtering models tend to assume the existence of housing submarkets, they are concerned with the link between new and secondhand housing markets and they particularly focus on the movement of households in relation to existing housing stocks. Thus, filtering studies are concerned with dynamic processes in the housing market, unlike the access-space model where the system is always assumed to adjust smoothly and instantaneously. In the final section it is indicated that filtering and access-space models are not polar alternatives and that they are, in many respects, reconcilable.

The social ecologists of the 'Chicago school' took great pains to stress that the simple ring structure produced by the competitive process was no more than a single snapshot of a dynamic process. The succession process, whereby households moved upward and outward in the housing system and by which neighbourhoods experienced a process of decline and decay, was equally stressed by the social ecologists. Although great emphasis has been placed upon the spatial dimension of his model and indeed it was initially viewed as a critique of the Burgess ring model, Hoyt made a major contribution to the economic studies of housing market dynamics (Hoyt 1939). Based on an empirical/inductive analysis of the changing patterns of land values and the movement of population in thirty-eight American cities, Hoyt provided the first major contribution to what may be labelled 'filtering' studies. In this section, the simple succession model outlined by Hoyt is examined, the implicit assumptions of the theory are uncovered and then the broadening and refinement of the filtering concept which occurred largely in the 1960s is analysed. More recent theoretical and empirical studies from the UK and USA are cited to indicate how filtering studies are now likely to develop.

The Hoyt model

Homer Hoyt's seminal contribution has largely been viewed as a contribution to urban spatial economics and, as a consequence, the important dynamic (time-related) dimension to this analysis has been insufficiently stressed. Hoyt argued that large cities were as much characterised by residential sectors as they were by residential rings. The basis of his argument is as follows. In the early phase of urban development, the most affluent and influential social and economic group were not sufficiently numerous to occupy a complete residential ring of the city. Instead, they tended to gather within a well-defined area or sector on one side of the city centre. The location of this high income group then became a reference point for successively lower income groups. The rationale for this assertion was that lower income households have a preference to live near to their peer groups. Thus, initially assuming a stationary urban economy, it could be expected that the neighbourhood of the dominant social, racial and economic group would produce rent gradients around the edge of the peer group sector. In time, relaxing the static assumption, new housing would be provided on the urban periphery. With the growing incomes of the rich allied to an endogenous preference for newness or novelty *per se* the peer group would move outwards to new suburban neighbourhoods. The houses vacated by the high income group would be sold at a discount and this would allow the next socioeconomic group to move in, thus providing vacancies in their price range. This movement and price change effect would be transmitted throughout the range of quality level submarkets until the lowest income group abandoned the lowest quality housing.

This inductively based model, which is riddled with implicit assumptions regarding housing consumers and the urban housing system, came to be known as the 'filtering process' and it has occupied an important place throughout the short history of housing economics. Thus, in the Hoyt model, the term 'filtering' is applied to both the observed pattern of movement and the specific process underlying the movement outcome. Whilst subsequent models relate the term 'filtering' to move-

23

ment patterns they either utilise or imply different assumptions about movement choice influences. Therefore it is appropriate to list the specific assumptions of the Hoyt model before considering the more general development of the model. The Hoyt model should not be viewed as a general theory of housing dynamics but rather it is a specific hypothesis which requires detailed specification and testing in different locations. Thus, in urban economics, unlike physical chemistry, there is no general principle of filtration. The specific elements of the Hoyt model labelled as 'filtering' are:

1. New building is suburban and geared to income growth in higher income groups.
2. Income growth by the peer group is utilised to pursue preferences for 'newness', 'status' and more space.
3. Changes in overall income distributions and population structures are not articulated in the model but income growth is assumed to occur for high income households.
4. Lower income groups have a preference to live near their peer groups.
5. By definition, price falls per unit of housing service induce upward movement, and there are no serious transfer costs precluding movement.
6. The behaviour of housing market institutions is abstracted, that is neither building societies nor estate agents etc. shape area choices.
7. The models are conventionally described in terms of optimising perfectly informed household decisions, there are no long-term problems of housing asset risk assessment and, in the short term, there are no housing search problems for sellers and buyers.

Quite obviously there are strong implicit and explicit assumptions about the housing market in the Hoyt model. But urban housing market analysts did not proceed to test and revise or generalise Hoyt's theory. Instead two main responses were forthcoming. First, there was a generally hostile reaction to the potential ethical implications of the filtering model. This led to a series of definitions and redefinitions of filtering as an outcome. Second, in the 1960s there was a conceptual response by Grigsby who provided a general matrix or framework in which to analyse observed movements across households and housing stock. Subsequently there have been technical rather than theoretical developments of Grigsby's framework.

Ethical criticisms. Although Hoyt had been primarily concerned with theoretical and empirical aspects of his work a series of commentators criticised the model, on the quite unreasonable grounds that Hoyt's employers (the Federal Home Administration) might use it as a policy framework (Smith 1970). The filtering model, as outlined by Hoyt, indicated that if new houses were to be provided in suburban locations for high income households then filtering moves would raise the quality of housing, at reduced prices, for all other groups. But this would imply that housing subsidy would be directed, either by producer or consumer subsidies, towards the higher income groups. Even if the mechanics of the Hoyt model were correct, empirically and theoretically, ethical objections could be raised because:

1. Subsidy was directed to high income groups.
2. The lower income individuals maintained a constant relative distributional relationship vis-à-vis other groups. Filtering policies did not encourage distributional equity.
3. The filtering mechanisms would only work very slowly, if at all.
4. The policy encouraged suburban oriented decentralisation.

The critics of the policy implications of the Hoyt model were then addressing a central argument of housing policy and not a minor theoretical issue. Filtering models have, at least implicitly, influenced policy for more than fifty years.

Considerable debate has surrounded the meaning of the term filtering. Hoyt's succession process stresses both the movement of people and the interrelated shift in property values. For instance Lowry (1960) correctly stressed the importance of non-moving households in any housing system and suggested a purely price related definition of filtering. That is, he suggested that it is property values which filter as relative price changes occur and such changes can occur without household movement. Developing the property related conception of filtering W.F. Smith has provided a commonly accepted definition that filtering is said to occur when property values decline more rapidly than structural quality. The postwar public housing programme in the UK (see Ch. 9) diverted attention from filtering concepts but they were still an important element in discussions of policy in the USA in 1979/80. For instance, the Proxmire proposal to redirect Section 8 assistance from low income families towards higher income supply policies, implicitly assumes that filtering is important and rapid.

Technical responses

An early indicator that housing market analysts were attempting to introduce too many processes into the Hoyt model, or alternatively were attempting to deduce widely applicable hypotheses from its specific assumptions, was the plethora of definitions of filtering. The Smith definition is, perhaps, an attempt to attribute ethical respectability to filtering.

However, these definitions had begun to divert attention from more general models of housing dynamics which would incorporate housing quality decline, the interaction of the new and secondhand markets, relative price changes and household movements. In 1963 Grigsby offered a more general analysis of the filtering concept and he was concerned to examine the empirical relationships between houses, households and household movement. Grigsby's work has been critical to the development of housing dynamics as it has provided a broad framework for subsequent research. The analysis presented by Grigsby is important and its major points are stressed as follows.

Filtering as outcome.   It stresses that filtering is an observed outcome, and that the pattern of filtering can be observed by presenting a matrix of household moves across different housing quality or price ranges.

Filtering 'up' and 'down'.   It follows from the above that households or areas may filter 'up' or 'down' the house price/quality range.

Filtering through submarkets.   The matrix model utilised by Grigsby stresses the importance of submarkets. The definition of submarket proposed by Grigsby, that houses are in associated submarkets if they are close substitutes for each other is not a widely acceptable definition of 'submarket'. For it could imply that there is a unitary market in which slightly different products are sold. A stronger definition of submarket would require that the price of a unit of housing service varied across space or quality sub-groups. Although the existence of sub-markets is implicitly assumed to exist by most housing market economists, there have been few attempts to identify such groupings. Indeed limited tests in the USA (Schnare and Struyk 1976) and in the UK (Kirwan and Ball 1977) reject the existence of submarkets in particular cities. But these empirical tests have not been convincing. For instance, in the context of Bristol, Kirwan and Ball allocate a small sample of transactions across a limited number of areas identified from census data. Not only does this census data convey little information about economic aspects of the housing market, but the spatial units chosen are rather large to effect such a test. They then, for each submarket, estimate the coefficients of a hedonic price function for each submarket and they conclude that the observed coefficients are not significantly different across the areas concerned. Leaving aside the limitations of the techniques involved (see Ch. 2) it is not apparent why the same hedonic function should be applied across all submarkets. Recent analysis of the housing markets in Glasgow and Aberdeen (Maclennan and Wood 1980a) indicates that small areas within an urban housing market, with relatively fixed housing stock, may display quite different inflation rates over short- and long-run time periods (see Fig. 1.7). This would suggest the existence of submarkets as a reasonable working hypothesis.

Filtering as an outcome of a variety of processes

The movements of households observed in Grigsby's matrices are an

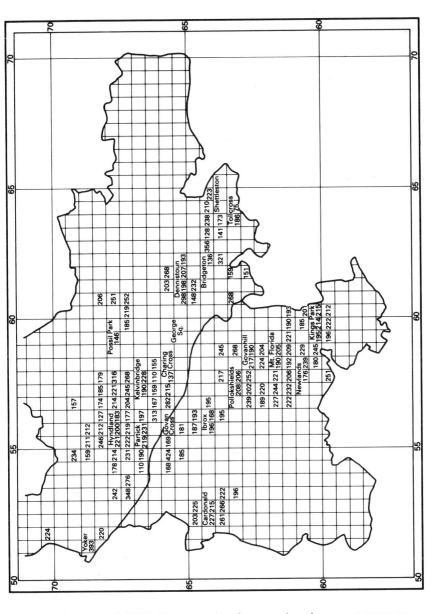

Source: Dawson *et al*. (1980). Figures are given for areas where there were ten or more sales in each year

Fig. 1.7   Small area (500 m²) price change relativities, Glasgow, 1976/72.

outcome of housing finance, supply and demand factors. That is, unlike the Hoyt model, it is not necessary to ascribe all movements to a single process.

The different processes inducing or permitting housing market movement were not analysed in detail by Grigsby, nor indeed by many subsequent analysts. Thus it is appropriate to consider which economic forces drive the dynamics of an urban housing market and to speculate on what patterns of movement may result.

John Stuart Mill has suggested two separate definitions of dynamics which are helpful in understanding the sources of movement in the housing sector (Mill 1848). First, Mill suggested that dynamics could be applied to an economic magnitude which was internally not at rest but which did not change its dimensions over the time period. A motor car at rest but with the engine running is a possible, if not completely precise, analogy. In the housing context, births and deaths occur, marriages take place, household separation occurs and properties may be demolished or built. As long as the structure of demand and supply does not change in aggregate, this internal dynamic will not be reflected in relative price changes for houses or neighbourhoods. Thus life-cycle related movements are also excluded from the conventional range of movements and turnover discussed in filtering studies; this may be an erroneous omission if population and or structure changes. If life-cycle stage and housing consumption are related, then changes in population structure will result in a change in the pattern of submarket supply and demand and probably induce a change in relative prices across submarkets.

It can be argued, however, that this first conception of dynamics is logically inconsistent if applied in the housing market. For change in the housing market is inherent, either because the quality of existing housing declines over time, or because fashion for novelty is a critical element in consumer satisfaction.

Thus it is Mill's second definition of dynamics which is particularly pertinent in the context of succession, namely where the relevant aggregates change in magnitude over time. In a full analysis of the housing system steady state and unbalanced growth models should both be considered and developed. However, here four potentially dynamic elements of changes and processes in the housing market are briefly indicated.

Income growth
The filtering process as outlined by Hoyt really requires a growth in household income for the peer group, or a fall in new house prices, if the high income groups are to make new house purchases. It seems a peculiar assumption that this income growth is restricted to the peer

group. If income were to grow and the relative distribution of income maintained then lower income groups could now afford to move into the homes formerly occupied by the peer group. Interestingly, such a movement is precluded from Smith's concept of filtering as it does not require a price fall. Under certain assumptions the second level group could move into the previous houses of the peer group and be associated with a price rise. For instance, if the distribution of income or wealth is not rectangular but, more realistically, normally or lognormally distributed then the peer group will be absolutely small in relation to the next income group. If there is a preference to live in the former houses of the peer group, that is, a new qualitative dimension is added to the choice set for the second level, then there may now be excess demand for these houses, assuming income levels expand uniformly. It is also possible that the distribution of income may shift over time and housing market pressures may be particularly felt in the value ranges/locations/submarkets potentially available to rapidly rising income groups. Smith's restrictive definition of filtering therefore excludes income related changes which may be an important source of mobility and changes in the relative values of neighbourhoods and indeed such changes may actually be required in Hoyt's filter model to initiate the process.

Population change

Population growth, with a constant distribution and per capita level of income, can have marked effects on the structure of demand. Rapid growth, without a change in racial or population structure, may alter relative prices within and between submarkets, depending on the attempted entry pattern of new entrants. Further, rapid growth may suspend any Hoytian filtering process, if there are supply side lags and if new entrants capture all the vacancies which are created by individuals moving from the initial housing stock. Population structure changes, especially where related to life-cycle and income effects can also affect relative prices. If there are marked discontinuities in the quality and price ranges between submarkets then population structure effects are obviously important. For instance, in the United Kingdom new household formation of first-time house purchase is commonly associated with buying flats and terraced houses. A rapid rate of new household formation will then be reflected in growing pressure on the cheaper end of the housing market in turn generating rapid rates of house price appreciation in such areas. Figure 1.7 indicates that in at least one major British city lower priced areas are associated with more rapid rates of price appreciation than higher priced areas. This outward and upward push thesis is at marked variance with Hoyt's filtering model of urban housing change.

Tastes and preferences

The nature of preferences is also critical in the Hoyt filtering process. Three elements of preference are important. First, it is assumed that the desire for newness or novelty is not income elastic but effectively an element of the choice set for upper income households. Second, the demand for space units is income elastic, for all groups. Third, that preferences to reside with, next to or apart from particular groups is given and fixed. Despite the 'situational' and uncertainty characteristics of neighbourhood choice the model of filtering is usually cast in terms of exogenously given and fixed preferences whereas 'Veblen', 'snob' and 'bandwagon' effects would seem to be an important consideration in this context. However, in more conventional neoclassical filtering models it is not clear why novelty, peer group and suburbanisation preferences should conform to Hoyt's assumptions. In recent years in Europe and North America the well-documented phenomenon of gentrification, whereby high income groups return to renovate and raise the prices of inner city properties is evidence that preferences for well-maintained older property catering to urban life style tastes can exist. Hoyt's preference assumptions may well have had a sound inductive base for the periods and places analysed. It could not be expected that they would have universal relevance and thus his succession model, or 'upward' filtering models, will have limited detailed application.

Supply factors

The filtering models do make the important connection between the flow of new house completions and the reassignment of the existing stock a central part of their analysis. New house building, combined with income growth and novelty tastes of the upper income group, is the driving force of the filtering model. There is a general assumption that new building is the only major force creating potential vacancies. However, if the structure of demand changes over time, without a lead from the top of the market, then vacancies may appear more frequently and turnover rates increase within given submarkets. For instance, if a marriage boom does create excess demand and price rises at the lower end of the market then, in time, the life-cycle/income growth process may move this peak of demand outwards with the area of origin suffering relatively falling prices. The potential instability of such a system is examined below.

These reservations apart, the general finding of British filtering studies, which assume a new building driving force, does indicate that new dwellings are relatively highly priced and inhabited by high income/socioeconomic groups. Vacancies do tend to create chains which are filled by lower income groups or new entrants (Watson 1973). However, Jones has demonstrated that such 'upward' movements by households are by no means inevitable (Jones 1978). There is no evidence from British studies that prices actually fall to induce upward movement. Thus none of these studies really tests the filtering hypothesis as defined by Smith. The longer-term test related to property values in Edinburgh, over a long period of time, by Richardson, does confirm a spatial evolution of land values consistent with Hoyt's sectoral thesis and suggests a Hoyt-like change in property values over time. It is true that the test does relate to a period of transport improvement, suburbanisation and urban growth in Edinburgh which was generally similar to those of Hoyt's city (Richardson, Vipond and Furbey 1975). It could not be claimed that the model provided similar results for Glasgow in the period 1971–8 (see Fig. 1.7).

The supply-side generalisations of the Hoyt and filtering models may not now be ubiquitously valid. New housing can be supplied for lower income groups and, in the United Kingdom, an increasing proportion of first-time house purchasers are now purchasing new houses. Further there is increasing governmental pressure, in British cities, to provide a variety of new house types in both inner and suburban locations. Novelty and peripheral location need not always be perfectly correlated. Further, as was noted in relation to the gentrification process, neighbourhood decline is not irreversible and maintenance and renovation expenditures (given initially appropriate relative prices) can lead to areas being recycled back up the ranking of residential areas.

Subsequent developments

Once the complex set of factors which determines household movement, turnover and area ranking (in terms of price) is taken into account then it is clear that the filtering model is not a general process and inevitable feature of urban development, but that different dynamic processes can, over space and time, underlie movement patterns. Thus Grigsby's analysis of filtering, as a housing market outcome, could have stimulated a research effort to understand housing market dynamics (probably related to the burgeoning literature on intra-urban movement patterns and processes). But whilst processes of movement and neighbourhood change have become important research issues in the 1970s, the main out-growths of the filtering literature have been technical rather than theoretical or empirical developments. Expanding on Grigsby's technique of matrix analysis the following developments have been important.

The assignment problem. Using a simple linear programming model, the objective function of maximising rent payments and an assumed developers' cost function, Smith has traced the hypothetical effects of altering housing or population structures in a filtering matrix. The empirical and policy relevance of the model was severely criticised by

Edel who suggested that market signals are sufficiently dispersed and diffused to render the assumption of a well-informed central planner irrelevant (Smith 1963; Edel 1972).

Housing chains. Analysts in Britain and North America have examined the number of subsequent moves which new housing construction generates. Studies of this kind such as Kristof (1965) and Lansing, Clifton and Morgan (1969) for the United States have suggested that each new house built will generate 3.5 further moves on average. This statistic, the housing chain multiplier (White 1971), has been somewhat lower (at around 2.5 to 3) in UK studies (Watson 1973). In addition Davies (1978) reports that Canadian studies have indicated shorter chains, that is lower value vacancy multiples, with values between 1.5 and 1.7. But such values are likely to be dissimilar over space and time.

Sophisticated models. More sophisticated attempts to model housing market dynamics by simulation or econometric techniques have been restricted to analysts in North America. A series of studies have examined household movement in relation to submarkets via Markov chain models (Bourne 1976; Clark 1965; Davies 1978), commodity quality hierarchy models (Sweeney 1974), and simulation models such as the National Bureau of Economic Research (N.B.E.R.) model (see Davies 1978). But the major drawbacks of all these exercises has been that they have not contributed to the specification of detailed housing economic models of intra-urban processes.

New directions in filtering research

A recent and important review of the filtering literature (Davies 1978) has presented a broad definition of filtering which, contrary to the stress of filtering as an outcome emphasised here, suggests:

> Filtering in the housing market is the process in which the real housing consumption of families or households changes over time, whether by the depreciation or renovation of the same dwelling unit or the choice of a different dwelling unit (which may be newly constructed or have experienced depreciation, renovation, or conversion from a different type). The process may involve changes in real incomes and in the relative price of housing services (Davies 1978: 139).

This definition effectively equates filtering and housing market dynamics.

At the present time there are two main theoretical developments which may contribute to a fuller understanding of housing dynamics. These stress the importance of neighbourhood or submarket factors in housing choices. In North America, policy concern for neighbourhoods has required analysts to develop models of housing demand and household movement (Segal 1979), which stress the effects of preference interdependences, for instance, racial prejudices or preferences, and area externalities on housing choice. At the present time such considerations have been introduced into the broadened and individualistic applications of the access-space model. But relatively little progress, which is necessary to shift to a dynamic perspective, has been made regarding the modelling of neighbourhood housing supply decisions and institutional influences on neighbourhood change. However, there is at least encouraging evidence that there is now an attempt to pull out empirically the matrices of Grigsby's model and to relate such changes to submarket housing conditions and processes.

The second and, at the present time, the most convincing attempt to model and measure neighbourhood change was undertaken by Leven *et al.* (1975). They argued that, in general, filtering models by assuming certainty, full information and optimising decision taking, rule out some of the behavioural factors and limitations which may be important in the household movement process. Further, although time is introduced into filtering models, insufficient attention is given to the importance of asset characteristics of housing.

The durability of housing as an asset means that purchase and sales decisions have to take into account future patterns of house prices and the value of annual flows of consumption services. The future cannot be known with certainty and risk and uncertainty may then become important elements in housing values and choice over time, with different groups or individuals being more or less risk averse. Expectations and attitudes towards risk on the part of households and institutions have a crucial role to play in the neighbourhood succession process.

Taking these factors into account, Leven *et al.* have stressed that whilst Hoyt's filtering model may have been an appropriate model of the sustained and gradual suburbanisation process prior to 1950, the present process of household movement and neighbourhood change has now evolved away from simple 'filtering'. The sudden and rapid decay of core and inner suburban areas in North American cities requires a more sophisticated and realistic model of household behaviour in the face of neighbourhood decline or expected decline or 'blockbusting'. Of course, studies of 'tipping' of areas due to racial changes have usually confirmed the existence of such sudden changes. British readers should note that this model may well be appropriate to inner city/core residential areas but certainly not to all inner suburban housing submarkets.

Leven *et al.* are sympathetic to the viewpoint expressed above that household movement is determined by an interaction of a complex set of submarket supply and demand factors (which may change over time) rather than the simple price/physical quality relationship of the filtering model. They then stress the great uncertainties and interdependencies which surround submarket supply and demand, and they outline an 'arbitrage' model of price change and household movement. The filtering models of the 1960s were somewhat unclear about the price adjustment process which induced filtering and the time period over which the effects on an addition to the housing stock spread throughout the submarkets. For instance, for peer group properties to be sold at a discount, the most plausible assumption is that all the peer group decide to sell immediately and move to the new housing stock. However, if there is a wide distribution of novelty, status and suburban tastes within the peer group then the turnover of existing stock may be relatively slow and, if incomes are growing, there may be no price fall. The assumption of rapid turnover and adjustment is much more likely if there are substantial interdependencies of utility or preference functions within a housing group or class. That is, a household's valuation of a house and their propensity to move or stay is dependent not only on the location of the house and its physical characteristics but also upon the attributes of the population in the perceived submarket or neighbourhood and upon the expected pattern of future house prices (von Boventer 1978).

Individuals may have very strong preferences either to reside with or separate from particular socioeconomic groups. If a non-preferred group begins to enter an area, *ceteris paribus*, then those with the strongest aversion to such groups may move out. Prices need not necessarily fall. However, if a bandwagon effect develops then a resident may find that a non-preferred group may be replacing a desired group. A threshold level of non-preferred entrants may be reached at which the resident, say the median preference resident, decides to move and as a result a very sudden increase in turnover is then experienced in which prices may actually fall. The process is exacerbated, accelerated and indeed made self-fulfilling if households or financing institutions begin to base their price expectations on the early inflow of non-preferred groups. Selling price expectations may be exponentially revised downwards as non-preferred groups enter, thus accelerating short-period turnover and effectively reducing prices. It is not possible to predict *a priori* a single pattern of price changes as a neighbourhood goes through the transition process. In the early stages non-preferred entrants may have to pay a premium to gain initial access to the area, prices may then fall depending on the rate of turnover but in the longer term prices could rise if the neighbourhood is effectively transferred to a submarket in which excess demand exceeded that of the initial submarket. The essence of this process, and also its theoretical *a priori* indeterminacy, springs from the interdependence of housing demand functions and future uncertainty.

British housing and urban research has generally not followed the

American lead in this avenue of research into neighbourhood dynamics. This may reflect an unhealthy complacency that such preference/prejudice based processes do not occur in British cities. Although such shifts in British cities are less dramatic (at least until the summer of 1981), there is undoubtedly a growing awareness of patterns of race, schooling, planning blight and environmental decay in housing location decisions. It may now be time to desist from casual and erroneous application of the historically interesting filtering model and directly investigate contemporary succession processes. It has already been suggested that household location decisions should not now be analysed within the narrow theoretical structure of the access-space model. Similarly it can now be stressed that the filtering models and the succession process should be analysed within the context of a housing choice model. In the next two chapters there is an attempt to assess which models or frameworks are applicable to the housing market.

2 Housing choices and housing demand

In Chapter 1 it was stressed that neither the access-space nor the filtering models were always appropriate frameworks for the applied economic analysis of housing choices. The models discussed previously have considered both the demand for and supply of housing. In the next four chapters there is an attempt to analyse housing supply, housing finance and housing demand in more detail. This chapter focuses on housing demand analysis using neoclassical equilibrium models and revealed preference theory. Problems associated with utilising this paradigm for housing market studies are discussed in Chapter 3 and an expanded research framework suggested.

Applying demand theory

The introductory chapter also indicated that the analysis of housing demand in access-space and neighbourhood succession models could be expanded, and indeed reconciled, by using a housing choice model as outlined on p 21. Before proceeding to examine the application of an expanded neoclassical model to microeconomic problems of housing choice it is pertinent to review the assumptions which underline the neoclassical consumer choice model.

Consumer theory and housing demand

In applying neoclassical models to housing demand analysis important assumptions are made regarding consumer behaviour, the nature of the commodity and the housing market. These are:
1. There are many buyers and sellers.
2. In relation to the aggregate volume of transactions the sales or purchases of each household are insignificant.
3. There is no collusion amongst or between buyers and sellers.
4. There is free entry into and exit from the market for both consumers

and producers.

5. Consumers have continuous, transitive and established preferences over a wide range of alternative choices of housing and non-housing goods.

6. Consumers and producers possess both perfect knowledge with respect to prevailing prices and current bids and perfect foresight with respect to future prices and future bids.

7. Consumers maximise total utility whilst producers maximise total profits.

8. There are no artificial (non-price) restrictions placed on the demands for supplies and prices of housing service and the resources used to produce housing service. For instance, house purchases are not constrained by finance rationing or the non-availability of preferred housing choices.

9. The market is assumed to be in equilibrium.

Assumptions 1 to 9 define a set of conditions sufficient for the existence of a perfectly competitive market in housing services. Within this framework the standard consumer choice model can readily be theoretically applied to housing. If the household has a rational and complete preference ordering defined over the array of existing commodities, then by maximising utility subject to the budget constraint equating household income with expenditure over the relevant time period, it is possible to express the quantity demanded of any particular commodity, in this case housing, as a function of income, the price of housing and the price of all other commodities. This relationship is the demand function and its parameters can, in principle, be estimated empirically.

These theoretically derived relationships, and their associated descriptive parameters – the price and income elasticity of demand – are then established empirically by examining observed market behaviour. That is, to relate housing consumption to price and income changes or variations, different observed choice outcomes are analysed. In such instances it is necessary to establish that variations in housing consumption reflect income and price changes (demand factors); therefore, for each observation the slope and position of the housing supply function have to be ascertained or assumed (to solve the identification problem). Thus, where income, price and housing consumption choices and shifts in the supply function are unknown, then price and income elasticities can be estimated from a time series study of a given market. At a given period of time, cross-section studies can be undertaken where incomes, prices, housing choices and supply conditions vary across space or across submarkets.

Problems in applying consumer demand theory

There are however two kinds of problem, which are not unrelated, that arise in the application of this strategy for assessing demand. These problems are, respectively, operational and conceptual difficulties.

Operational problems

The estimation of housing demand functions is beset by four main problems. First, since submarkets may exist in the urban housing market, an application of the above technique requires a prior, or simultaneous, identification of submarkets. Second, in many submarkets housing supply arises from the turnover of secondhand housing stock and this turnover depends on demand influences on existing residents. Thus housing supply and demand, in most submarkets, will generally be simultaneously determined and identification problems will be commonplace. Third, and this issue is elaborated under the heading of conceptual difficulties, where housing is a complex commodity multiple attributes are traded in the market for which individual prices are not observed. Fourth, recognising the complexity of housing markets, detailed data on individual transactions is required. In the North American context, Quigley (1978) has stressed the richness of such available data. In the United Kingdom suitable census data, for houses and households, does not exist.

If these operational difficulties can be overcome it is possible to derive utility and demand functions for housing in the usual way. But there are a number of characteristics of housing which suggest the need for modifications to this model. These features, which are deemed to be of particular significance, are grouped under four headings:

1. As a durable asset housing structures provide both consumption and investment services and they are usually purchased with loan finance.
2. Housing is a complex, multi-dimensional commodity.
3. The standing stock is characterised by 'situational' attributes, defined in spatial or social terms, which generate interdependence elements in household utility functions.
4. In the housing market, even in equilibrium, there are likely to be frictional and search costs which are significant enough to influence housing choice.

1. Durability, income and investment considerations

The durability of housing units is a dominant characteristic of the standing stock. This characteristic has a direct bearing on the factors determining the demand for housing and it influences the specification of the housing utility function and the income constraint. Since housing is a durable commodity it is plausible to argue that households will have

38

a long-time horizon in making decisions about housing expenditure. It may be further deduced that if the household is to be consistent, then the income measure referred to when making this decision is unlikely to be current income, but will be some 'averaged' measure of former levels of income and expected future earnings ('normal income'). In fact this is an operational rather than a conceptual problem for the applied economist and a variety of assessments of permanent income may be made (Struyk 1976). The critical conceptual problems arise, even where the housing market is in equilibrium, if the housing and capital markets are not in joint equilibrium. In such instances, which are empirically relevant in the UK (see Ch. 7) (Maclennan and Wood 1980a) and perhaps in the USA (Fair 1974) loan institutions may ration household expenditures. Further, where housing assets appreciate more rapidly than other assets and appreciation rates are higher than the mortgage rate then permanent wealth, if it is defined to include imputed housing income or wealth, will depend partly upon housing expenditure choices. If such occurrences are likely then demand estimation models require a simultaneous modelling of demand, supply and finance sectors of the housing market.

Regarding household preferences for housing, the significance of housing as an asset makes necessary the distinction between the stock of capital assets in the form of structures existing at any moment of time and the flow of housing services per period of time which that stock is capable of yielding. There are clearly therefore two housing markets. There is a demand and supply of a consumer good which can be termed housing service, and there is also a derived demand and supply of an investment good which can be termed housing stock. Though the two markets are integrally related, by choosing to rent households can participate in the market for housing services alone. However, unless there is a focus of analysis purely on the market for rental housing services it is inappropriate, as is implicitly accomplished in the simple consumer choice model, to ignore the derived demand for houses as assets.

The household active within the house purchase market must make two closely interrelated decisions with respect to its demand for housing. First, the level of housing services required for consumption purposes must be selected and, second, the stock of housing units or assets to be held for investment purposes is chosen. These investment considerations may confound the normally expected inverse relationship between current price and quantity of private housing services demanded. Here it is important to make a distinction between new entrants to the market and existing owner-occupiers. For those first-time purchasers who are at the financial margin of choice it is safe to presume that any increase in current price will make purchase less financially viable despite any prospects of capital gain encouraged by current upward changes in house prices. However, for existing owner-occupiers who intend to move, house price inflation provides a capital gain which helps prevent contraction of demand due to a higher current level of prices.

When the moving home-owner perceives that capital gain plays a large part in helping to reduce trading down in the face of upward changes in current prices, he will presumably actively consider the future expected values of the prices of the prospective properties. The expected value of these prices will (in relation to the current and anti-cipated values of the mortgage rate, general price level and interest rate on securities and deposits) determine the expected rate of return on these properties vis-à-vis non-housing assets, a relationship which is clearly of importance with respect to constrained choice.

Struyk conceptualises the two roles of the owner-occupier and investor by positing two interdependent demand functions, one for housing services Q_d^s and the other for housing stock Q_d^k (Struyk 1976). These functions are

1. $Q_d^s = f(Y, fam, Psa, Psr, \pi, Q_d^k)$
2. $Q_d^k = g(Q_d^s, r_0, r, W)$

As is conventional, Q_d^s is expressed as a function of Y, permanent income; '*fam*', life-cycle and family characteristics; *Psa*, the price per unit of housing services; π, the price of all other goods than housing; *Psr*, the price of rental housing services the closest substitute; Q_d^k enters because 'the household in question may actually be consuming more or less services than it would in the absence of the investment considera-tion'. Note also that Q_d^s enters the Q_d^k function as 'we would expect at least that Q_d^k would be great enough to provide services sufficient for the minimum living requirements of the family'; r is the rate of return available on other investments, W is the household's wealth and r_0 is the rate of return on the housing unit in question.

As long as the level of desired housing consumption services and desired stock holdings are consistent then the model is easily solved. But housing consumption and investment motives could conflict (see Ch. 7). The household as consumer wishes to maximise utility, but as investor he will choose from the choice set that housing unit with the maximum net present value (NPV) of expected net returns (where the discount rate used will be the opportunity cost of the expected capital outlay). The NPV of expected net returns will enter the budget con-straint of the utility maximisation problem. If the flow of housing services, Q_d^s, yielded by the solution to this problem is greater than the level of housing services provided by that Q_k^d which maximises NPV, we have an element of indeterminacy.

It may be possible to avoid this problem by suggesting that Q_d^k is chosen to maximise NPV subject to the additional constraint that

$Q_d^k \geq Q_d^s$. However, it is an illegitimate step to consider Q_d^s to be known before the relevant NPV measure can be included in the budget constraint.

One possible solution is to collapse all investment consideration into the budget constraint of the utility maximisation problem, that is, we remove housing stock as an argument in the utility function, leaving only housing services in the function. It is then implicitly assumed that there is no utility to be derived from owning housing assets *per se*. Thus, the ownership of housing assets only confers benefits indirectly via the budget constraint. This can be done by deflating the prices of the housing units in the household's choice set by their NPV of expected net returns. From the utility maximisation procedure a demand function can be derived for housing services which will depend on the determinants in (1) plus: the expected rates of return in the household's aspiration set, the expected rates of return in other sectors of the housing market and economy as a whole, the discount rate and W, household wealth. Accepting Muth's definition that one unit of housing service is that quantity of service yielded by one unit of housing stock per unit of time, this can easily be translated into a demand function for housing stock.

It is also possible that the housing consumption decision may select a desired stock or flow of services, Q_d^s, which will fall below the level generated by the optimum investment stock Q_d^k, either because increased house size generates housing disutilities (fear of being felt ostentatious, dislike of very low density living, etc.). In this instance there is a trade-off between present consumption and future wealth.

Few studies of housing demand have broached these important aspects which are, of course, critical in inflationary economies.

2. Housing attributes and housing complexity
It is generally recognised that housing is a multi-dimensional commodity. This implies a view of housing as a 'composite demand for a flow of services embodying a variable mix of characteristics rather than for identifiable units of a commodity'. Theoretically the standard consumer choice model can be modified to allow for this problem; instead of treating housing as a single commodity entering as an argument into the utility function, the latter becomes dependent upon the identifiable or perceived attributes (e.g. accessibility, quality of environment, number of rooms, etc.) of housing and all other commodities consumed (Rosen 1974). It is then possible to derive demand functions for individual attributes which will be functions of income, life-cycle characteristics etc. and various prices, amongst which will be the implicit prices of attributes. However, it is shown below that the identification and measurement of these implicit prices in applied analysis are problematic.

As Odling-Smee (1975) has noted, the explicit recognition of the complex nature of housing and the allowance for significant differences in household preferences questions the appropriateness of the assumption that housing can be thought of as a bundle or scalar, which is measured in terms of housing services. In particular, if the units of housing services are defined as a constant monotonic function of the quantity of attributes contained in a house then it is easy to give instances in which the crucial axiom of non-satiation which underlies modern demand theory is violated: Imagine a situation in which house A has more units of housing services than house B, but an individual (household) who associates a relatively high level of utility with those attributes in which B is relatively more abundant, prefers B to A. If housing were thought of as a scalar, the non-satiation axiom would be violated. The desirable analytical properties of the conventional model of consumers' behaviour would not be valid in a world where individuals derived different amounts of utility from different attributes of housing.

Since the early 1970s, therefore, it has become commonplace in housing demand analysis, following the lead of the N.B.E.R research studies to attempt to estimate implicit prices and demand functions for individual housing attributes. Such studies have become dependent upon hedonic price index studies and there is a continuing disquiet amongst some applied economists (Maclennan 1977a; Rothenberg 1979) that the technique has major limitations. Here, following Freeman (1979) the details of the technique are outlined, the assumptions employed identified and some critical questions raised.

The hedonic method. The discussion of hedonic prices for housing presented here is a paraphrased version of a recent and clear exposition of the technique provided by Freeman (1979). Freeman, a proponent of the technique who has particularly utilised hedonic prices in relation to establishing demand functions for environmental attributes, argues that;

> The hedonic technique is potentially applicable to any attribute which differentiates houses in the eyes of potential occupants . . . If these things matter to people and their levels vary across the array of available housing, then the interaction of supply and individual preferences can affect the pattern of house prices (Freeman 1979: 193).

Therefore hedonic indices can be used to reveal the implicit prices of goods which are not explicitly traded but which are characteristics of traded goods.

The estimation of attribute demand functions, therefore, follows a two-step procedure. First, the implicit prices of characteristics are estimated by the hedonic technique. This assumes that, for an individual or group, if there are variations in house prices paid, P, and variations in characteristics, C, across houses then the marginal implicit price for the attribute is the first derivative of price with respect to characteristics. That is, a marginal price schedule is derived for the characteristic. More formally, the hedonic function has the form

$$Ph_i = Ph (Si_1 \ldots Si_j, Ni_1 \ldots Ni_j, Qi_1 \ldots Qi_j),$$

where Ph_i is the price of house i, Si_1, Ni_1, Qi_1 refer respectively to housing attributes grouped, as is commonly done, under locational, neighbourhood and internal attribute headings. In turn

$$\frac{\partial Ph}{\partial Nk} = P_{Nk} (N_k),$$

is the implicit or hedonic price function differentiated with respect to the characteristic N_k.

The simple linear formulation of the hedonic function can, of course, be altered. In the simple linear formulation there is the implication that the implicit price of an attribute is constant for all individuals and over all levels of consumption of characteristic K. If the function is non-linear, then this may reflect an assumption of diminishing marginal utility to the consumer from additions of the characteristics. Similarly, the characteristics may not affect utility and implicit price separably but may interact. The selection of the form of the hedonic price regression is discussed below.

The second stage of demand equation estimation is to assume that the individual housing consumer is a price taker and is therefore faced with an array of implicit marginal price schedule for various characteristics. The household then maximises utility by moving along each marginal price schedule until marginal willingness to pay for each attribute is equal to its marginal implicit price.

This equilibrium condition, for the individual, can be shown diagrammatically as in Fig. 2.1. Here the schedule $P_{NK(NK)}$ represents the marginal price schedule for characteristic K derived from a price regression. The schedules, $W_{i(NK)}$ and $W_{j(NK)}$ represent the marginal willingness to pay schedules of two different individuals i and j. The marginal willingness to pay, or inverse demand function, for each household is assured to be a function such as

$$W_i = W (NK_i, M_i, A_i)$$

where W_i is the marginal willingness to pay for the characteristics, NK_i is the amount of K consumed by the individual, M_i is income level and A_i are other demand determinants such as age, family size, etc. Thus, for each household, an observed implicit price point, such as i or j, in Fig. 2.1, is taken to be a point on the willingness-to-pay function. Therefore, it is possible to observe such a series of points if, for

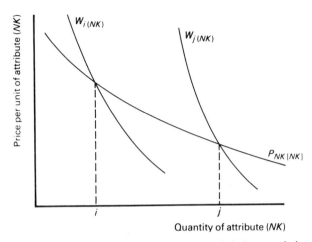

Fig. 2.1 Equilibrium choices for non-traded characteristics: two individuals (i, j)

instance, there is variation in income across households. Thus, an income elasticity could be identified for characteristic K. Similarly, if price variation can be established, price parameters may be generated.

However, Freeman is careful to cite, even in the context of his optimising, equilibrium assumptions, that inverse demand functions cannot always be revealed in full.

1. If the hedonic price function is assumed to be linear then marginal implicit prices estimated do not vary with quantity consumed. It follows therefore that a price elasticity cannot be estimated although income elasticities can be observed.

2. When all individuals have identical incomes and preference functions then only a single point on the inverse demand function can be established.

In general, however, it will be necessary to make assumptions about the supply functions for housing characteristics to allow the demand system to be identified.

3. If the supply of characteristics is infinitely elastic then the hedonic price regression provides a direct estimate of the demand function – that is the quantity demanded at the fixed supply price.

4. If the supply of characteristics is infinitely inelastic the hedonic price regression generates inverse demand functions – that is the willingness to pay for a fixed quantity supplied.

5. If the housing supply schedule has some finite elasticity value, that is, both supply of and demand for the characteristic are a function of price, then a simultaneous equation approach to demand estimation is required. Although this latter case is most likely to prevail in the

housing market, simultaneous estimation techniques have rarely been utilised in housing demand studies.

The major assumptions. In order to derive, and indeed give meaning to, hedonically based price and income elasticities Freeman has to make four major assumptions:

1. Consumers can make complex optimising decisions.
2. The housing market is in equilibrium.
3. There is continuous variation in the supply characteristics of a given attribute.
4. The housing market operates as a unitary whole.

The continuity and unitary market assumptions can be relaxed without major consequences. For instance, if house size did not vary continuously, but in discrete steps, a stepped implicit price function may only marginally distort results. Further, in an urban housing market, if there are a number of observed submarkets, the hedonic regression could be applied within each submarket. Indeed, this may be an important source of attribute price variation. If hedonic studies are not adequately structured with respect to consumer sub-groups or housing submarkets then sources of estimation and aggregation bias can occur. For instance, it is self-evident that preferences will differ across sub-groups of households and submarkets. In the absence of *a priori* knowledge with respect to how and to what extent preferences differ, researchers have been forced to assume the problem away via the adoption of an assumed equilibrium unitary housing market. Given the latter's segmented nature this *ad hoc* procedure inevitably results in aggregation across sub-groups and submarkets where both the value of parameters and the functional form differ. The marginal valuation thus yielded by the hedonic technique will be a relatively meaningless average.

To show this more clearly, suppose there is a local housing market in which there are n 'active' buyers and n 'active' sellers differentiated by income. The estimated hedonic index $P(K)$ for any one attribute is the locus of n tangency points at which the offer and bid curves of the n sellers and n buyers are tangential. Unless utility functions are invariant across all market participants, separable in both attributes and other commodities and homothetic then the slopes of the offer and bid curves at the points of tangency will differ, that is, the marginal valuations for any one attribute vary across individuals. Consequently, the estimated coefficient (marginal valuation) for any attribute in a linear hedonic price regression which pools data will be a linear sum of the true coefficients for each individual. The weights will depend upon the attribute values consumed and offered by each individual buyer and seller.

If, however, it could justifiably be assumed that utility functions are separable, homothetic and identically so across all buyers *and sellers* the offer and bid curves of all individuals would have identical shapes with income and utility level acting purely as shift factors. *P(K)* could then be interpreted as a unique price schedule facing all market participants. As Harris and Edwards (1978) point out this has an unfortunate theoretical and empirical drawback because it constrains the income elasticity of demand for each attribute to unity. It is important to recognise that in this case the choice of a particular demand model has imposed strong *a priori* notions or constraints which are *built in* and will *interact* with the data thus influencing the results yielded.

But the assumptions of equilibrium optimising behaviour are not tenets of faith which all housing economists would profess. If complexity, infrequency of purchase and search costs all affect consumer behaviour in a housing market in disequilibrium then the conditions required to make sensible use of hedonic techniques may not prevail. These issues are discussed in Chapter 3, here it is sufficient to note that hedonic techniques are not applicable to such housing markets without biased outcomes.

The durability, complexity and spatial fixity of housing all tend to generate compartmentalisation or segmentation of the market (and the strong likelihood of disequilibrium tendencies). A well-recognised source of disequilibrium in the housing market is the inelastic nature of the supply of particular types of housing in particular locations (even in the long run). These tendencies are compounded when the assumption of *a priori* perfect information is relaxed and costs of searching are recognised. It may then be inferred that observed prices are unlikely to be equilibrium values; the question which then arises is whether or not we are observing a demand (bid) price, supply (offer) price or indeed a price which lies off both schedules. A naïve 'attribute regression' ignores this problem and disallows any supply side influence.

If, as seems likely in the secondhand market, sellers are the mirror image of buyers in the sense that they are subject to similar financial and informational constraints it would be inappropriate to assume away their influence on prices. Further, it would be wrong to presume that the offer schedules of sellers have the same shape and are identical to those of buyers. Where the offer schedules of sellers are incongruous with the bid schedules of buyers the disequilibrium state we refer to above will pertain. In the absence of a tâtonnement market clearing process, market forces will not instantaneously remove this disequilibrium and false trading (that is, trading at non-market clearing prices) takes place. The estimates of a hedonic price regression capture these influences but can tell us little about how and over what likely time period equilibrating processes take place.

It can also be argued that even where the optimising and equilibrium assumptions seem reasonable that the hedonic technique is beset with problems. The most critical of these is the selection of the content and form of the hedonic price regression. How are the elements to be entered, linearly or non-linearly, separably or non-separably? How do researchers know what 'differentiates housing in the eyes of the consumer'? According to Quigley (1978) this is an empirical matter, but how is this empirical assessment to be made? Is the best-fit hedonic regression to be selected? But is this not dangerous econometric practice when many of the right-hand side variables are highly collinear? In selecting the form of the hedonic regression, which always fails to consider the housing time inputs cited by MacDonald (1979), it becomes apparent that housing economists do not know, and have not studied, the housing production function relationships between housing attributes and satisfactions. Thus citations of the Lancaster approach to housing demand are generally theoretical window dressing and there is no real effort to examine the model empirically. Given the present state of knowledge on household production functions the structure and content of hedonic regressions must always arouse concern.

The second major drawback of hedonic models, given their own assumptions, as applied to housing is that they pay no regard to differences in the quality of housing attributes. The hedonic applications restrict their attention to variations in total housing service quantity, which derive from variations in the quantity of characteristics present. Ironically, quality differences have been consistently ignored.

These specific criticisms of hedonic models, concern regarding their underlying assumptions and a suspicion that supply and submarket conditions are seldom appropriately controlled for, has resulted, on the part of the author, in a sceptical view of received estimates of income and price elasticities (see below, Maclennan 1977a). But before examining these estimates further characteristics of housing as a good require to be examined.

3. Spatial and social 'situational' aspects

Although social scientists, and particularly sociologists, have long recognised that individuals make group decisions and that goods may impart status, with status increasing with price *per se*, economists have made little attempt to analyse such potentially important characteristics of housing.

Given the spatially fixed location of housing, then jointly supplied with any housing unit is the socioeconomic character of a neighbourhood and the physical nature of an environment. It is important to stress here that once a household has acquired the tenure rights of home-ownership or rental housing the jointly supplied neighbourhood and environmental attributes supply monetary and psychic costs and benefits which to a great extent originate externally to that household. That is, the effects of these attributes are in practice difficult to internalise. As such, the benefits and costs of these 'external' attributes can be conceptually distinguished from the satisfactions derived from the use of the physical asset yielding housing services. However, though conceptually distinct, it is important to note that the satisfaction yielded by the purchased tenure rights to home-ownership or rental housing will not be independent of the jointly supplied neighbourhood and physical environment, and thus, spatial preferences are an important determinant of the demand for housing.

Analogous to the treatment of 'internal' attributes (i.e. those attributes associated with the structure of the housing unit), the external attributes such as quality of environment, socioeconomic status of neighbourhood, *etc.*, can be directly entered into the household's utility function. Demand functions for these external attributes can then be derived (Segal 1979). However, the role played by status in the housing decision is a complex one. Status will influence tenure choice, attribute choice and the location decision via the consumption and investment decisions of the reference or peer group(s) to which the household aspires. The reference group plays a dual role; first, it has use in an informative role as a means of defining and ordering the preferences of the household, thereby reducing the cost and effort required from the household in order to define or learn its own preferences and tastes (given imperfect information); second, the household derives direct satisfaction from emulating the consumption pattern of its reference group. This effect can be captured by weighting or ordering housing attributes in the household utility function according to the consumption pattern of the reference group to which the household aspires. This suggests the possibility that bandwagon effects may be of significance in explaining shifts in housing demand across submarkets (von Boventer 1978). That is, these effects refer to the extent to which demand for housing attributes or certain combinations of housing attributes are increased due to the fact that others are also consuming the same attributes or combination of attributes. In such a context, rising prices may not deter upward movement if the household is determined to pursue a particular group. Thus price elasticity would be reduced. More extreme effects could occur, which may result in positive price elasticities (that is, increasing housing purchase becomes associated with rising real prices) if there is a 'snob' effect, particularly with inflationary expectations. Such factors could help to explain the relatively low price elasticities noted below. But status, peer group and inflation effects have not been adequately specified in housing demand studies.

4. Frictional costs

In the discussion of the difficulties of hedonic indices, above, it was argued that market disequilibrium, or even frictional factors in a market in 'statistical' equilibrium, could influence housing demand.

Search costs and strategies and disequilibrium features of the housing market are discussed in detail in the next chapter. Here it is sufficient to note that they have been excluded from all estimates of housing demand parameters. This omission could be important as search costs influence budget constraints and search expectations may influence choices.

Estimates of housing demand parameters

The preceding discussion of the housing commodity indicated that in a neoclassical approach to understanding housing choice a variety of influences on specification of models for empirical estimation should be considered. Asset characteristics necessitated a 'permanent' income approach and the inclusion of asset demand influences. Commodity complexity required the estimation of implicit attribute prices and a focus on individual characteristics of housing. Situational or status effects required a group related specification and frictional and search costs required an identification of entry costs. When these broader considerations are raised the adequacy of existing census data (even in the United States) for estimating well-specified housing demand functions become doubtful. The variety of types of data available, allied to the choice of theoretically based specifications has meant that a diverse series of housing demand estimates has been made both in Britain and the USA. In this section a brief review of house price studies, income elasticities, own price elasticities and other parameters estimated in housing demand studies is presented.

House price studies
Empirical investigation of hedonic house price regressions have proliferated since 1965, though the flow of output has reduced, fortunately, in the late 1970s. A review of the significant studies is presented in Ball (1973) and criticised in Maclennan (1977a). In general, these house price studies provided support for the notion that house prices were determined by locational, neighbourhood, racial, historical, physical and structural factors. These results are pervasive in the literature regardless of the specification of the hedonic regression and whether a multiplicity of individual attributes or selected 'composite' factors (derived from principal components analysis) are utilised. But, in general, the supply side of the housing system was not identified in such regressions and, as a result, they produced no valuable insights regarding housing demand.

Estimated income elasticities
Despite the theoretical arguments in favour of their inclusion, asset demands for housing, peer group effects and search and entry costs have been consistently excluded from estimating equations. As a result

the rapidly developing literature on this topic has focused on improving the specifications of income terms, incorporating price effects and on estimating demand functions for individual attributes.

The literature on estimating the income elasticity of demand for housing has passed through three discernible stages which have focused on macroeconomic time series estimates, cross-section studies with improved income specifications and, more recently, the introduction of implicit prices and estimation of characteristic demands.

Macroeconomic studies. Time series studies relating income and housing expenditure were conducted in the early 1960s (Reid 1962; Muth 1960). Elasticities exceeding unity were generally established and similar studies in the United Kingdom (Whitehead 1974) have identified flow elasticities near to unity and stock-adjustment estimates of 2.8.

Permanent income improvements. By the early 1970s a sufficient volume of microeconomic, cross-section demand studies had been undertaken to justify a review and reconciliation by de Leeuw (1971). The individual studies reviewed there had derived a variety of income elasticities, ranging from 0.6 to 1.3, using a variety of specifications. Several important sources of this variation were identified by de Leeuw. First, de Leeuw noted that elasticity estimates were higher where permanent replaced current income specifications. It was argued that, in the current income specifications, transitory 'losers' of income would not reduce housing consumption and transitory 'gainers' would not raise long-term housing expenditures. As a result, whilst observed or actual income varied, housing expenditures did not. Consequently there was a downward bias in observed elasticities. This bias could be removed either by grouping data, which would (by assumption) cancel out transitory gains and losses, or by relating housing expenditure to total household expenditure (Muth 1960; Vipond and Walker 1972). With these procedures, de Leeuw demonstrated that permanent income elasticity estimates were higher. Subsequent studies (Carliner 1973; Kain and Quigley 1975) which attempt to estimate permanent income for the individual household, hence avoiding grouping, have produced elasticity estimates of a lower value than those observed from grouped data. However, these individually based permanent income specifications still generate higher elasticities than those pertaining to current incomes.

Several other sources of difference were noted by de Leeuw. He argued that estimates for rental housing lay consistently below owned housing estimates and he noted that the focus of survey data on moving households produced an upward bias in elasticity estimates. For the latter group respond more, or more rapidly, to rises in income. Taking all these differences into account, de Leeuw argued that the received studies could be reconciled to yield an income elasticity of between 0.8 and 1 for owned housing.

Unfortunately existing British studies have not been similarly reviewed and reconciled. Although they appeared somewhat later than the articles reviewed by de Leeuw, British studies have used generally similar techniques and also concentrated on moving households. Again, permanent elasticity estimate values have been higher than for current incomes.

A low estimate, of 0.4–0.6, was obtained by Vipond and Walker (1972) from Family Expenditure Survey data. Other studies of national or local building society data have generated higher elasticities. For instance, for somewhat dated (1961) data Wilkinson estimated an elasticity for owned housing of 0.81 for current income and 1.53 for permanent income (Wilkinson 1973). Byatt *et al*. (1973) established a permanent income elasticity lying between 0.75 and 1.25 for owners and 0.6 for renters.

Price specification improvements and simple characteristics. The developments discussed in this section have reflected the introduction of hedonic price techniques into housing demand studies and, as a result, they have been largely North American. Of course scepticism regarding the use of hedonic prices must also be reflected in a concern for their use in this area of research.

The first application of the hedonic technique to improving income elasticity estimates was to identify price variations for housing attributes. In estimating a true income elasticity, as opposed to an outlay or expenditure elasticity, it is important to assess whether variations in observed housing consumption reflect income differences across households or variations in prices of housing services across houses. For instance (Straszheim 1975; King 1976) analysts desire to establish how an attribute's implicit price will vary over a housing market. This is usually accomplished by assuming that the implicit prices of particular attributes vary smoothly in the housing market, usually around employment centres. The empirical validity of this assumption is questionable and it is interesting to compare the limited claims made for this technique by Straszheim, who asserts that it is primarily pedagogic, with those of Kirwan and Ball who assert a much stronger interpretation of similar results for the Bristol housing market (Kirwan and Ball 1977).

The proliferation of studies with different implicit price assumptions prompted Polinsky (1977) to review critically studies of income elasticities in urban housing markets and to attempt their reconciliation. Polinsky's study has already been succinctly paraphrased by Quigley (1978). Quigley asserts:

Part of the reconciliation reflects 'standard' econometric problems, the particular specification and measurement of housing prices relative to the prices of other goods employed in various studies. In part, however, the reconciliation emphasises theoretical issues in housing markets – the inherent jointness in the housing consumption and location decision and the meaning of housing 'prices', between as well as within markets. Polinsky's analysis considers the effect of specification errors upon price and income elasticity estimates arising: (a) from samples of individual households within a housing market; (b) from samples of individual households drawn from several housing markets; and (c) from averaged data drawn from several housing markets. The theory of residential location suggests that higher-income households will consume more housing and will locate where housing prices are lower within a housing market. On the other hand, higher-income households are more likely to live in cities with higher average incomes and housing prices. Thus:

1. If housing demand is price inelastic, estimates of income elasticities obtained from the bivariate regression of housing expenditure on income in sample 'a' will be biased downwards (since housing expenditures will fall as price decreases with distance and higher-income households will choose more distant locations).

2. Estimates of income elasticity obtained from the bivariate regression on sample 'b' will also be biased, the intra-city residential location pattern imparting a downward bias, but this time reduced by the magnitude of the inter-market effect (i.e., the positive bias imparted, assuming price inelasticity, by neglecting the positive relationship, on average, between income and housing prices across cities).

3. Similarly, if a regression is estimated for sample 'b' between housing expenditures, income and some average metropolitan price index (e.g., from BLS budget data), the downward bias in the estimated income elasticity is larger (since the average price term holds the inter-market effect constant to the extent that across cities, incomes and prices are correlated). Of course, if prices and incomes are perfectly correlated (completely uncorrelated) the bias is equivalent to case 1 (case 2).

4. Finally, in the case 3 regression above, the estimated price elasticity based upon the average prices is, in general, biased upwards.

The reconciliations pursued by Polinsky suggest that the income elasticity of demand estimated from models with improved income and price specifications will fall in the range of 0.7 to 0.9. This range lies slightly below that suggested by de Leeuw. However, this may reflect a variety of causes. For instance, Polinsky's assumptions regarding spatial price variations may not be universally relevant or it is possible that the income elasticity of demand for housing, as measured in cross-section studies, actually is falling over time. In a recent study, Polinsky's price specification improvements did not improve elasticity estimates and the observed range fell below that suggested by Polinsky (Stegman and Sumka 1978).

The second main use of hedonic techniques has been to break down total house prices into expenditures on specific attributes. The analysis of individual attributes of housing was, prior to this development, restricted to studies of property size and quality (David 1962; Wilkinson 1973). It is intuitively plausible that since housing attributes satisfy quite different wants ranging from basic shelter to sophisticated interior decoration, that characteristics will have a different price and income elasticity of demand from each other. A series of North American studies have begun to examine individual attribute elasticities. The income effects on demand for living space, neighbourhood and housing quality (and for different racial groups) were analysed by Kain and Quigley (1975) and Straszheim similarly investigated the demand for tenure type, house size, lot size and age of structure. Straszheim found that average income elasticity of demand was 0.46, 0.26, and 0.12 for total expenditure, lot size and number of rooms respectively. Further studies by King (1976) produced somewhat higher elasticities for site and interior space (0.54 and 0.64 respectively) and with the interior space elasticity exceeding lot size. The study by King also indicated very high elasticities for improved structural features and faculties (2.04) and for interior and exterior quality (1.72). British studies of quality and size have produced disparate estimates for house floor area. Estimates range between 0.24 (Ball and Kirwan 1977) and 0.82 (Wilkinson 1973). The overall elasticity estimated by Kirwan and Ball was in the range of 0.7 for all purchasers, and between 0.2 and 0.3 for new entrant purchasers. A recent cross-section study, which is discussed below, for new entrants in Glasgow produced, depending on specification selected, a range of estimates from 0.25 to 1.15 (Maclennan and Wood 1980b). An even wider assessment of attribute elasticities, (Diamond 1978) generated elasticities in excess of 2 for access attributes and for spaces in neighbourhoods with low crime rates and a negative elasticity was generated for topographical features (hilliness).

These recent developments in estimating income elasticities are interesting and helpful in formulating housing models and policies. But there are still difficulties to be faced if the hedonic technique cannot be sensibly applied and if the market is subject to frictions in disequilibria. In a recent analysis of the relationship between housing expenditure and income, Maclennan and Wood (1980b) attempted to control for a number of factors usually omitted from such estimates. The house price variable was re-specified to allow for different mortgage sizes, rates of interest and tax allowances which were non-linearly related to income levels. In addition structural improvements and property tailoring undertaken within six months of entry to a house were discounted into the price term. Further travel to work costs and frictional entry and search costs were included in the expenditure term. On the income side of the equation, the explanatory variables commonly included such as income, occupational status were supplemented by crude proxies for liquid wealth and asset demand factors. In addition, the sample of home buyers was subdivided into individuals who were financially rationed by building societies or other lenders and a second group who did not fully utilise their borrowing capacity. This subdivision indicated a concern that observed housing expenditure patterns reflected building society lending rules rather than purchaser preferences. The detailed results are presented elsewhere (Maclennan and Wood 1980b) but re-specification produced two broad conclusions. First,⸱the rationed sample had a significantly lower elasticity than the non-rationed, suggesting that cross-section studies may be under-identified if they exclude financing concerns. Second, re-specification of price and explanatory variables raised estimated elasticities on outlays from 0.25 to 0.51 for the rationed group and from 0.47 to 1.15 for the non-rationed group. The authors concluded with a negative assessment of the theoretical and empirical usefulness of aggregate expenditure studies which ignore disequilibrium or frictional factors and expressed surprise, not at the diversity of results generated by such studies but rather at their apparent similarity over space and time.

Price elasticity estimates
The determination of price elasticities of demand for housing relies, in aggregate or for individual attributes, on hedonic price identification. Several of the studies discussed above have also generated price elasticities often lying in the range of -0.6 to -0.8, and with price elasticities for site size somewhat larger (-0.8 to -1.09) in relation to quality and interior space attributes (-0.15 to -0.25) (King 1976; Straszheim 1975; Kirwan and Ball 1977).

Thus in aggregate terms, housing demand studies have suggested that the demand for housing is mildly inelastic with respect to both price and income changes and that differences in estimates from Britain and the United States should not be overemphasised on current evidence.

Other influences on demand
Although the empirical evidence is less systematically developed than for price and income effects, cross-section studies have generally examined the effect of household size, life-cycle stage and race on housing expenditure. Household size and life-cycle effects have been established to have a clear effect on housing expenditure (Straszheim 1975; Kirwan and Ball 1977) but the effects of race are still open to debate (MacDonald 1979).

Additional approaches to assessing housing preferences

Most economic analysts of the housing system have pursued an understanding of housing choices by the application of revealed preference models to observed market outcomes. More direct attempts to establish household preferences by interview techniques have been viewed as non-rigorous, hypothetical and worthy of immediate rejection. However, since some reservations have been expressed regarding standard techniques of demand assessment it is pertinent to review what 'preference' studies may reveal. In particular interview studies eliciting attitudinal responses to different housing and neighbourhood attributes could help in formulating hedonic price functions (Onibokun 1973). Further, if housing market search processes are as important as is suggested in the subsequent chapter, 'preference' studies could be used to reveal housing choice 'aspiration sets' which help explain the pattern and costs of search adjustment (Maclennan and Williams 1980).

It is only 'behavioural' models of residential selection and movement that have tended to stress the significance of directly assessing locational and neighbourhood preferences (Quigley and Weinberg 1977). These 'behavioural' models have stimulated research into residential preferences the bulk of which has been undertaken by urban planners and urban geographers, who utilise mental map and area preference studies. The latter are no more than an interview application of hypothetical methods of demand measurement to one dimension of the urban housing market. The studies generally proceed by selecting a large number of individuals to rank a set of named areas in order of preference. Factor analysis is then applied to identify groups of like individuals; variation in ranking over these groups is then related to such factors as age, local experience or spatial information of respondents.

In so far as these studies are recognised as a method of testing the hypothesis that information will influence the ranking of named areas, there can be few objections. However, it is inappropriate and misleading to interpret the hypothetical interviewee rankings 'hyporanks' as area preferences. This is a consequence of using methods of preference analysis which are economically non-rigorous and ambiguous and thus inadequate in economic terms.

To show this clearly it is necessary to examine the strict meaning of the terms choice and preference in economic usage. Preferences relate to the concept of underlying tastes which exist *independently* of constraints and which are formalised within economic analysis in the form of a utility function. As such, preferences are conceptually distinct from choices which are the outcome of the interaction of tastes and constraints. In order to interpret 'hyporanks' as preferences the former must clearly be elicited independently of perceived constraints.

There are three major methodological objections to the use of mental map and area preference studies for the identification of housing preferences.
1. The problem of defining points or areas in terms meaningful to interviewees.

2. The behavioural realism of the ranking process and the differential ability of individuals to make any ranking.
3. The interpretation of choice criteria and the influence of non-informational constraints on 'hyporanks'.

Problems of areal definition

Of relevance here are two conditions which must hold if 'hyporanks' are to be correctly interpreted as preferences; first, the elements of the relevant urban area be clearly defined and second, individuals have an equal ability to assign identical areas of urban space to a particular place name. Within the simple consumer choice model of economic theory this is analogous to the assumptions made that each point in the consumption set represents a unique commodity bundle, and that all consumers either have identical perceptions with respect to the elements of the consumption set or have perfect information on consumption possibilities. As stressed earlier in this chapter the spatially dispersed nature of residential areas, their multi-dimensional nature and the fact that in general households only rarely enter the housing market give us sufficient *a priori* reason to believe that these conditions will not even approximately hold.

Behavioural realism in the ranking process

Though mental mapping and urban perception studies have the avowed aim of introducing behavioural realism into analysis of urban housing markets, the actual survey procedure employed in many preference studies completely violates any assumption of limited cognitive capacity of interviewees. By asking individuals to evaluate and rank a very large set of urban areas or neighbourhoods (normally 25–40), 'hyporank' studies are emulating the equally unrealistic assumption (in the housing market context) of the simple consumer choice model that all individuals have a *complete* and *rational* preference ordering defined over consumption space. To expect individuals to rank 25–40 areas, in terms of several residential criteria, and further to expect consistent and rational ordering is to pose insurmountable demands on human cognitive capacity. In a study of the furnished rental sector in the City of Glasgow, of 288 representative students who were asked to rank up to 9 areas, 37.8 per cent considered themselves unable to offer a single 'hyporank' (Maclennan 1977b). This suggests that the orderings of conventional mental map and residential preference studies do not have any real economic meaning, the relevant areas being merely rearranged as a logical exercise rather than carefully ranked.

The interpretation of choice criteria and the influence of non-informational constraints on 'hyporanks'

The contention herein is that the hypothetical nature of the method-

56

ology employed prevents interpretation of 'hyporanks' as preferences; not faced by the harsh realities of the market situation, where preferences are revealed by choices made with respect to specified and variable constraints (income, relative prices, information, *etc.*), 'hyporanks' and ranking criteria are conceived with respect to a perceived set of constraints which the individual takes as given. Maclennan's sample results reveal that 'hyporanks' and stated criteria vary with both perceived real financial constraints and hypothetical financial constraints. It is also worth noting that perceptions with respect to other forms of non-informational constraint are also likely to influence 'hyporanks'. First, if residential area preferences are not strongly separable from all other housing attributes and commodities, then 'hyporanks' and stated criteria will vary according to the aspired consumption patterns of individuals; second, if preferences are price dependent (the snob hypothesis) then the perceived rent and price gradients defined over the relevant urban area will be an important factor; lastly, perceived supply constraints may also be an influence. Maclennan found that the propensity of areas to be included at particular levels in the 'hyporank' structure was positively related to the furnished rental supply capacity of an area, the latter being the tenure form chosen by the vast majority of students.

If, as suggested, 'hyporanks' are not preference orderings economically defined, can there be any worthwhile place for this methodology in the microeconomic research of urban housing markets? On a more optimistic note, area preference studies could play a role in models of housing choice which stress the role of imperfect information and housing market research. As the development of labour economics has shown, behavioural and neoclassical economic models are not irreconcilable, particularly when allowance is made within constraints for imperfect information, uncertainty, search costs, *etc.*

It was noted earlier that expectations and perceptions regarding the nature of areas and the constraints facing an individual are crucial in determining 'hyporanks'. It is clear that in two applied studies of housing market choice processes 'hyporanks' were really defining an aspiration subset of the whole area, which could quite conceivably form the basis for housing search procedures (Maclennan 1977b; Maclennan 1979a; Maclennan and Wood 1980c). In a world of imperfect information and uncertainty initial perceptions of constraints and preferences are collapsed into aspirations whose empirical counterpart are 'hyporanks'; search procedures will lead to a more detailed knowledge of both constraints and preferences and thus revision of aspiration levels. 'Hyporanks' have economic meaning with this search adjustment framework.

Conclusion

When the assumption which has been maintained throughout this chapter, that housing markets clear instantaneously and in equilibrium is relaxed it is apparent that techniques of analysis to supplement conventional economic models may be required. Indeed the same considerations may call into question the adequacy of neoclassical demand analysis as a framework for housing choice research and thus imply that income and price elasticity estimates are not an adequate set of parameters for describing or predicting housing choices.

3 An expanded framework for the analysis of housing choice and demand

Problems of modelling housing choice

The general thrust of the previous chapter has been to analyse and criticise particular economic models of the urban housing market. However, each model has been evaluated as not being a generally applicable theory of housing choice and demand. With respect to the access-space model it was argued (Ch. 1) that whilst it may act as a fruitful paradigm for the equilibrium analysis of residential spatial structure, the model makes rather specific and empirically unjustifiable assumptions regarding the objects and processes of housing choice. In turn, the filtering model was evaluated as being a series of specific, inductively based hypotheses which may have applicability in some locations and periods but which cannot serve as a general model of urban housing demand or housing market dynamics. Standard equilibrium micro-economic models for demand analysis have been transferred with amendments for housing durability and complexity to the urban housing context.

It was suggested in conclusion to Chapter 2 that a continuing commitment to the assumptions of optimising behaviour in simple competitive markets which are frictionless and in equilibrium, results in housing demand theory remaining an unconvincing framework for the theoretical and policy analysis of particular housing market phenomena. This doubt arises for, at least, three main reasons. First, there is empirical evidence to indicate that neither consumers nor markets behave in accordance with the assumptions of the simple neoclassical model. Second, even with this qualification, the approximate estimates from conventional demand analysis could still be useful guides for formulating the broad direction of policy. But hedonic price and income elasticities are now being adduced in evidence regarding sensitive issues requiring relatively precise answers. For instance they are applied to such questions as the potential compensation for environment damage, the identification of submarkets, or whether blacks pay more for housing services. Third, it is increasingly realised that such models ignore housing market processes. This is a critical omission because there are some housing market problems which are process related. For instance racial or sexual discrimination, which are notoriously difficult to identify from the analysis of observed choices, may occur in the housing choice process and, more generally, waiting or searching for housing may constitute a housing problem worthy of policy action. Thus, instead of interpreting housing outcomes according to prior theoretical assumptions regarding housing market process, the market clearing process, and its effect on choice outcomes, should be a focus of applied economic research.

The housing market – some likely features

There are several features of the housing market and housing as a commodity which suggest that the market clearing mechanism will not conform to simple Marshallian or Walrasian assumptions. Such salient features (1 – 7) are listed below.

1. Individuals transact in the housing market infrequently. Whilst non-moving households may acquire a broad, continuous stream of housing market information, from the mass media or friends transacting in the market, the specific information required for purchase will only accrue with purposive search. The average household transacts in the market only once every seven years in Britain. More rapid mobility rates are only commonplace in the furnished rental sector and for the early life-cycle stages of the household. As a result the quality of information stored in the individual's memory is likely to decay over time. That is, there is a 'forgetting' curve.

2. The problem of consumer memory loss is compounded by changes in the housing market in the non-moving period. Even if the broad quality, neighbourhood, locational and relative price characteristics of the market remain constant over time, in any market search period the household is likely to face a random draw of vacancies from the existing stock. Thus, property characteristics, prices, and vacancy rates may change over different market periods. That is, the housing market renders specific, detailed information redundant. For instance, in the privately rented sector the probability of finding a vacancy, of a given type in a particular area, may change on a daily basis (Maclennan 1979a), and in the owner-occupied sector recent British experience (in 1973 and 1978) has shown that house prices may rise by 10 – 15 per cent in a three month period and over such a period relative prices within a single housing market may become distorted across submarkets.

Further, with larger periods of non-transaction, the dynamics of the housing market may alter the quality, neighbourhood characteristics, relative accessibility and relative prices of large areas of the housing stock. This tendency to make historical information redundant will be reinforced where market change occurs via disequilibrium processes. Thus, the rapid redundancy of price and availability information in the housing market combined with the infrequency of purchase or movement will generally result in potential movers having imperfect information.

3. Imperfect information and the possibility of making a 'false' trade need not, however, result in a search process. However, since housing is the major act of consumption and investment good purchase for most households a sub-optimal purchase may result in severe losses of consumer satisfaction or household assets. The latter cannot be redeemed by instant removal although subsequent movement could adapt consumption levels. But the search and financial costs of effecting a purchase, for legal fees, realtors or removal costs, are likely to make recontracting and movement expensive. Such costs may range between 5 and 10 per cent of the total price of a house, particularly where movement entails both selling and purchase costs. Thus the consumer will generally wish to evaluate each house prior to purchase.

4. The complexity of housing also exacerbates the problem of evaluation of possible purchases in the housing market. A household may accept a description of an orange or some other simple commodity relayed to them impersonally but the household generally has to view and assess the complexity of each individual housing unit. In addition some of the attributes of the commodity may be complex and difficult for the consumer to assess. For instance assessment of structural stability or likely rate of price appreciation may be sufficiently difficult that the consumer's evaluation may have to be enhanced by the assessment of 'experts' such as surveyors or building societies or estate agents. This aspect of housing market search implies that households can, given their imperfect information, be subject to influence, even manipulation, by housing market professionals. At the extreme such institutions may shape households' tastes and choices.

5. The burden of housing evaluation is exacerbated by the spatially dispersed nature of housing vacancies. Particularly in larger urban housing markets, the spatial separation of purchasing opportunities adds to the time, travel and psychic costs of housing search.

6. The house purchase process requires individuals not only to evaluate dispersed housing offers and to successfully pursue (in the owned sector) a search for loan finance but it also necessitates the placements of bids. The actual form of the housing market transaction may vary over space and time. For instance buyers may personally respond to a fixed price offer of sale (particularly in a buyers' market) or they may enter a direct bargaining process with the seller. If such bargains are agreed they may be legally binding or they may be informal. It is the

latter characteristic of the English pricing system that gives rise to gazumping when buyers or sellers renege on non-binding contracts. In the Scottish system sales generally take place by presenting sealed bids to the seller's agent, with the latter usually accepting the highest bid. Open auctions of housing are now uncommon. Thus, the generally prevailing systems of selling housing, and its associated search effort conform neither to a well-behaved Marshallian market nor a Walrasian auction.

All these search and bidding processes associated with transacting in the housing market generate frictions but they may remain relatively constant over time if the housing market evolves in a stable fashion. But they will be exaggerated and assume greater significance if a seventh likely characteristic pertains in the market. That is, market disequilibrium may be commonplace.

7. The fixity of the secondhand housing stock and its relatively slow rate of turnover (partly related to recontracting costs) is likely to mean that submarket demands may change more rapidly than supply. As a result disequilibrium may be pervasive and it will be exacerbated by the asset and peer group price effects alluded to in Chapter 2. Further, lagged new supply completions and the possibility of disequilibrium in the market for housing finance are all likely to contribute to housing market instability.

In this chapter there is an attempt to provide a framework for analysing such important operational characteristics of the housing market. Two elements of this approach are critical. First, it is essential to develop a broader conception of equilibrium relevant to the housing market and, second, a research framework for analysing the process of housing choice is required.

An appropriate concept of equilibrium

The particularly important characteristic of housing market models is that they are beset by the traditions and methods of equilibrium analysis. Indeed, faced with a newly developing field of interest in economics, it is not surprising that the analyst may resort to the use of the established theoretical framework. Thus, in the housing context, in models of tenure choice, income elasticities or in the access-space model a state of long-run competitive equilibrium is assumed to exist. It is hardly novel to challenge the use of this fundamental assumption in housing economics. The case against the assumption has been strongly and succinctly presented by Whitehead and Odling-Smee:

> The concept of equilibrium in the conventional sense is particularly inappropriate in the urban housing market because such factors as transactions costs and information costs are of more than usual importance. Economic models of urban housing will yield satisfactory

predictions of real world phenomena only if they take such factors into account (Whitehead and Odling-Smee 1975).

Quite clearly, substantive issues for housing market theory and policy slip into the yawning crevices on the 'ice covered terrain of the Walrasian economy' (Hahn 1973).

However, this dismissal of the possibility of housing market equilibrium is perhaps too strong and it is rooted in a restriction of the use of the term 'equilibrium' to describe the stable states of competitive neoclassical analysis. Alternative concepts of equilibrium can be developed which do not imply the existence of perfect economic order and the absence of market frictions. It is, therefore, important to define what is meant by equilibrium and here it is appropriate to consider an alternative definition proposed by Hahn. He suggests that a state of equilibrium can be defined to exist when the behaviour of economic agents becomes repetitive. That is, when individual agents are no longer learning in the market or revising plans or intentions (Hahn 1973). The traditional notion of housing market equilibrium may be too narrow for applied analysis because it assumes that rational plans and feasible actions are instantly reconciled and there is no protracted sequence of market learning and plan revision. Hahn argues that it is

> reasonable to require of our equilibrium notion that it should reflect the
> sequential character of our actual economies, [and that] this in turn
> requires that information processes and costs, transactions and
> transaction cost and also expectations and uncertainty be explicitly and
> essentially included in the equilibrium notion. [Essentially] it will be a
> condition of the agent being in equilibrium that he is not learning (Hahn
> 1973: 12).

The outline of the salient characteristics of the housing market given above suggests that individual learning and plan revision will be a characteristic of consumer behaviour in the housing system.

But will disequilibrium be characteristic of the system at a more aggregative level and over a period of comparable episodes? The notion of individual equilibrium advanced by Hahn can be applied to the more aggregative market level. At any point in time information stored will be decaying, new price and vacancy signals will be generated and there will be a flow of more or less well-informed buyers and sellers into and out of the market. If these flows remain constant then the expected values of search effort and plan revision will remain constant for the market as a whole. That is, the form and length of the equilibrating sequence will not change from period to period. Thus the market, even with its informational imperfections, can be said to be in a state of balance or equilibrium. This notion or state of equilibrium would be reflected in a set of structurally stable equations describing successive periods.

In the housing market with housing stock decay, income growth, changing population structures, *etc.*, the underlying economic environment is constantly changing, and this may be the relevant context for many important housing market problems such as the 'arbitrage' process discussed above or house price inflation or new supply provision. In such cases market signals and sequences will change and a state of disequilibrium may be defined to exist until new constancies are established. Where underlying market parameters are subject to change what has to be established is the nature of the learning, information seeking, plan revision and consumption adjustment strategies of housing market participants. If these processes remain stable, or change in a predictable fashion then Hahn's more widely defined equilibrium notion may still be useful in a dynamic context. This broader approach to equilibrium has two implications. First, the competitive equilibrium models remain as a special case, there is no need to vilify them or use them as straw men. Second, the wider definition of equilibrium is ripe for empirical and theoretical development, and not just in housing economics.

An alternative approach to housing choice

Although Whitehead and Odling-Smee were perhaps too general and unspecific in their attack on the notion of equilibrium analysis in the housing market, it is also the case that they have accurately identified appropriate lines of development. The period since the publication of the Whitehead/Odling-Smee critique has not, however, been marked by the appearance of extensive theoretical and empirical research stressing information and adjustment processes in local housing markets. Rather, as indicated in the previous chapters, over this period the theoretical framework for urban analysis has proliferated and strengthened under the umbrella heading of the 'New Urban Economics'. This framework could be labelled 'old growth economics' (with subscript (*s*) replacing subscript (*t*)), but more kindly it may be regarded as a rigorous theoretical expansion of the von Thunen/Alonso model. Theoretical and empirical analysis of the housing market is still dominated by the access-space model – old or new, simple or complex. The inadequacy of the equilibrium assumption, traditionally defined, may be obvious but the alternative is apparently not.

In this chapter, it is intended to outline the first tentative stages of an escape route from the simple neoclassical equilibrium box. Compared with the grand elegance of Arrow-Debreu equilibrium theory, the approach may seem, at first sight, somewhat piecemeal and non-rigorous. The approach is drawn generally from the seminal contribution of Hahn and more specifically from two sources which have much in common. These are, first, models of mobility and spatial search behaviour developed in urban geography (Moore 1972; Clark 1980) and, second, the information and adjustment models of the 'new' microeconomics (Phelps *et. al.* 1970; Pissarides 1976). The latter development is particularly important as it abandons the assumption that market analysis is concerned with a simple commodity exchanged in a Walrasian auction. It also emphasises that attention has to be focused on levels of imperfect information and adjustment processes. These are areas of theoretical and empirical research which have 'for long occupied a slum dwelling in economics' (Stigler 1961) and it is, therefore, difficult to identify *a priori* convincing simple models.

Despite Stigler's metaphorical allusion to the housing market, almost all the economic research concerned with market search has been confined to the labour market. During the last twenty years a series of models and empirical tests concerned with information gathering, job-search duration, reservation wages, learning strategies, *etc.*, have been evolved. Although some of the broader concepts and methods of this research have relevance in general to the housing market the detailed emphasis or specification of labour market adjustment models cannot be transferred directly to housing. For instance, in the labour market studies, the spatial structure of the market, the existence of submarkets and commodity or factor complexity have not been accorded the status which they would require in housing studies. In addition, it is usually assumed that the individual has a known probability distribution of likely wage offers and that offers received are storable from search to search. Such assumptions, even if they are valid in the labour market, are not, it is argued below, appropriate in the housing context.

In the long term, the application of a similar paradigm in the housing market may reveal results and insights which would allow a more general set of market models to be developed. But, since it has already taken twenty years to generate a series of widely used labour market models there is an implication that it may take a long period of housing market research before such an approach can produce its own generalisations or empirical regularities. In the meantime, researchers in the field must begin to tackle the problem and not postpone a shift of perspective indefinitely.

It is the contention here that the analysis of housing choice and demand should follow the Marshallian strategy of applying economic principles within a structure of concepts and assumptions which are relevant and general to the problem on hand. Such a strategy wherein the assumptions deemed permissible may vary within sub-parts of the

65

overall discipline has the implication, as suggested in Chapter 1, that general equilibrium models will be difficult, even impossible, to construct. Instead, a series of detailed partial analyses of the urban economy will build up a general and relevant level of understanding which may exceed the understandings derived from general equilibrium models which start with a series of overgeneralised assumptions. Such an emphasis is clearly related to the purpose of this volume, which is to understand the economics of the housing system. Thus a choice of paradigms rather than hypotheses is being discussed. However, at this stage it would be premature to label the framework of choice which is outlined below as being a paradigm of housing choice. A paradigm must consist of a set of well-defined and accepted concepts and research techniques which form a sufficient basis for hypothesis derivation and testing. But housing economic research, apart from the models previously rejected, has historically been so limited in extent that a widely accepted framework is not yet a possibility. Instead, in the remainder of this chapter a possible framework for the economic analysis of housing markets is outlined.

Framework characteristics

The framework proposed has the following characteristics.

(a) The framework is relatively loose and does not make important *a priori* assumptions regarding the objects or processes of choice. Further a specific spatial structure of the housing market is not assumed to exist *a priori* nor is neoclassical equilibrium a necessary component of the conceptual organisation.

(b) The conceptual framework does make some broad assumptions regarding the structure of the housing choice decision.

(c) Whilst the framework can be said to be behavioural in that the decision structure is outlined and in that it allows the relevant objects of choice to be identified no prior assumption is made regarding the behavioural processes by which the stages of the choice decision are linked. The boxes, representing the choice process sequence, are outlined in Fig. 3.1 and may be linked by either optimising neoclassical connections or by sub-optimal or satisficing modes of behaviour. However, the appropriate specification of the structure of the housing choice decision should mean that 'behavioural' and 'neoclassical' models should no longer be seen as polar alternatives but that they tend to converge as the decision structure is appropriately specified.

(d) The direct linkages between individuals and housing market institutions are identified.

(e) To make the framework operational and measurable certain additional conceptual boxes are introduced. For instance the concept of pre-search 'aspiration' is potentially more readily identifiable than the concepts 'preference' and 'constraint'.

The structure of the framework

The framework of housing choice and demand which we now outline is an extension and formalisation of the 'mover-stayer' model which has been widely used in the analysis of population migration, shopping behaviour and labour market analysis, and can be applied to tenure and/or location choice. The focus of the analysis is the individual or the household which is a more detailed level for analysis than the 'representative individual' of standard microeconomic theory.

The decision to enter the market

The sequences of the model can be initiated as follows (see Fig. 3.1). The household is initially assumed to be receiving a given utility or satisfaction in their present dwelling. Each member of the household has a series of activities, requiring inputs of time or resources, which are related to the characteristics of the house, location and neighbourhood. The individuals within the dwelling may not be equally satisfied or dissatisfied with existing housing provision. For a movement to be contemplated either the household as a coalition or the key household decision taker must perceive a minimum threshold of housing dissatisfaction to exist. The impetus to change may accrue over a lengthy period of time as the household may recognise its existing mismatch of housing characteristics and household activities but be precluded from movement by high transfer costs. Equally, when they purchase a dwelling, the level of housing services generated may concur not with the presently desired level of housing services but some future optimum requirement (for instance young childless families moving to larger housing prior to the conception or birth of children). So far this implies the need to develop a theory of household rather than individual decision taking and that household consumption of housing immediately prior to or following household movement does not reflect presently desired optimal levels of housing consumption services.

The decision to actively enter the housing market and evaluate alternative housing opportunities may be 'triggered' by a variety of factors. Entry 'triggers' may be predictable long-term events such as increasing income, change in family size or secular relative price changes across submarkets. Such well-defined trigger factors are reflected in, respectively, studies of the income elasticity of housing demand, life-cycle theories of housing consumption and the filtering model. Less predictable, for the individual, are windfall gains such as inheritances, the advent of undesirable neighbours or accidental changes in family size (increases as well as decreases!).

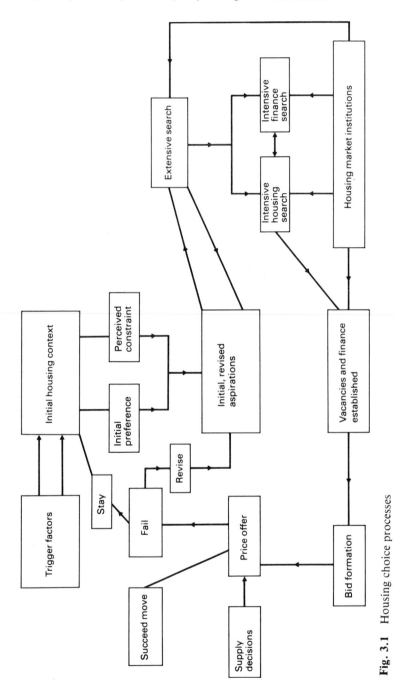

Fig. 3.1 Housing choice processes

Entry points

Apart from instances where perceived changes in the price, quality or availability actually trigger entry the household must select an intended entry point or range. That is, the household decision takers then are required to evaluate perceived alternative houses according to their incomes, other constraints and preferences. However, the processes of making such evaluations are complex in the housing market and we now try to indicate the probable characteristics of this complexity. The household is assumed to have some form of preference function for different attributes of housing. However, the extent, structure and stability of the household utility function cannot be assessed or known *a priori* by the researcher. Households may not, historically, have experienced a wide variety of housing conditions and as a result well-defined preference functions known with certainty may only exist for the household if small changes in income, price or spatial location are being considered. But such small changes may be unlikely to trigger attempted movement. When interurban housing moves are considered then quite clearly newcomers to an urban area will be unlikely to have a meaningful preference ordering over alternative neighbourhoods. Such uncertainty of preference effects could also be important for moves within a large complex urban housing market. It can, therefore, be expected that any housing search process will not only yield housing price, quality and availability information but will also extend the preference function of the household or indeed shift its position. The preference schedule may either be extended or shifted by search activity.

The components and structure of the household utility function, as discussed in relation to hedonic price regressions also cause some problems. Theoretical models have tended to oversimplify the content of the household's utility function — for instance, the emphasis of the access-space model on size and location and the filtering model on 'newness' and social factors. Empirical studies, although disquiet has been expressed in relation to their detailed methodologies and conclusions, have suggested that a variety of structural, locational and neighbourhood characteristics of the house provide satisfaction. The approach, as most theorists realise (MacDonald 1979), which views housing as a complex commodity with various attributes which satisfy quite different wants such as shelter, living space, status, elegance or capital accumulation seems, *a priori*, to be more reasonable than a simple neoclassical model. However, as has been stressed in the preceding chapters, there is no empirical evidence regarding which housing attributes singly or interactively, actually satisfy which wants. Rather than imposing or implicitly assuming the particular form of the utility function *a priori* it should be an important research question to establish which housing attributes are important to households and, further, how such sources of satisfaction vary across different household groups. Proponents of house price studies will respond that this is indeed the objective of their research. However, for the technical reasons outlined above, clearly their objections are not reasonable. Instead, it may be vital that the importance of attributes is identified directly by research rather than inferred from *ex post* market data.

There are three ways in which attempts could be made to make a more satisfactory selection of functional form. First, following Pesaran and Deaton (1978), the differences between functional form and their significance could be ascertained. Second, Doling's method of 'content analysis' could be employed (Doling 1977). He suggests that the important attributes of housing are those which advertisers of property use consistently. This suggestion remains untested. Finally, since the general approach to housing market analysis outlined here emphasises a survey based research strategy, it may be helpful (as indicated in the previous chapter) to ask respondents to rank or attach an importance index to the characteristics of housing which influence their choice process (see Onibokun 1973; Jones 1979a). There still remains a problem of identifying aspiration and preference functions.

The household may also be uninformed on the constraints which will influence the house selection process. At the prior to search stage, the consumers may know their household income but they may be unaware of how lending institutions will use this figure as a basis for purchase decisions. Further, since the house moving process is intermittent and actual selling prices of houses are not always revealed to purchasers then the consumer will be uncertain about the real purchasing power of household income. This uncertainty is compounded for households who are trading up or down within the owner-occupied sector when the selling price of their currently held housing assets has not already been established. Income uncertainty, imperfect knowledge regarding the pattern and level of excess demand, and search cost uncertainty will all influence the house selection and evaluation strategy of the household. It is reasonable to characterise the prior to active search phase of the housing selection process as being concerned with the formation not of choices or preferences but of 'aspirations'. Aspirations can be defined as being targets, on a limited number of objectives, which the household perceives that it can attain. On the basis of partially informed preference orderings and perceived purchasing power the household will form views or aspirations regarding the feasible price range, size, location, neighbourhood, asset appreciation and search cost characteristics of the house which it could move to. If this considered aspiration, which may be equivalent to the so-called 'preferences' discussed on pp 56–7, exceeds present housing satisfaction then an active search process will commence. In a world of perfect information and centralised Walrasian auctions there is no need for the concept of aspiration, as preference and constraint immediately interact, to form choices. But the Walrasian bidders live in the market, not houses.

This concept of aspiration brings us directly to a consideration of the search and adjustment processes which operate in clearing the housing market.

The housing search process

The above reasons represent a convincing argument for including search processes and their related costs in a model of housing choice. In addition, it should be emphasised that, in the owned market, the household is pursuing interdependent search processes for housing and housing finance. However, in the absence of a wide basis of empirical research, it is difficult to generalise about the major characteristics of the housing search process. Instead a tentative outline, based on limited empirical backing, is now suggested. The search process can, conceptually, be divided into at least three distinct phases (Fig. 3.1). In the stage of initial aspiration formation, which predates active search, the individual has a changing stock of imperfect information of a generalised nature about the housing markets which stems from the media etc. In addition, individuals with previous experience in the housing market will have a stored set of facts and 'models' regarding the operation of the housing market. For instance, newcomers to a local housing market with experience elsewhere will have a conceptual notion of the operation of the housing market based on experience elsewhere. At the same time, and especially just prior to the active search period, the individual will receive an array of relatively 'noisy' messages regarding the local housing system. For instance, casual information may be passively gathered regarding local housing on the journey to work, in discussions with friends or relatives or from newspapers and local media. This is an important phase of the housing choice process which is extremely difficult to research convincingly. The second phase of search is denoted by the onset of considered scrutiny of different alternatives. In this phase of search the individual will not search randomly but rather order the pattern of search in relation to broadly defined initial aspirations and perceived constraints. As in the labour market (Rees 1966) information can be consciously gathered from a variety of sources and examination of properties, prices and areas undertaken (Maclennan 1979b). It is in this phase of search that aspirations and perceived constraints first begin to be reconciled with probably realistic choices, that is the aspiration set is narrowed or expanded to include only apparently feasible alternatives.

But there may be theoretical problems in modelling this phase of search precisely. For in the earliest searches households, particularly

71

those who are not risk averse, may pursue possibilities rather than probabilities (Maclennan and Wood 1980c). This implies that households in the course of the search process may use different forms of behaviour − that is, their rationale in assessing search plans may change. Aspirations may be revised and feasibility established with the assistance of selling agents within the system such as estate agents, solicitors or financing agents. The extent to which such institutions provide advice regarding prices, expected prices and 'area' quality may be important influences which condition the search pattern of the individual. Given the characteristics of the housing market listed above, the influence of institutions on individual choices may be extremely important and these are discussed in relation to 'red-lining' in Chapter 5.

The third phase of the search process, detailed intensive evaluation of specific properties within selected price ranges or submarkets, may not always be distinguishable in practice from phase two. However, conceptually it may be viewed as the evaluative phase when a small number of properties are examined in depth with a view to offering a bid. The controlling role of the financing and uncertainty reducing institutions in the housing market are likely to be at their most significant in this phase of housing search. This phase is akin, in the owner-occupied sector, to individuals paying to have houses surveyed and convincing lending institutions to provide funds to the specific property in question. In most instances it could be expected that individuals undertaking this search phase will not further revise aspirations but instead move to the bid formation process. In making this search process the household may become aware of the effectiveness and costs of using particular information networks. The pattern of networks may vary across individuals and change with shifts in excess demand or the duration of the search process. Information acquisition strategies have been examined in housing and labour markets and their significance has been empirically confirmed (Rees 1966; Mackay and Reid 1972; Maclennan 1977b). But the supply of housing market information, and its transmission throughout the market, are only now being researched. Some tentative results (Clark and Smith 1980) indicate that the level and type of information (on price, location, quality, *etc.*) varies with market conditions. Information supply and demand vary with the state of the market. Apart from direct information acquisition costs, the household will incur costs of foregone time and movement expenses in visiting houses. Of course these costs will also depend on the market conditions prevailing but it would be wrong to assume that they are always insignificant.

Further, and substantial, search costs are likely to arise in forming and placing a price bid. As indicated above the bid formation process in the housing market is, once again, subject to substantial institutional influences which vary across space, time and sectors. An open auction system would obviate the difficulties of protracted gazumping experienced in England or the price formation problems of the closed bid system often used by Scottish solicitors. In the latter system the seller may have a reservation price, but the bidder is totally uncertain about the sealed bids of competing potential buyers and thus the purchaser, again on the basis of advice or past experience, has to estimate rather than observe the degree of excess demand for a specific house. Undoubtedly the bidder, under both the above systems, will consider the potential costs of failing to purchase the house with a bid. The expectation of further search costs, the prospect of further short-run rapid rises in house prices and fears regarding future credit availability may all probably tend to inflate the size of a bid. It is hardly surprising that the housing market tends to be rapidly inflationary in periods of expansion of loan finance. 'Animal spirits', in the housing sector, almost always generate short-run real rises in house prices. If the bid is a failure then there may be, as at earlier stages in the search process, a marked revision in aspiration levels and resultant search activity. This arises for several reasons. First, new price expectations or beliefs may be revealed by the bidding process or expected real search cost may rise and the information characteristics of the system may alter, even in the period taken to form and offer a particular bid.

It is of considerable importance in the analysis of the housing market to understand how individuals acquire new information but also to comprehend how this information is used to revise housing consumption strategies. In a simple market, when price bids fail to effect a trade then the consumer may either raise the price bid or purchase less of the relevant commodity. In the housing context, since there are aspirations over the multiple characteristics of housing, the household may adjust price bid, location, neighbourhood, house quality, house size, etc. This complex series of adjustments implies, first, that price signals which would induce new supply of the most preferred bundle of effectively demanded housing may become diffused and, second, that policy analysis requires an understanding of complex adjustment patterns. Further, if the market is in disequilibrium, then this framework indicates that a simple flow of demand conception of the market will be inappropriate. That is, if the market is not cleared, then backlogging may occur with likely rises in search costs and durations (Bowden 1978). Regarding backlogging and dimensions and costs of adjustment in the housing market this discussion has, for ease of exposition, referred to the complex house purchase decision. However, a similar mode of analysis can be used in the private rental markets. The results of such applications are discussed in Chapter 7 for the owned sector and Chapter 8 for rental housing.

In selecting a vacancy and in forming a price bid which it is believed to be acceptable to the seller of housing, the searching consumer provides a direct link with the supply side of the housing system, as indicated in Fig. 3.1. The supply of new housing services is discussed in detail in the following chapter, but the supply of housing is directly and indirectly related to the housing search model outlined above. For instance, the supply price of housing and the flow of supply onto the market may be influenced, not only by the prices offered to suppliers but by the number of searchers flowing through a given area. And of course, for the purchaser who is moving within the housing market, there is also a sale to be made. That is, their overall housing transaction consists of a house purchase, finding finance and finding a purchaser for their own house. It would be revealing to ascertain how this joint search is ordered over space and time and how it is affected by market conditions. For moving owners of housing effective, supply and demand are highly interdependent. By way of example, a household may choose to stay at a particular house rather than move not because they cannot find a competitively priced vacancy elsewhere but because they are unable, or expect to be unable, to sell their existing house at their reservation price within some acceptable time period or limit of seller search costs.

The observed results of a shortage may yield important insights. It is argued, however, that the directions of adjustment and the process of adjustment *per se* are often what are labelled as housing problems – for instance gazumping, repeated bidding, search costs, reduced inter- or intra-sectoral mobility are process related problems. Since the form and extent of housing problems is largely conditioned by the detailed adjustment process we feel that the proposed framework is a more suitable approach to the analysis of housing choice than the standard models.

Conclusion

Quite clearly the scheme for the analysis of housing choice which is outlined above is more detailed and disaggregated than the conventional models of housing choice and demand. To the sceptical reader it may appear to be no more than a set of 'empty economic boxes' which are and will remain unfilled because of the expenses of observing housing market processes. The usefulness of the framework as a conceptual model for applied housing research is yet to be ascertained. However, even at the present stage of development the following arguments can be advanced in its favour.

1. The model lays stress upon directly identifying, via preliminary household studies such as 'preference', importance, 'aspiration' or

household activity pattern analysis, likely arguments in the housing choice set.

2. The model stresses the importance of market processes and indicates the diversity of possible adjustments within the housing sector. It does not assume away the problems of housing market processes.

3. The role of housing market professionals and institutions is allowed for.

4. Although the framework is consumer oriented links are made to the housing supply system and, in particular, the interdependence of secondhand supply and housing demand are emphasised.

5. In addition, the framework can be linked to existing models and measurement techniques. For instance, an acceptance of the neo-classical access-space framework merely requires (Fig. 3.1) that the housing market search and adjustment 'boxes' are excluded. If the full search adjustment model is used, then income or expenditure elasticities can be estimated *ex post* and allowance made for search costs or entry conditions which influence observed expenditure levels. Further, if equilibrium (in the broader Hahn conception) pertains in the market, such frictional influences on housing expenditure parameters may remain stable.

6. The framework's emphasis that individual equilibrium may take some time to obtain, or that overall equilibrium may not pertain, implies that empirical research has to be carefully structured. For instance, there is no longer a simple dichotomy between movers and non-movers in a housing market. At any point in time, particularly for younger or more mobile households, a large proportion of non-movers may be actively seeking to move but are sustaining a protracted search process (Maclennan and Wood 1980a).

There is no doubt that the use of access-space and neoclassical models has contributed insights for housing theory and public policy. But, there are important economic aspects of housing markets which they have not been able to discuss satisfactorily or, more seriously, which they have detracted attention from. It is only by embarking on a long series of widespread and systematic studies of housing choice processes that richer insights, for theory and policy, will be gleaned. The framework outlined here is only one of several possible approaches which minimise the significance of prior deductive assumptions. But it has clear possibilities for development.

4 Supply in the housing system

The preceding two chapters have focused their attention on models of consumer choice in the housing sector. Although this chapter is considerably shorter this emphasis in no way reflects the great significance of the supply of housing. The brevity of the supply section in this book arises from three considerations. First, general housing market characteristics such as disequilibrium, submarket structure and imperfect information have already been discussed and here they are only alluded to in the context of supply decisions. Second, specific aspects of supply decisions in the access-space model and in secondhand housing markets were introduced in Chapters 1 and 3. Finally, at least in relation to the United Kingdom, there are few empirical estimates of supply side parameters available for discussion.

The structure of the argument in the previous chapters was progressed by first discussing relatively simple neoclassical models of consumer demand and then introducing increasing complexity into demand estimation. In this chapter, although the overall objectives and conclusions reached are similar, the structure is reversed. First, the broad operational characteristics of the construction industry and construction firms are outlined and then applied economic attempts to analyse housing supply are discussed. In conclusion, the need for an expanded applied economics of the residential construction and rehabilitation sector is argued.

Housing supply

Definitions

In any economic analysis which is centred upon market systems of provision, price signals play the critical role in reordering the consumption and production plans of consumers and suppliers of products. Thus, in examining the supply side of the housing system the focus of interest rests upon how the flow of housing services supplied in the market will vary with house price changes. That is, in conventional price theory, analysis is concerned with flows of goods or services in the market at a point in time. Accepting, for the moment, a flow related definition of housing supply, it is apparent that the rate at which new supplies enter the market can vary with the new house building completion rate or by raising or lowering the rate of flow of housing services from existing stocks of housing. Thus housing supply, even with this simple definition, is likely to be a complex phenomenon with new suppliers or suppliers from existing stock facing different supply technologies or factor prices. That is, new supply and conversion supply may require separate, but interdependent, analysis. Further, since supply reactions will inevitably reflect decision implementation and construction lags, the time period over which supply adjustments are to be analysed must be considered. The market period, following conventional microeconomic terminology, is by definition that period in which flows remain fixed. The short run allows variable factors of supply production to be varied and in the long run, by definition, all inputs and outputs may change. Thus, the general term 'housing supply' is not particularly helpful and analysis has to be directed to specific supply sectors (new or conversion, *etc.*) over indicated time periods (short run or long run). Although the most satisfactory conceptual model of housing supply probably relates to a model of the flow of housing services from new and previously existing stock at any point in time, it is difficult to envisage how such a flow or flow adjustment model might be specified and tested. More usually supply analysis is undertaken using a stock adjustment model, where the major concern is with the rate of new additions to housing stock, conversions, improvements and, at the other extreme, housing demolitions and depreciation. The stock adjustment models are the dominant, but not sole, concern of this chapter.

The economics of the construction sector

British economists have had a long-standing interest in the residential construction sector. However, this interest has generally been expressed with regard to macroeconomic modelling of the behaviour of the national economy. This concern has been empirical rather than theoretical, and new housing stock adjustment has been the major research interest. Conversion and rehabilitation, flow adjustment and supply adjustments within urban economies have not been subject to systematic economic analysis. The research agenda for the housing supply sector in North America, as is indicated below, has, on the other hand, generated a considerable volume of empirical and theoretical studies of supply in urban housing markets. But in Britain the microeconomic foundations of housing market supply behaviour were seldom, if ever, considered to be of importance *per se*.

Macroeconomic significance

The somewhat simplistic concern with the aggregate demand effects of construction activity is perhaps understandable given the size and (at least historically) cyclical susceptibility of the sector. In 1976, in the United Kingdom, the construction sector produced 15 per cent of gross domestic product and employed an estimated 2.5 m. employees. Housing construction is estimated to contribute about one third of overall construction sector output. Clearly housing construction is an important macroeconomic magnitude and although the macro-economic aspects of the housing market are not the subject of this book, some introductory comments are pertinent.

The construction sector is extremely susceptible to the policy actions of central and local governments. Fiscal restraint, reflected in cuts of or restraints on public expenditure, has usually a rapid effect on the public sector building effort, and generally, in Britain, public and private sector starts move together (Table 4.1). Monetary restraint has generally been reflected in rises in minimum lending rates which have had a pronounced and rapid effect on construction activity because of its almost total dependence upon bank credit to finance construction. These general observations on the size and cyclical characteristics of the construction sector have recently been confirmed for the UK (O'Dea 1977) and they are at variance with patterns observed in the USA (Evans 1969). In the period prior to 1975 the British construction cycle had a pattern significantly different in detail from the series for aggregate capital formation in the economy as a whole, although the sector was generally pro-cyclical. The British construction cycle responds very quickly to decreases in interest rates in the downturn phase, leading the main series by about one year. The series for construction shows relatively high variability around a rising activity trend with marked peaks and troughs.

These fluctuations in housing starts, completion lags and housing completions are indicated in Table 4.1. Quite clearly the late 1970s has been a period of marked recession in residential construction activity, following the record levels of housing output observed earlier in the decade. The sharply cyclical character of the sector reflects the inter-action of economic policy with the detailed production processes and input and decision structures within the sector. At the same time such a pattern of fluctuation and 'stop-go' in output also forms the environ-ment in which construction decision takers must operate and the uncer-tainty generated undoubtedly influences expectations and reactions within the sector. Such influences must be borne in mind as this discus-

Table 4.1 Housing supply in Britain

	Private housing starts (UK)	Local authority housing starts (UK)	Slum clearance E.W. and S.	Values of construction output (£m. current)			Housing repair and maintenance as % of total housing spending	Extended time lag – start completion (GB) pub. (mths) pvte	
				New housing public	New housing private	Housing repair and maintenance			
1965	214,466	188,742	76,200	541	658	484	29	16	0.9
1966	197,241	192,622	83,387	594	652	518	29	16.3	12
1967	237,687	199,923	90,239	670	705	565	30	15.1	12.1
1968	204,768	177,645	90,354	731	782	627	30	15.1	12.3
1969	171,463	156,716	87,080	727	743	639	30	16.3	13
1970	169,154	137,647	85,149	690	737	686	32	16.7	13.7
1971	212,108	122,122	90,611	687	941	765	32	16.8	12
1972	232,190	104,857	84,616	697	1,218	946	33	17.7	11.5
1973	219,847	91,297	80,036	867	1,672	1,279	34	20.2	13
1974	109,604	124,392	55,128	1,122	1,467	1,504	37	20.9	16.4
1975	153,733	139,785	63,044	1,482	1,543	1,658	35	17.9	20.1
1976	158,361	133,663	57,984	1,795	1,798	1,788	33	16.5	17
1977	138,582	96,835	46,518	1,751	1,867	2,106	37	17.7	17.6
1978	161,597	79,519	38,885					19.1	17.7
1979	144,261	57,412	37,036					21.2	17.8

Source: *Housing and Construction Statistics.*

sion shifts to a microeconomic perspective first of the industry then firm levels of disaggregation. This approach emphasises, at least initially, the supply of new housing, but rehabilitation and conversion activities can be subsequently introduced.

The industry level

The construction sector in the British economy has been subject to two recent and comprehensive surveys (Hillebrandt 1974; NEDO 1977). The main characteristics of the industry can be briefly illustrated by updating a concise description offered by Whitehead (1974). The undernoted characteristics of the industry are important.

Industrial structure

The industry has an industrial structure which could be described as being deconcentrated and there are a large number of very small firms. There are some statistical pitfalls in comparing the size structure of the industry at different points in time, but Table 4.2 indicates that this size structure has remained quite stable over the time period 1964–76. However, this scenario of structural stability and low concentration is perhaps less obvious at the level of individual or regional housing markets. For instance, although a regional housing market may contain a variety of firm types such as small local firms, medium sized local firms, branches of national companies and headquarters of building giants (Phillips 1973), the number and range of firms able to respond to local opportunities at a specific time period, taking into account the ongoing commitments of existing firms, may be limited. Thus, an apparently competitive industrial structure may, at the local level, display imperfections in responses. There is also growing evidence that, at least in some British regions, the larger firms are now producing an ever-increasing share of residential construction output even if the number of such firms is now declining.

The statistics presented for the size structure of the industry do not necessarily imply that local housing market supply will be provided by atomistically competitive supply. Neoclassical analysis of housing supply has, as one might expect, considered the ownership structure or concentration characteristics of the industry as being a likely guide to supply behaviour. A deconcentrated pattern of ownership was interpreted as ensuring the safe use of a model of a competitive market immediately adjusting to housing market conditions with perfect information. This equation of market structure and economic behaviour, which is examined in detail below, has historically been used to predict the locations, density and timing of new housing supply.

Rather than adopt this simplistic approach which suppresses problems and uncertainties inherent in the supply process, in this chapter a

Table 4.2 Private construction firms, by size, Great Britain, 1965–78

	1965	1970	1973 A	1973 B	1975	1978
0–1	18,488	20,355	17,785	29,563	28,131	28,551
2–7	38,774	33,118	32,574	43,962	39,079	42,007
8–13	10,581	7,946	8,342	9,311	8,516	9,092
14–24	7,164	5,358	5,853	6,315	5,667	5,712
25–34	2,648	1,982	2,224	2,364	2,058	1,945
35–59	2,798	2,062	2,203	2,298	2,050	1,918
60–79	894	720	707	743	674	620
80–114	790	616	675	697	609	549
115–229	1,040	820	856	872	801	733
300–599	290	233	239	246	234	224
600–1,199	149	132	125	125	127	115
1,200 +	80	78	80	80	71	54
All firms	83,696	73,420	71,663	96,576	88,017	91,520

Source: *Housing and Construction Statistics.*

more detailed examination of housing construction within the firm is pursued in an attempt to develop a reasonable set of generalisations regarding the supply process.

Low productivity growth

The construction sector has low levels and growth rates of labour productivity. It is generally considered that the continued survival of a large number of small construction firms reflects the fact that construction is essentially an on-site activity which must use traditional and specialised labour inputs and materials and which allow few scale economies to emerge in the production process. In some respects the site supervising firm, or general contractor, comes very close to the Coasian (Coase 1937) notion of a firm. That is, Coase perceives the firm to be a decision locus responsible for organising and co-ordinating a large number of contracts for specialised inputs over fixed but varying, production periods (this theme is developed below). Industrialised building, at least in the United Kingdom, had largely been restricted to the public sector. Even within the public sector, industrialised building seldom exceeded more than a fifth of starts or completions in a given period and between 1974 fell from 18.8 per cent of public starts to 4.6 per cent in 1979 (in a considerably reduced volume of public sector starts). Though it is true, however, that in the private sector there is an increasing tendency to substitute inputs which have been produced in off-site situations of potential scale economies, for on-site production. For instance, plasterboard replaces on-site plastering, prehung doors and aluminium window frames reduce on-site joinery inputs, *etc.*

However, the capacity of the construction sector to further develop off-site preparation is largely related to the ability to produce and sell standardised output. Craven (1970) suggests that such adjustment is largely restricted to firms which are already large scale and which build semi-detached and terraced houses on large-scale sites (usually on the suburban fringes of cities). Smaller, more local companies are restricted to producing diversified output on smaller sites.

Sources of finance

Related to this smallness of size and low productivity growth, is the dependence of construction firms on bank finance. This may explain, at least in part, the susceptibility of residential construction to the vagaries of fiscal and monetary policies.

Speculative building

The finance of construction is only one of several factors contributing to the instability of the industry. Most residential construction is speculative. That is, producers generally do not build to order, but instead adjust housing starts and completions in relation to demand conditions and price and cost expectations. When demand is on the downswing firms may lengthen completions lags, by reducing overtime, *etc*, and may quickly reduce starts. For instance in the 1970s, average completions lags for the private housing sector varied from 15–21 months (Table 4.1). Financing arrangements demand this rapid adjustment, and the low fixity of labour inputs enable it. By such rapid adjustments construction firms may lessen or indeed forestall completely price reductions on their speculative output nearing the completion phase. In periods of demand expansion, speculative builders may require to have firm price expectations before raising completion rates and initiating new starts. Since general monetary expansion has a very rapid effect on housing demand (MacAvinchey and Maclennan 1981), it is not surprising that house price rises accompany monetary expansion as the supply response decision is subject to numerous lags.

These are all important characteristics of the housing construction sector. But they are in no way a recent set of phenomena. In an analysis more than two decades ago, Carter (1958) attributed the preponderance of small firms to the 'smallness of jobs', the ease of entry into the sector for craftsmen and the ease of buying specialised services. At the same time he observed that construction was a complex-phased production process in which there were no apparent economies of scale, whereas self-site supervision led to obvious managerial economies. At that time Carter described the construction industry as 'an untidy and shambling giant, with some difficulty in co-ordinating the movement of its limbs so that it may move forward' (Carter 1958: 73). This description still seems apposite. Therefore, although the industrial economics characteristics of the construction sector yield some insights, it is important to consider in more detail the production decision which actually faces a representative construction firm.

The construction firm

It has already been suggested that economic analysis of the construction sector in the UK is extremely limited and this lack of knowledge reflects an inadequate understanding of the basic decision making units within the sector. 'Surprisingly little is known about the way decisions are made in individual firms, or the effect these may have on opportunities for owner occupation' (Murie, Niner and Watson 1976: 149).

In this section it is intended to draw attention to the complexity of the construction process. It is hoped that this detailed view of a construction firm will point out the extreme reductionist thinking which lies behind the simple neoclassical presentation of the building industry as being composed of a series of perfectly competitive firms through which economic 'causes' (house price changes) smoothly trigger supply responses.

Just as the previous chapters have stressed the need for the analysis or adjustment processes in the housing choice decision of household, so this section draws attention to the inherent imperfections and uncertainties of the construction processes which condition the pattern, over time and space, of housing development.

The planning and co-ordination problems which a large-scale housing developer faces – smaller firms may face a smaller range of less acute decisions – are outlined in Fig. 4.1. It is assumed that the firm has some objectives related to profitability or firm growth or relative market share. The specific objectives pursued are not, at this stage, important, but it is assumed that firms are concerned with revenues from sales as well as costs.

Demand assessment

First the firm must have some conception of the demand for housing in a particular area. The likely selling price, the size, style and location of potentially saleable houses must be assessed and it is assumed that the firm will observe the flow of searchers, prices, price inflation rates and vacancies noted in the choice framework. If the firm speculates regarding the future pattern of demand, that is, it starts housing in advance of demand and completes building as demand emerges, then clearly the inflationary effects of expanding housing demand may be minimal. Builders' expectations and attitudes towards risk are clearly important in formulating demand estimates. If construction becomes an increasingly cyclical activity, then builders may become more averse to speculative building. To reduce uncertainty in demand estimates it may

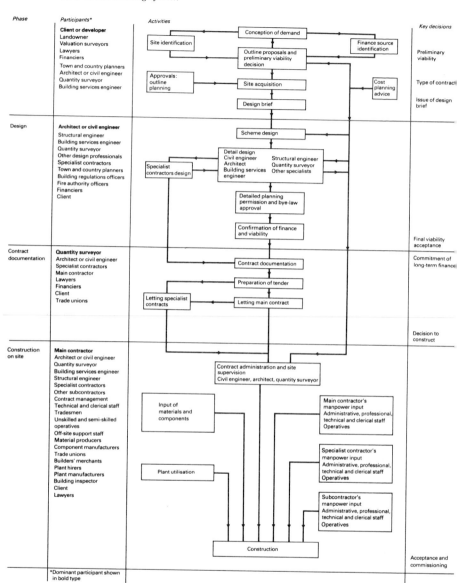

Fig 4.1 Traditional construction process for new building and civil engineering works. Source: *NEDO* 1977: 4–5

The following notes appear at the foot of the figure:

1. This is intended only to demonstrate an outline of the traditional construction process without attempting to detail the many activities, duties and relationships involved. These may be found in other publications such as the RIBA plan of work for design.

2. Many variations are possible on the traditional construction process: – some activities may be omitted, e.g. in private housing where the developer is also the contractor; – the order of activities may be different, e.g. the site may already be owned before the project is conceived; the contract may be let before design is started, for some types of contract.

3. Although the flows between activities are all shown as one-way, many of them will be two-way.

be that builders only react to housing prices which are obvious and sustained. That is, they react following sustained house price inflation, thus imparting an inflationary bias into the housing system. They may also reduce sales uncertainty, as is discussed below, by building house types in locations which cater only for the median preference group, or further, they may sell houses prior to actual construction with some commitment to restrict cost rises in the construction period. There is some evidence that advance sales have become increasingly important in the last decade.

Problems of demand estimation, or likely saleability of supplied construction, may also arise if the firm is contemplating a new style or location of production which radically departs from previous experience. That is 'new products' generate particular problems of project evaluation. Thus, in the United Kingdom context, construction firms have only recently begun to construct smaller new homes in inner city locations. And, in relation to the rehabilitation of older properties, companies have been more willing to compete in government sponsored rehabilitation schemes than through pure private enterprise. Of course, problems of site assembly, clearance costs, *etc.* may have exacerbated the problem of demand assessment in relation to cheaper housing.

Even where the firm is able to identify a clear profit opportunity in the housing system with some certainty there still exists a major decision uncertainty. That is, in a deconcentrated industry, a profit opportunity for one firm may exist for all others. In essence, builders may be uncertain about how competitors will react to generalised profit incentives. This argument has been used by G.B. Richardson (1959) to indicate that models of perfect competition do not contain signals which guide particular firms. The principle seems most appropriate in the multi-firm, small-scale construction sector. If all builders respond to an increase in prices oversupply may result and widespread losses may be generated. Again builders may adapt to this uncertainty by delaying adjustment until price rises reflecting excess demand are widespread or pervasive. Alternatively the growth of larger more concentrated building firms or an increase in control over land supplies, via land-banking, could reduce the difficulties of assessing competitor behaviour and in reducing this form of uncertainty a smoother expansion of output could be obtained. Alternatively some localised form of indicative planning may be required in the industry.

Thus the first planning stage for the construction firm of firm-specific demand estimation is not well understood and has not been researched in Britain. Instead economic models, in Britain and the United States, continue to make naïve or rational expectations assumptions regarding the firm's assessment of housing demand.

Project planning

Once an initial set of demand or sales estimates warrant further investigation the firm has to establish the price and availability of factors of production. Land costs and availability have to be ascertained and the likely future pattern of interest and wage rates established. In addition, since housing development forms a critical part of urban development, planning procedures exist to fashion the size, location and style of developments in a manner consistent with public interest and developments in other sectors of a local economy. Acquiring development permission (Table 4.3) may take some time and other lags frustrate immediate developments.

To reduce the reaction/speculation period, builders may hold a stock of land for which planning permission and designs have already been obtained. Land-banking would be normal practice for construction firms in a secularly growing or decentralising urban housing market. But the full range of decision problems for the firm would occur in rapid growth areas, as for instance in relation to housing development to cater for the oil development areas of North East Britain. Consider a project in such an area. Demand estimates are sufficient to induce development. In the early phases of project planning the construction firm has major activity phases in the capital and markets and has to undertake planning and consultative discussions with private and public sector professionals. At the same time project design may commence and the designs selected are vital as they influence the quality, quantity and phasing of the use of men and materials on the construction site.

At this stage the development and evaluation of the construction firm's plans are particularly dependent upon linkages with the markets for capital and land. The full panoply of problems facing decision takers within construction firms can only be understood by briefly considering linkages to these markets.

Capital for housing construction. Larger building firms may finance new construction projects with share capital or retained earnings. However, the peculiar size structure of the industry, as mentioned above, makes a substantial proportion of it reliant upon bank loan finance as small firms do not have assets for reinvestment. Further, the loans required to finance construction activity are large in relation to builders' assets, such as land and partly built houses. In this respect, the much criticised practice of land-banking by builders may not only allow an early start to construction activity but also reduce problems of raising building finance. Given this dependence on bank finance, which fluctuates rapidly in availability and cost with variations in monetary policy, and also taking account of the problems of speculative building, bankruptcies in the building industry (Wilkinson and Archer 1977) are

Table 4.3 Lags in the construction sector

(a) Characteristic times involved in the various phases of the construction process (years)

	Conceptual phase	Design and contract documentation phase	Construction on site phase
Public sector housing	1–4	1–3	1–4
Private sector housing	$\frac{1}{2}$–6	$\frac{1}{2}$–4	$\frac{1}{2}$ – $1\frac{1}{2}$

(b) Maximum rate of increase possible in material supply

	Stocks	Alterations in rate of working existing capacity		Additions to capacity		
		Production units with spare capacity	Moth-balled plant	Small plants	Large plants	'Planning problems'
Less than 1 month	Temporarily up to 10%	—	—	—	—	—
3 months		Up to 10%*	—	—	—	—
3–12 months		Up to about 30%†	Up to about 30%†	—	—	—
1–2 years				3% or more	—	—
2–3 years					3% or more	—
5 years						3% or more

* Provided that there is adequate spare capacity and skilled staff have been retained.
† Provided that there is adequate spare capacity.
Source: *NEDO*, (1977: 6, 63).

not uncommon in recession phases. Indeed at the time of writing, the use of a high interest rate policy to reduce inflation has resulted in record high levels of firm bankruptcies and record low levels of housing start in the UK and the USA. Indeed there are some remarkable asymmetries in the financing of the supply of and the demand for housing in Britain. The financing of demand, by building societies, is carefully monitored by government and rises in mortgage rates and fluctuations in available funds have prompted government intervention to restrain rising mortgage rates. At the same time, savers are encouraged by tax concessions to deposit loans with building societies (Ch. 5). By way of contrast building firms have to compete for bank finance, and the mortgage rate may often lie (due to 'stickiness' or government intervention) below bank rate and there is no synchronised effort to make supply side funds available. Thus, at least in the last decade in the UK, financial system imperfections have left builders short of costly funds in periods when building society borrowers were faced by a scenario of available funds and relatively low mortgage rates. The implications for house price inflation rates should be apparent.

In the late 1960s one of the major national builders (Wates) quite rightly stressed that a stable supply of new house building required a stable flow of building finance, preferably from large institutional investors, but such finance has not been forthcoming. Wates also stressed that the Rent Acts (see Ch. 8) in the United Kingdom encouraged builders to sell all the houses which they developed. If builders were to take some of their profits in retained houses, these appreciating assets plus their stream of rental payments would ensure that builders had substantial collateral for further developments. At the same time, firms could stabilise construction employment by increasing maintenance on retained properties when demand for new starts and completions was low. Given the desperate straits of the UK housing building sector by the late 1970s these suggestions seem worthy of reconsideration.

The land market and the planning system. In urban economic analysis the land market is ascribed the crucial role in shaping the supply of housing. In the access-space trade-off model (see Ch. 1) spatial variations in land prices are principal determinants of lot size and building density (Evans 1973). In Marxian analyses of the housing system the land market is ascribed an important and complex role in social and economic processes over space and time (Catalano and Massey 1978). Here it is stressed that the land market is only one of several complex subsystems in the environment of the building firm and thus comment on the market is restricted.

Land and land preparation costs form an increasingly important component of new housing costs and prices. Small sample statistics published by the Nationwide Building Society, by region, show the percentage of plot price in selling price as indicated in Table 4.4. More definitive figures for Scotland indicate that this proportion rose from 9.5 per cent in 1971 to 15.7 per cent in 1976. For the UK the DOE land price index (1970 = 100) rose to 300 in 1973, had fallen back to 200 in 1975 and did not begin to rise again until 1977, but had reached an index of 366 by the end of 1979 following a mini-boom in 1978 and 1979.

Table 4.4 Average prices of new property on which the society approved loans in the first quarter of 1977

Region	New properties			
	Average prices (£)	*Change in indices over past year* (%)	*Average values of sites* (£)	*Site values as proportion of price* (%)
London & S. East	16,213	(+10)	3,635	22.4
Southern	15,533	(+9)	3,565	23.0
South Western	12,490	(+9)	2,163	17.3
Midland	13,026	(+13)	2,884	22.1
Eastern	12,841	(+11)	2,611	20.3
North Western	12,679	(+13)	2,373	18.7
North Eastern	11,272	(+11)	1,968	17.5
Scotland	14,625	(+11)	2,144	14.7
Wales	12,692	(+9)	1,981	15.6
Northern Ireland	15,856	(+21)	1,923	12.1
United Kingdom	13,586	(+11)	2,692	19.8

Source: *Nationwide Building Society Occasional Bulletin* 141, April 1977.

Attempts to disentangle the relationships between the earlier land price and house price booms of the 1970s have been somewhat unconvincing. Was there a sudden realisation of landowner monopoly power? Did rises in house prices follow as a consequence from rising land costs or did land prices soar as the result of anticipation of housing development? In the UK these are still open and important research issues. Whatever the order of events, monetary expansion in the UK resulted in speculative rises in land prices, reflecting in part the relatively restricted supply of development land.

Clearly the price elasticity of land supply is generally low but it varies by submarket and housing sector. For instance, in the period 1967–76 land prices in Scotland rose by a factor of 15 in the city areas, by a factor of 5 in the oil regions and by a factor of 3 in other areas. In the period 1976–8 the national land market was in a state of virtual collapse with the volume of transactions and price levels low in comparison to the early 1970s. In part this may be due to land-banking and the DOE estimated that in 1978 builders were hoarding land adequate for 350,000 new starts (roughly equivalent to three years of construction activity). The construction industry claims, however, that land stocks held by builders are currently some 25 per cent below desired levels, and that land-banking is essential for the orderly progress of the industry. As a response they further add, that the Community Land Act, Development Land Tax and local government reorganisation have so disrupted the supply of land for building that current sales are of a low order and are in general locationally marginal unserviced land.

From the academic viewpoint these somewhat polemical 'assertions' have no status other than as hypotheses. At the present time discussion of the relationship between housing and land markets in the UK is somewhat long on 'hypotheses' and considerably short of 'research'. Specialists in this area of urban economic analysis, particularly land economists, may feel that the brief treatment of land attributes derisory significance to the land market. No such implication is intended, the present volume requires a comprehensive consideration of construction and the land market is only one of several significant influences on the residential development process. It is enough for our purposes to note that land planning controls generate lags in developers' responses, that planning standards may raise development costs, and that fluctuations in and a rise of land prices have resulted in land prices becoming an increasingly important and fluctuating element in builders' costs.

When land and capital market trends are taken into account and planning permission granted, contracts are prepared and finalised and on-site construction is then, finally, able to commence. This delay in building starts may, as indicated in Table 4.3, take from eighteen months, at the very least, to five years. Over this time period, demand estimates may be revised and the availability and cost of inputs markedly altered. The construction firm, at the very most, can only hope that it has made a 'best first move' when it starts a construction project.

Construction
The actual construction phase may take from twelve months to four years to complete and the completions rate may be used as a variable by the firm to adjust to changing demand conditions. As noted above, in periods of brisk demand the completions rate may be accelerated by overtime working, etc., to ensure quick sales, and in periods of recession in the housing market reduced labour inputs per unit of time will allow a slower completion rate so that builders may avoid the policing and financial costs of holding stocks of vacant completed houses.

Undoubtedly the construction firm requires substantial managerial skills to reach efficiently the stage of project development when construction can actually commence. But the actual organisation of construction requires considerable effort to phase and implement a whole series of small-scale contracts. Table 4.5 indicates the great variety of trades and skills, often provided by small subcontractors, required to produce a house (see Fig. 4.2). This large number of small-scale inputs suggests that inefficiencies and indivisibilities in labour use are likely to be a characteristic problem in the industry. This complexity is exacer-

Table 4.5 Employment of site operatives for various market sectors of new work (site man-days* per £1,000 contract value at 1970 prices)

| Trade groups | Housing | |
Trades	Private	Public
Structure		
Bricklayer	9.1	9.0
Roofer	1.1	0.9
Steel erector	—	0.3
Erector	—	
Glazier	0.2	0.2
Others	0.2	—
Total	10.6	10.4
Carpenter	8.3	7.9
Services		
Plumber	2.8	2.5
Heating	0.2	0.8
Electrician	1.8	2.5
Others	0.2	0.4
Total	5.0	6.2
Finishes		
Plasterer	4.2	3.7
Painter	4.5	4.6
Floorlayer	0.5	0.5
Others	0.8	0.4
Total	10.0	9.2
Other		
General labourer	14.5	16.8
Plant operator	2.0	1.1
Scaffolder	0.8	0.3
Steelfixer	—	0.3
Welder		
Pipelayer	0.2	0.8
Drainlayer		
Tarmac/Asphalt	0.2	0.2
Others	0.8	0.4
Total	18.5	19.9
Gen. Foreman	3.3	3.0
All trades	55.7	56.6

* $8\frac{1}{2}$ hours per day ($5\frac{1}{2}$ days per week) for building
Source: *NEDO*, 1977: 29.

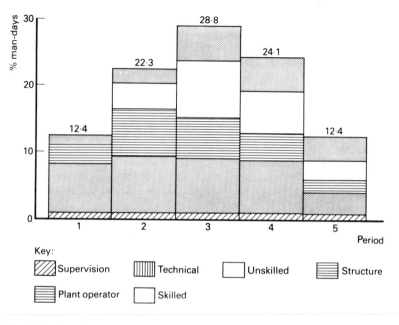

Fig. 4.2 Complexity of phasing labour inputs for construction.

Source: *NEDO,* (1977: 6, 63.)

bated by the specific phasing required for on-site construction with, for example, structural workers being required predominantly in the middle phases of development. Clearly a large-scale site operator with a large number of houses at various stages of completion can use specific labour inputs more systematically than smaller firms. Smaller firms, and indeed many larger firms, overcome this problem of technical variations in demand for specific skills by extensive short-term sub-contracting. However, efficiency of labour use, in these cases, may only be obtained by exacerbating the difficulties and delays of setting up the construction activity via a myriad of small contracts. Small, non-unionised firms, may overcome many of these phasing difficulties if employees perform a variety of tasks. For instance labouring, joinery, roofing and finishing which may require specific trade inputs in union-ised firms may be undertaken by the same individuals in smaller firms.

The task of organising inputs of construction materials is similarly complex. At this stage of development the major linkages of the con-struction sector are into the labour market and the market for construc-tion materials.

The labour market. Reference has already been made to the mix of skills and subtle phasing of labour inputs required in the construction. It was further suggested that the complex pattern of labour inputs posed problems for improving efficiency in the sector. It is this issue of efficiency, and more particularly efficiency wages which are highlighted here. Clearly sustained wage inflation poses particular problems for planning and management in an industry with low productivity growth and a relatively irreducible share of labour inputs in the physical production process.

Low productivity growth in housing construction has always been a concern in the UK (Carter 1958; Whitehead 1974; NEDO 1977) and has also been a source of comment in other economies (Stegman 1970). This low productivity growth has been variously attributed to poor management, to the failure of technological progress to be introduced at the design stage and to conservative labour practises in the labour force which has particularly high turnover rates. All these arguments seem plausible but detailed empirical verification is, once again, lacking.

The inflationary experience of the 1970s has made the productivity issue of particular significance. Construction sector wage statistics indicate that wage rates in the sector expanded at approximately the national average rate until 1977, though recent experience has seen construction wages fall well below national levels. In general, construction hours worked per week exceed average hours per week and the index of industrial production suggests that output per man in the construction sector lags behind the national average. This low rate of output per man cannot, of course, be assumed to arise because of low-skilled manpower. Land conditions, capital used and management skills all affect average output per man (or machine or acre). Strenuous efforts have been made to seek out productivity improvements in building, and in particular off-site mass production of components (see above) is viewed as a potential, but limited, source of productivity gain. However, Stegman, citing the Baumol model of sectoral unbalanced growth, was not optimistic about the potential for improving productivity in America in the 1970s;

> . . . industries do not choose to be low technology but that productivity growth over the long run is only possible in industries where labour is primarily an incidental requisite for the attainment of the final product (Stegman 1970: 108).

The construction industry is an industry where labour inputs are clearly fundamental. Thus, in an era of comparative wage bargaining if construction wages rise faster than efficiency then, as a consequence, product (house) prices must rise. Further, at least in the United States, the limits to off-site production inputs may well have now been reached and further labour productivity gains are not available to stabilise house price levels. Increased standardisation of housing output is also resisted by potential consumers who, with rising real incomes, increasingly desire product differentiation.

In the United Kingdom, at present, construction wages have fallen well behind national trends as construction unemployment has risen rapidly and cyclically. It is only to be hoped that the present recession does not lead to the induced obsolescence of labour and entrepreneurial skills and capital equipment which is currently unemployed. For high rates of new household formation, reflecting past demographic and new social trends, are likely into the mid-1980s. Expanding demand and a collapsed, depreciating housing supply industry create the conditions for yet another house price boom.

Materials. The influences of the capital, land and labour markets on the housing construction industry have been recognised by economists working in the areas of monetary, labour and land economics. However, the significance of materials has been less well recognised and this is an important omission. Material inputs commonly constitute at least 40 per cent of the value of construction output and thus form an important linkage between the industrial economy and the housing sector. Clearly productivity performance and capacity adjustment behaviour of material supply industries will have an important bearing on inflationary propensities and builders' reaction rates in housing construction.

These problems became more apparent when the nature of materials inputs for the construction sector are considered. Aggregates for roads, flooring and foundations are extracted from sites or quarries which are only expanded or initiated after considerable scrutiny from the planning system. In periods of expansion delays often exceeding eighteen months may be encountered in the planning process. With respect to cement, there are problems in periods of both expanding and contracting demand. When demand for cement is falling producers have a limited stock-piling capacity as cement cannot be stored for periods exceeding three months. Thus, when a subsequent expansion commences, not only are there limited stocks available, but further, producers have to be convinced that the expansion in demand will be sustained before expanding productive capacity. Even if producers expectations are elastic, the development of major new capacity may take four to five years with 50 per cent of this delay being due to the problems of acquiring planning permission. In the UK cement deliveries had fallen by 14 per cent per year between 1973 and 1977, then rose by 3 per cent in 1978 and 1979 but have since reportedly dropped considerably. The supply of bricks is compounded by similar difficulties and is particularly sensitive to fluctuations in housing demand as production is primarily for housing construction and because, in periods of recession, the cost structure of operating plants is such that capacity usage of less than 80 per cent is usually uneconomical.

Similar problems arise in relation to the provision of other inputs such as steel, glass and soft wood but they are less severe because of importing possibilities and because housing demand is a lower proportion of the final demand for such products. In conclusion it should be stressed that unstable demand for house-building materials may generate increasing unit costs of production in periods of recession and rising prices and lags in increasing output in periods of expansion. Further, local or regional shortages and surpluses of building materials, at least for aggregates, stone, cement and bricks, will cause particular difficulties as these commodities have a low value to bulk (weight) ratio and are therefore costly to transport across regions.

The above discussion has suggested that the construction industry is particularly susceptible to short-run variations in macroeconomic policy and that the industry faces, because of low productivity growth, difficult operating conditions when wage inflation is pervasive. Further, a series of major links into the markets for land and materials were identified. The materials market was seen to be subject to substantial lags in increasing output and the land market was viewed as being subject to phases of destabilising speculation in inflationary economies. Thus, apart from the inherent difficulties of assessing demand, the construction firm is faced with a constantly changing environment of factor prices and availabilities. Hopefully this description has been illuminating *per se* but it has a further purpose, namely, to provide a back cloth against which the theoretical and applied economic models of construction can be evaluated. In the subsequent section the two main approaches to theoretical and empirical analysis of urban housing market supply are discussed. These are, neoclassical models of housing supply, including access-space models and models of the behaviour of residential developers.

Microeconomic analysis of housing supply – neoclassical models

In Chapter 2, the major assumptions required for the existence of a competitive housing market were outlined. The neoclassical and access-space models retain such assumptions for housing supply analysis. But, for present purposes, the nature of the firm, the characteristics of factor markets and the housing production function have to be examined in more detail.

Factor and product markets. It is assumed that the firm operates in factor and product markets which are atomistically competitive and where, by some means undefined in such models, general market price signals or profit opportunities can be interpreted in a firm specific fashion.

The firm.   The firm, in these models, exists primarily as a logical construct to transform price signals into output adjustments. The firm has perfect information regarding present and future events and it ranks projects only in terms of profitability. The firm, at a given location, is assumed to be a price-taking profit maximiser. The existence of such assumptions allows the precise output level of the firm associated with a particular product price to be identified deductively insofar as the firms' production function is well behaved, well known and single valued.

The production function.   The production function is the relationship between inputs into the production process and their associated outputs. It is a physical relationship. Taking into account the prices of factors of production, firms (assuming they are completely X efficient and operating on the production possibility frontier) will select the most efficient combination of factors available. To produce a unique output and output adjustment pattern for the firm, it is assumed that the production function is single valued and well behaved. That is, isoquants are continuous, convex to the origin, and of a known shape. Further the relationship between output and expansion of factor inputs (returns to scale for the firm) is assumed known. This is equivalent in consumer theory to assuming that a well-defined utility function exists. If all these conditions pertain for the housing supply firm then a precise theoretical relationship between product price and firm output can be established. For the competitive builder a unique housing supply function will exist for the individual housing firm in the short and long term although, since the analysis does not define the number and characteristics of existing and potential firms the industry supply can only be deduced in the short run. The main concern in neoclassical analyses of housing supply, analogous to the estimation of demand elasticity parameters, is to establish the values of two critical, summary parameters. These are (a) the price elasticity of supply which can be defined to be the percentage change in the quantity of housing supplied for a given percentage change in housing prices; (b) the elasticity of factor substitution, which is the percentage change in factor proportions utilised for a given percentage change in relative factor prices.

Access-space models

Taking this set of assumptions, neoclassical economists have, in the United States, developed theoretical models and empirical analyses of urban housing supply. Essentially these models form the supply side of the access-space models and this section is an elaboration of Chapter 1, pp 14–15.

Using the neoclassical access-space framework Muth (1964, 1969) developed a sophisticated and seminal model of the housing production decision. This model has been used to formulate theoretical specifications for the estimation of price elasticity of supply of housing both in the short run and long run and for the elasticity of substitution between land and non-land inputs to housing production. In this instance the use of the term 'short run' relates to supply decisions facing housing producers when some input, usually dwelling structure, is already fixed. The 'long run' relates to periods when all factors of production are variable. Of course Muth's access-space model assumes, at least initially, that all production choices are determined instantaneously in conditions of long-run competitive equilibrium on an undeveloped urban surface. In such instances the theoretical 'long term' is achieved instantly. As is discussed below, when the phrase 'long run' or 'long term' relates to the supply adjustments which occur in a housing market over a long-time period, say greater than 5–10 years, a quite different set of problems is raised.

Theoretical framework

Although Muth's model is highly abstract, and indeed it may assume away some of the fundamental market imperfections, operational uncertainties and lags which pertain in the construction industry, it has a useful pedagogic value in stressing the possibilities of factor substitution in urban housing production. In particular, by assuming that the price of non-land inputs remains constant within an urban area, Muth demonstrates the effect of variations on the price of urban land on housing output. Muth's analysis of the optimum pattern of housing inputs and outputs in a city is developed in two stages. First, the conditions for firm equilibrium are used to derive the equilibrium land rent gradient and, second, the reaction of a single competitive firm to this rent structure is established.

Following simple profit maximisation rules for the neoclassical firm, Muth states that the standard conditions for firm equilibrium apply. That is, if the firm's profit function has the form

$$\pi = pQ(L,N) - rL - nN, \qquad [1]$$

where π is firm's profit, p and Q are respectively the price and level of housing output (which is a known function of inputs), L is land input and N non-land input and r and n are respectively the prices of units of land and non-land inputs. For a position of profit maximisation to pertain, necessary conditions are

$$\frac{d\pi}{dL} = P\left(\frac{dQ}{dL}\right) - r = 0$$

$$\frac{d\pi}{dN} = P\left(\frac{dQ}{dN}\right) - n = 0 \qquad [2]$$

That is, the marginal cost (prices) of a productive factor equals its marginal revenue product.

To take account of the spatial dimension of the urban housing system Muth argues that overall equilibrium also requires locational equilibrium. That is: 'firms choose their locations in such a way that their incomes cannot be increased by a move' (Muth 1969: 49). In essence Muth wishes to show that the rent per unit of land is competitively bid-up for any location which appears to offer supernormal profits to any of the identical firms. Thus locational equilibrium implies that the profits of firms are constant over space as competition for land units instantaneously erodes excess profits. Thus the total differential of equation [1] is

$$d\pi = (Q\,dP - L\,dr - N\,dn) + (p\,dQ - r\,dL - n\,dN) \qquad [3]$$

But if at each location the firm is in profit maximising equilibrium then, from equation [2],

$$r = P\left(\frac{dQ}{dL}\right)$$

$$n = P\left(\frac{dQ}{dN}\right)$$

substituting for r and n in the second parenthesis of [3] then yields

$$P\left(dQ - \frac{dQ}{dL}\,dL - \frac{dQ}{dN}\,dN\right) = 0$$

since, by definition, $dQ_i = \dfrac{dQ}{dL}\,dL + \dfrac{dQ}{dN}\,dN$

But since locational equilibrium is assumed to prevail, this implies that $d\pi = 0$. Therefore, the first parenthesis in equation [3] becomes,

$$(Q\,dP - L\,dr - N\,dn) = 0$$

or $\qquad dr = \dfrac{Q\,dP}{L} - \dfrac{N\,dn}{L}$

or $\qquad dr = \dfrac{Q\,dP}{L} - \dfrac{N}{Q}\cdot\dfrac{Q}{L}\,dn$

or, expressing changes in natural logs,

$$\log dr = \frac{1}{P_L}\log dP - \frac{P_N}{P_L}\log dn \qquad [4]$$

where P_L and P_N are, respectively, the share of the value of land ($P_L = \dfrac{rL}{PQ}$) and non-land ($P_N = \dfrac{nN}{PQ}$) inputs in total revenue. This implies that the price of land will be bid up to an equilibrium rent wherever prices, P, signal increased profits until locational equilibrium is restored. Assuming a positive relationship between centrality and potential profitability Muth indicates that the land rent gradient will fall away from the centre of the city.

The second stage of the analysis is to indicate how this variation in the price of land inputs influences input and output structures for the housing producer. Muth proceeds as follows. Assume a simple production function,

$$Q = Q(L,N)$$

Further, by assumption, factor payments exhaust firm revenues. That is

$$PQ = rL + nN \qquad [5]$$

To examine variations in the value of housing output per unit of land input, Muth divides equation [5] by L, the number of land inputs. That is

$$\frac{PQ}{L} = \frac{rL}{L} + \frac{nN}{L} \qquad [6]$$

Differentiating [6] yields

$$d\left(\frac{PQ}{L}\right) = dr + n \cdot d\left(\frac{N}{L}\right)$$

or

$$d \log\left(\frac{PQ}{L}\right) = P_L\ d \log r + P_N\ d \log\left(\frac{N}{L}\right) \qquad [7]$$

The elasticity of substitution, σ, between any two factors of production is defined to be the percentage change in factor proportions used produced by a given percentage change in relative factor prices. Expressed in natural logs,

$$\sigma = d \log\left(\frac{N}{L}\right) \Big/ d \log\left(\frac{r}{n}\right)$$

$$\therefore \quad \sigma\ d \log\left(\frac{r}{n}\right) = d \log\left(\frac{N}{L}\right)$$

Substituting for $d \log\left(\frac{N}{L}\right)$ in [7] implies

$$d \log\left(\frac{PQ}{L}\right) = P_L\ d \log r + P_N \sigma\ d \log\left(\frac{r}{n}\right)$$

Since n is assumed to be constant

$$\text{d} \log \left(\frac{PQ}{L} \right) = \left(P_L + P_N \sigma \right) \text{d} \log r \qquad [8]$$

Substituting for d log r, from [4] a further expression can be derived,

$$\text{d} \log \frac{PQ}{L} = \left(1 + \frac{PN}{PL} \sigma \right) \text{d} \log P$$

or $\quad \dfrac{\left(\text{d} \log \dfrac{PQ}{L} \right)}{\text{d} \log P} = \left(1 + \dfrac{PN}{PL} \sigma \right) \qquad [9]$

Empirical studies

The left-hand side of equation [9] is, expressed in log terms, a measure of the price elasticity of the value of housing output per unit of land. From this expression Muth is able to deduce that the elasticity of housing value per unit of land will be higher the greater is the significance of the share of land in housing output. Thus, where the city's house price gradient is also known, the variation in the value of housing output per land unit is easily shown to be $(1 + \dfrac{PN}{Pn})$ σ multiplied by the price gradient. The formulation of equation [9] has given rise to empirical estimates of a number of the parameters in the equation. In particular, σ, the elasticity of substitution, has been widely estimated in North America. For instance, Muth argued that if the share of land inputs, P_L, was of the order of 0.05 (in the current British context it would lie between 0.10 and 0.15) then the estimated elasticity of value of housing output would be around 20 if σ was close to unity.

A variety of estimates of σ have been produced in the United States, and this variation reflects differences in data, prior assumption and estimation technique. Four major studies of single housing markets (Muth 1971; Koeneker 1972; Rydell 1976) have found estimates of σ lying between 0.5 and 0.75. All of these estimates have lain significantly below unity. However, a higher estimate of σ has been obtained using improved equation specification and estimation methods (Sirmans *et al.* 1980; MacDonald 1979). Instead of assuming that σ is constant at all levels of output or at different factor mixes (which would imply a Cobb-Douglas or CES production function) Sirmans *et al.*, have assumed a variable elasticity of substitution (VES) production function, and established σ to lie in the range of 0.925 to 0.664. Further, MacDonald (1979) implies that a series of omission and measurement errors in all the above tests lead to a down-bias in the estimates of σ, and in a small study for Chicago estimates a σ not significantly different from unity.

The theoretical framework developed by Muth was particularly designed to examine intra-urban variations in housing output. But the framework has been expanded by Bradbury *et al.* (1977) to apply to a series of markets or submarkets in a given metropolitan area (Boston). Bradbury's model contains two important empirical advances. First, in her equivalent of equation [9], price variation does not arise from a systematic intra-city price gradient but is, rather, observed over the period 1961 to 1971 for 89 zones of the Boston Standard Metropolitan Statistical Area (SMSA). Second, and this is an important theoretical point previously noted in Muth (1964), Bradbury does not assume that all land in particular zones or submarkets is simultaneously developed. That is, at any point in time already developed land will coexist with land currently being developed and vacant land. This vacant land, which has a parallel in land-banking in Britain, reflects the decisions of landowners to speculatively hold land 'off' the present market. It is hypothesised that as land demand in a zone grows rising opportunity cost of land-holding will induce speculators to supply land. Thus, to take account of this vacant land effect and to relate estimates to volume rather than value of output per unit of land an equation similar to [9] is derived of the form

$$\frac{DQ}{Q} = \left(\frac{Pn\sigma + eL}{P_L} \right) \frac{\mathrm{d}P}{P} + \left(e_{L,J} \frac{\mathrm{d}J}{J} \right)$$

where Q, P, Pn, P_L and σ are as previously defined. Here e_L is the price elasticity of the supply of vacant land and $e_{L,J}$ is the elasticity of supply of land to non-housing land uses, and $\frac{\mathrm{d}J}{J}$ is the percent change in such other land uses. In this way the supply of land is entered directly into the theoretical arguments and empirical estimates. Further, in their estimating equations proxies for restrictive land zoning policies on the part of local governments are introduced. Although Bradbury's disaggregated estimates have been subject to criticism on grounds of specification (MacDonald 1979) and interpretation (Quigley 1977) the overall estimates for the price elasticity of new housing supply are probably valid. The elasticities 'range from 0.87 in the open suburbs to almost zero (0.0007) in the dense centre (*sic*) city' (Bradbury *et al.* 1979: 72). In addition housing supply was also seen to be responsive to variations in vacancy rates. That is, housing suppliers respond to quantity as well as price signals. Other microeconomic studies of a broadly similar form to those of Bradbury *et al.* have produced a similar range of price elasticities of housing supply. In a cross-section study of thirty-eight metropolitan areas de Leeuw and Ekanem, (1971) explained variations in prices and output of rental housing via a reduced form equation which incorporated supply and demand influences. By introducing prior estimates for the values of demand related coefficients, they estimated that price elasticity of supply would lie between 0.3 and 0.7 (for a criticism, see MacDonald 1979).

Can real long-run elasticities be deduced?

The applied studies of decadal changes in house prices and supply do make a genuine attempt to estimate real time related 'long-run' elasticities. Further, the applied character of these longer time period studies makes a relatively useful approach for the analysis of these policy questions, particularly when compared with studies focused on estimating σ in access-space models.

But, it is not entirely apparent that the access-space theoretical framework is appropriate for real long-term analysis. Even if the assumptions of competitive factor and product markets, optimising firms and well-behaved production functions are maintained, a long-term supply model is difficult to deduce theoretically. First, returns to scale for an individual firm have to be ascertained. Second, even if there are constant returns to a single firm, what assumption is to be made about the industry as a whole? Are entering marginal firms, as Muth implies, as efficient as existing firms? How is the entry and exit process for firms into and out of the industry to be determined? Moreover, if the discussion of the construction firm as a decision taking unit is taken into account, what theoretical deductions can be made if the output or factor markets are less than perfectly competitive? What if the firm is faced with uncertainty, or if new production technologies can be devised or learned? In such circumstances, which probably characterise the housing industry in Britain, a reasonable theoretical model of the firm is unlikely to be capable of deductively generating a single valued supply curve *ex ante*. If stable statistical relationships between house price changes and housing supply can be observed *ex post* then they may reflect equilibrium in the wider sense suggested in Chapter 3. That is, an equilibrium or stable relationship between house prices and output may exist if housing producers do not change the emphasis they place on price or vacancy signals, or if rates of learning do not change, or where degrees of factor and produce market imperfection do not alter. But, as in the analysis of consumer choices, it is not enough for the applied economist to attempt to establish such empirical constancies. Rather, more detailed analysis of decisions, problems and processes in the housing industry may indicate the nature and extent of imperfections and, as a result, suggest ways in which the operation of the market could be improved.

Short-run estimates

The same criticisms apply, if somewhat less forcefully, to attempts to examine how housing producers undertake 'short-run' supply responses. That is, where housing production firms, or owners of existing stock attempt to convert or modify existing stocks or flows of housing. Again, the label 'short run' derived from production function analysis may be misleadingly inappropriate. Conversion and improvement decisions may be made regarding housing investments which may endure for more than thirty years.

The analysis of equilibrium housing supply in the access-space model usually, but not exclusively, focuses on new construction. As indicated earlier macroeconomic studies also have an emphasis on examining new house building. But in most developed economies the reconstruction and maintenance of existing housing structures is becoming increasingly important. For instance, from Table 4.1 it is apparent that major improvement and reconstruction work affects an increasingly large number of houses, and private and public sector repair and maintenance expenditure accounted for 37 per cent of total housing investment in 1977.

In presenting a comprehensive analysis of the housing supply process it would be essential to link new housing supply to turnover of and investment and maintenance in secondhand housing. The filtering model in Chapter 1 draws attention to supply aspects of turnover, improvement and maintenance expenditures. Since turnover has been discussed in the previous chapter, here it is intended to concentrate attention on how the supply of housing, in stock or flow terms, may be maintained or increased by recombining existing land and capital with other variable inputs.

Reconstructing housing

The short-run supply decision which faces existing property landlords or owner-occupiers covers a range of questions. An existing dwelling unit, following Ingram and Oron (1977) can be characterised as providing locational, neighbourhood or structure quality services to the household. The household, via individual housing investment decisions, cannot alter the relative location of the house nor the pure public goods aspects of neighbourhoods. But it is possible to alter structure quality services and those neighbourhood effects which arise from the size, style or condition of housing. Clearly there exists a range of different structure services (aesthetics, comfort, shelter, privacy, *etc.*) which flow from different structural aspects of a house. For simplicity, however, it can be assumed that a single service flows from structure quality.

The structural services which flow from a dwelling arise from the inputs of fixed land and capital and, in addition, the use of labour, organisational and capital inputs. This additional capital has a spectrum of durabilities and substitutabilities. That is, the house is a combination of fixed land and capital, with other smaller scale capital inputs capable of being removed, replaced or added. For analytical purposes Ingram and Oron suggest that structure quality services can be subdivided into structure capital and quality capital. Structure capital is the minimum input of fixed land and long-term capital with a small short-term depreciation rate required to provide a given dwelling structure. Quality capital is added to structure capital to raise the output of quality services and it is not particularly durable and depreciates rapidly.

With an existing dwelling, structure capital is only removed or altered if, respectively, demolition or conversion are contemplated. Quality capital can be varied, in the short term, and it is the target of short-run operating decisions, maintenance and improvement expenditures. If, following previous analysts, the reconstruction firm rather than the construction industry, is the focus of analysis, then it is possible to generate models of optimum reconstruction investment decisions.

Dynamic programming model

A sophisticated neoclassical approach to modelling housing reconstruction is illustrated in an optimal control dynamic programming model for a competitive firm (Dildine and Massey 1974). The full analytics and implications of this model are not discussed here as the mathematical exposition is sufficiently technical to lie beyond the grasp or experience of the likely reader. In essence, Dildine and Massey assume that the firm has perfect foresight and knows present and future technologies, input and housing prices. With that knowledge the firm then wishes to select the sequence of operating, maintenance or incremental investment decisions which will maximise the net present value of services from the existing dwelling. This objective for the firm is indicated in the function

$$
V = \int_{0}^{T} \left(P_{(t)} h_{(t)} - q_{(t)} M_{(t)} \right) e^{-Pt} + Se^{-PT}
$$

where $P_{(t)} h_{(t)}$ is gross rent at period t, $q_{(t)} M_{(t)}$ is maintenance expenditure at t, S is the terminal value of the dwelling and P is the discount rate. V is the resultant net present value.

The achievement of this objective function is assumed to be constrained only by the technological relations embodied in the known production function and the known time path of input prices. Taking these production relationships into account, at any time period the rate of change housing services yielded by a dwelling will be

$$\frac{dh}{dt}_{(t)} = D\left[M_{(t)}, h\right] - S_{(t)} h_{(t)}$$

Using dynamic optimisation techniques it is possible to indicate that the level of maintenance and improvement services will be higher the greater is the price of housing, the lower are the prices of inputs of units of maintenance and the greater the elasticity of substitution between fixed and variable inputs.

This model is not considered further because, not only is it inherently complex but it embodies an excessively optimistic view of intertemporal foresight on the part of housing producers. In this respect, the approach of Ingram and Oron is somewhat more realistic. They assume that households in any decision period have well-defined expectations for housing reconstruction costs and service output prices over a limited five year period. Thereafter, they assume that households linearly extrapolate fifth year expectations into the future. Further, as real time unfolds, households replan at each annual interval. Using this theoretical approach Ingram and Oron consider three decisions facing the household.

The operating decision

Since, in the present period, it is assumed that current maintenance expenditures only affect subsequent housing output, the household is only able to raise present housing service outputs of quality capital by increasing operating inputs, O_t. For instance, household heating services can be increased by using more fuel with the existing heating system. In general at the present time

$$Q_t = Q_t(O_t, \bar{K_t})$$

For the landlord, given this production function, input prices and output prices, then operating inputs are varied until

$$dR\frac{(O, \bar{K_t})}{dO} = P_0$$

For an application of a similar model see the discussion of the effects of rent controls (Ch. 8).

The maintenance decision

Here Ingram and Oron allow maintenance inputs to have long-term effects, they recognise the need for borrowing to finance expenditure and they note that the rate of depreciation forms a technical limit to the extent to which maintenance services may be negative in any period. With the exception of the five year expectation period, they then define an objective function to maximise the net present value of housing services of the house which is similar to Dildine and Massey. This objective function is then maximised subject to the constraints of the production function and the maximum negative depreciation rate in order to select the optimum operating and maintenance policies which will produce the desired level of housing stock five years hence. In this stationary state the desired stock requires that

$$\text{d} \, \frac{(R - P_0 O)}{\text{d}K} = P_K$$

Structure conversion

In the longer term it is of course possible to alter structure capital inputs. That is, conversion of the dwelling from one structure type to another can occur. Ingram and Oron model this decision by assuming that optimum maintenance and operating input decisions are made for each structure type. The reconstructor then has to select the structure type yielding maximum net present values of returns to the fixed inputs. That is

$$V = \overset{X}{\underset{t=0}{\Sigma}} \, (R_t - P_0 \overset{X}{O}_t - P_m \overset{X}{M}_t - F_T) \, \frac{1}{(1 + v)^t}$$

Further, in selecting the optimum structure, allowance must be made for conversion costs. A conversion from structure type i to type j, which would be the structure yielding maximum net present values, would only occur if

$$V_J - C_{ij} > V_i,$$

where C_{ij} is the cost of converting existing structure i into structure j. Similarly new housing construction would replace existing dwellings if

$$V_n - D > V_i,$$

where V_n is the net present value of new housing returns and D represents demolition and site clearance costs.

The optimum decision conditions are given specific form by assuming that the housing reproduction function is well behaved and of the CES variety. They then derive long-period 'guesstimates' for Boston, of the elasticity of substitutions. They estimate that it is 0.6 for high rise dwellings and nearer unity for smaller dwellings. Clearly a great deal more rigorous empirical research is required on this topic.

Problems of this approach

Rothenberg (1977) has raised some pertinent concerns about this type of housing reconstruction model. For instance, he argues that technical characteristics of housing need to be considered in more detail, demolition services should directly enter the production function, and that the assumption of constant continuous substitution of reproduction inputs to raise structure services is unlikely to be reasonable. In addition, he argues, that the production relationship is likely to show decreasing returns to scale and that this analysis has to be expanded to the industry level. And, further, at the industry level what is the nature of the reconstruction industry — are there product or factor market imperfections or substantial uncertainties? Finally, Rothenberg correctly draws attention to the possibility of credit rationing preventing improvement and conversion. Indeed it is probably in inner-city areas, where the latent demand for property redevelopment and conversion is highest, that lending institutions will be most risk averse and least likely to lend funds. Apart from corroborative evidence presented in Chapter 5, this criticism can be sustained by the work of Williams (1976) who observed in Islington that institutional renovation capital was not widely available until several wealthy gentrifiers sustained their own conversion and improvements costs. In such areas uncertainties of response by other suppliers of housing could be likely to depress levels of improvement activity. That is, individual A is unlikely to improve dwelling exterior unless he anticipates that a sufficient number of other suppliers will make similar decisions resulting in visual improvements of neighbourhood. But an individual cannot attain such an improvement by his own housing market actions. The existence of such externalities and interdependences is important for housing reconstruction in older urban areas and analysis cannot afford to ignore it indefinitely.

But studies of the economics of actual housing improvement and conversion in the context of a housing supply model are sadly lacking in Britain. Though there has been some concern to establish theoretical formulae for appraising improvements (Needleman 1965). In the United States the analysis of the Boston area by Bradbury *et al.* (1977) was expanded to consider new and conversion supply with demolitions simultaneously and she concludes that;

> Decadal changes in zonal units through conversion-demolition are largely a function of the same expected revenue and cost measures that reflect the number of existing structures and of different type, age and condition in the zone that are available for conversion or ripe for demolition (Bradbury *et al.* 1977: 82).

For single units, the conversion price elasticity was estimated to be 0.146 but negative elasticities, reflecting demolitions, pertained to other structures. Ozanne and Struyk (1978) have recently generated similarly low elasticities, in the range 0.2 to 0.3, for changes in services provided within a fixed set of housing. In the Ozanne and Struyk study, supply price variation for given housing attributes is assumed to arise due to the existence of spatial subdivisions in the metropolitan housing

107

market. Assuming the validity of the hedonic technique, the expenditure on a given property is then broken down into the implicit price of attributes and quantity of attributes consumed. Taking the same property, appropriately decomposed into price and attribute terms, at decade intervals yields a position of quantity and price changes. The estimated equation yielded low price elasticities in the range of 0.07 to 0.22. With minor revisions and adjustments these estimates were revised to the range 0.2 to 0.3. They did not differ significantly for owners and landlords. Taken together, North American studies imply that the elasticity of conversion and improvement supply is likely to be low at around 0.3, and is less than half the value of estimated elasticities for new supply. But, a great deal of scepticism must surround such estimates and it has been argued throughout this discussion that neoclassical empirical studies have adopted a simplified view of the construction firm and industry which is in conflict with the characteristics of the industry outlined in the first section. But some analyses, with a less general or restrictive theoretical framework, have researched issues regarding housing supply and these studies are now briefly examined.

Other microeconomic studies

A series of studies with less restrictive, and less explicit, assumptions about firm behaviour have analysed temporal aspects of supply dealing with the timing of development decisions (Porter and Davies 1976) or the capacity of the industry to respond to price changes (Wilkinson and Archer 1977). These studies begin to link microeconomic analysis of housing supply decisions to macro-model building and also begin to question some of the simplistic decision taking behaviour attributable to the building firm in strict neoclassical theories. The work of Wilkinson and Archer is illustrative of both these types of development. They successfully adapt a macro-model supply function developed earlier by Whitehead, to take account of uncertainty effects on suppliers of housing and the capacity of the industry to adjust to price signals. By examining the validity of an instantaneous supply response mechanism they raise questions regarding how developers behave in the face of uncertainty.

It is perhaps fair to suggest that knowledge of the construction sector is currently so limited that it is difficult for researchers to select *a priori* behavioural objectives and rules for housing suppliers. Again, more convincing deterministic models of housing provision could be developed if the underlying behavioural basis was clarified. Clearly construction is not an economic activity whereby adjustments and behaviour can be predicted from an atomistic industrial structure.

Residential developer behaviour

The final class of supply model discussed here is models of the residential development process. An early and important analysis of the residential development process in Britain was made by Craven (1970). He viewed the private developer as being a significant and under-researched agent in the process of housing supply and urban development. With respect to South-East England he examined the view that the speculative builder was essentially a planning 'bête noire' and was responsible for building estates full of 'little boxes', destroying the rural fringe and creating urban sprawl. Craven found this view somewhat overstated and, instead, suggested that the builder is 'a catalyst who interprets, albeit inaccurately, major forces in the urban environment'. In general the developer is more constrained by planning processes than by demand. Market research was seldom undertaken by housing suppliers. He did, however, conclude that the price and availability of land, planning controls and the provision of infrastructure had important influences on decisions regarding the location and timing of development. Unfortunately the early work of Craven has not been capitalised upon in the UK.

Most recent studies of developers' decisions have been undertaken in North America, particularly Canada. In a recent survey of two Canadian empirical studies Goldberg (1978) stresses that a variety of factors influences the locations chosen by developers. Land prices, as would be consistent with any economic model of the housing market, are important but land availability is also critical. In addition the role of government, by zoning land or providing sites serviced with sewerage facilities, *etc.*, can influence both the location and costs of development. Further, they stress the complexities of and uncertainties surrounding the developer's decision. In particular, he maintains that land-banking is of limited extent because of the uncertainties of development and the high opportunity or interest costs of holding land. Such findings, of course, may vary from city to city. Indeed, if governmental planning restrictions on developers are relatively scarce, then the models suggested by Bradbury *et al.* may be a reasonable framework for analysing housing supply. But there remains the suspicion that most econometric models of urban housing supply have only introduced spatial dimensions of analysis by oversimplifying problems that arise from the existence of time.

Conclusion

A behavioural approach to the residential development has much to commend it. It clarifies the objectives of the developer and makes quite clear the market imperfections and uncertainties which surround the development decision. Further, it makes apparent the important interactions between private developers and the planning system. An examination of such studies, which do not set out with an unrealistic, preconceived notion of the firm, makes it quite clear that housing analysts and policy makers cannot be content with simple competitive models of housing supply. Analogous to our conclusions on housing demand, it is obvious that simple neoclassical models cannot be accepted as reasonable approximations to reality. The housing supply curve is as difficult to identify, measure and interpret as housing demand. A more precise understanding of the housing supply system would contribute to housing theory, the development of housing policy, the overall modelling of the urban economy, and interpretation of the macroeconomic role, both in relation to output and inflation, of the housing system.

5 Housing finance and the housing market

(with G.A. Wood).

In previous chapters the durability and budget significance of housing expenditure has been stressed and attention drawn to the capacity of housing market institutions to influence housing search strategies and outcomes. Thus an understanding of the behaviour of financial institutions and the mechanics of the mortgage market are integral to the understanding of the economics of the housing system. In this chapter it is intended, first, to identify major sources of housing finance and, with respect to the building society sector, to indicate its overall economic significance. Second, the broad characteristics of the building society 'industry' are examined and the major concerns of societies identified. This empirical and historical background is then used to discuss theoretical and econometric models of building society behaviour. In the past, in Britain, such studies have been concerned with examining building societies as an aggregate in order to develop macroeconomic models or estimates. These models are discussed and then a series of microeconomic issues regarding individual society behaviour at the local housing market level are considered.

Building societies and housing finance

Building societies are a distinctive institution in the British housing system. Originating from small 'clubs' of savers who would successively finance the construction of their own dwellings, and then terminate, building societies are now legally defined and registered non-profit making financial institutions. As indicated Table 5.1, not only do they dominate the overall provision of housing finance but, as shown by their assets structure in Table 5.2, their activities are heavily specialised into the housing finance market.

There are fluctuations over time in the relative significance of building society lending (ranging from 75 to 95 per cent of loan finance in the 1970s) with local authority lending acquiring a counter-cyclical role

Table 5.1 Loans for house purchase to the personal sector 1968–77 (£ m.)

Year	Building societies	Local authorities	Other public sector	Banking sector	Insurance companies	Building societies loans as % Total
1968	860	9	15	25	71	88
1969	782	− 18	16	− 5	83	91
1970	1,088	72	10	40	36	87
1971	1,600	121	12	90	13	87
1972	2,215	97	20	345	2	83
1973	1,843	260	41	290	123	72
1974	1,490	502	113	90	120	64
1975	2,768	534	133	60	68	78
1976	3,618	50	103	60	14	94
1977	4,096	− 21	28	120	23	96
1978	8,709	159	n.a.	285		95

Source: *Financial statistics.*

until 1980. Since then commercial banks have raised their market share to more than 7 per cent. Building society lending varies across and within housing markets. For instance, in the Scottish context, 95 per cent of loans in the city of Aberdeen in 1977 originated from building societies, but only 54 per cent were similarly funded in Glasgow. Further and supporting evidence from English cities (Bristol, Birmingham, Leicester, Newcastle) indicates that there are marked small area variations in the significance of financial sources. In Glasgow, for instance, the share of different 600 m^2 zones could range from 10 to 80 per cent.

These intra-urban variations in the significance of different sources of housing market finance are examined further below. At this juncture a focus on aggregate trends over time is maintained. After a year of record growth in assets (21.6 %) in 1977, the assets of building societies expanded by 15.6 per cent to £39,358 m. in 1978. These growth rates were by no means exceptional as in the decade 1967–77 the average annual growth rate of assets held was 16.5 per cent per annum (see Table 5.2).

The building society movement's ability to sustain growth in assets depends largely upon successful attraction of savings from the personal sector. It has been suggested (Hadjimatheou 1976) that growth may be more difficult to sustain in the future because the rise in total savings with building societies has come from a rise in the number of savers, rather than an increase in the level of the average savings account. The recent trend in shares and deposits with building societies is depicted

Table 5.2 Building Societies, use of funds.

Year	Total assets (£ m.)	% Change of total assets	Mortgage assets (7‡ m.)	% Mortgage assets/total assets	Reserve assets as % ratio–of total assets	Liquidity rate
1967	7,446	18.1	6,038	80.8	3.8	18.1
1968	8,298	11.4	6,901	83.3	3.8	15.9
1969	9,289	11.9	7,705	82.7	3.7	16.1
1970	10,819	16.5	8,752	80.5	3.6	18.4
1971	12,919	19.4	10,332	79.7	3.7	19.1
1972	15,246	18.0	12,545	82.1	3.6	16.5
1973	17,545	15.1	14,532	82.6	3.5	16.3
1974	20,094	14.5	16,030	79.8	3.4	19.2
1975	24,204	20.5	18,802	77.7	3.3	21.1
1976	28,202	16.5	22,565	80.0	3.5	18.3
1977	34,288	21.6	26,427	77.0	3.7	21.6
1978	39,723	15.9	31,715	80.0	3.8	18.4
1979	45,709	15.1	36,629	80.1	n.a.	18.0

Source: *Report of the Chief Registrar of Friendly Societies 1977, 1979.*

in Table 5.3 and substantiates this point. For the more than four fold increase in shares and deposits during the decade 1967–77, 84 per cent of that increase can be attributed to a growth in the number of savers while only the remaining 16 per cent is the contribution of increase in the average share and deposit account size. Although mortgage assets also experienced more than a four fold increase over this same period, the factors underlying this growth present a rather different pattern. An increase in the number of borrowers was responsible for 45 per cent of the rise in mortgage assets while the remaining 55 per cent was contributed by growth in average mortgage size. This is a clear reflection of the high house price appreciation rates over this period.

The structure of the industry

The continued growth in the size of total building society assets has not been accompanied by a growth in the number of building societies. Instead, the number of building societies has been declining since 1890 and, moreover, most rapid growth has been experienced by larger or, particularly in the mid-1970s, merging societies. Table 5.4 indicates the constantly growing dominance of the larger societies within the housing capital market. The size structure for a single year, 1978, in Table 5.5,

Table 5.3 Mortgage borrowers and investors with building societies 1967–77

Year	Number of borrowers ('000)	% change in number of borrowers	Number of share investors and depositors ('000)	% change in number of share investors and depositors	Average share and deposit balance (£)	Average mortgage balance (£)
1967	3,166		7,993		874	1,895
1968	3,334	5.3	8,797	10.1	885	2,057
1969	3,470	4.1	9,700	10.3	899	2,208
1970	3,655	5.3	10,883	12.2	939	2,382
1971	3,896	6.6	12,223	12.3	997	2,639
1972	4,126	5.9	13,549	10.8	1,063	3,027
1973	4,204	1.9	15,057	11.1	1,104	3,440
1974	4,250	1.1	16,497	9.6	1,131	3,758
1975	4,397	3.5	18,593	12.7	1,231	4,262
1976	4,609	4.8	20,703	11.3	1,285	4,880
1977	4,836	4.9	23,296	12.5	1,387	5,449
1978	5,108	5.6	25,780	10.7	1,452	6,179

Source: *Report of the Chief Registrar of Friendly Societies*, 1977; *Building Society Year book* 1977.

shows this concentration in more detail and, since there were 316 societies in that year (estimated to have fallen further to 289 in 1979), the large number of very small firms is also apparent.

Although it can be misleading to compare simple concentration ratios over different sizes of economic system (as larger systems may be functionally or geographically compartmentalised), it is pertinent to note the size structure of the housing finance sector in the USA. The degree of deconcentration in the USA is in marked contrast to that of the British context. This difference is important. In the USA it may be quite legitimate to assume that the housing capital market is relatively competitive, if subject to regulation, and primarily influenced by government through monetary policy changes. In Britain, however, the degree of concentration has facilitated the development of a price-fixing cartel, the Building Societies' Association, for interest rates with diverse associated forms of non-price competition. In addition, central government uses a variety of methods to affect the housing finance market via the cartel ranging from interest rate changes to moral suasion. Whilst this macroeconomic price or interest rate fixing cartel may have facilitated policy implementation for and econometric modelling of the housing finance market in Britain there has been, in the last decade, a growing awareness that such concentration may not always serve borrower or lender concerns. These issues are raised in the concluding microeconomic section.

The building society

Building societies are non-profit making firms which exist to borrow relatively short-term capital, in competition with other savings institutions and to relend them for long period loans to purchase housing assets. An understanding of the different sectional interests within societies and some of their operational targets can be gleaned from examining the flows of finance and asset structures for the building society movement as a whole.

The major activities of building societies are shown in Table 5.6 where the consolidated balance sheets for 1977 and 1978 are summarised. In total, shares and deposits account for over 94 per cent of total liabilities. In the 1970s, in an attempt to lengthen the duration of individual investments, societies have offered an increasing range of 'capital bonds'. Ordinary deposits are more liquid than capital bonds and generally attract a lower rate of return, while capital bonds attract a higher rate of return. An attraction to both shareholders and depositors are tax concessions. Tax is paid by building societies to government on behalf of investors and is thus treated as a distinct component on the liability side. The tax rate applied, known as composite rate, is invariant across savers and is calculated by the average of the marginal

Table 5.4 Concentration in the Building Society industry 1930–77: share of total assets held by societies in different size groups

Year	Total number of building societies	Largest 5		Next 5		Largest 10		Next 10		Largest 20		All total assets (£ m.)
		Total assets (£ m.)	Share of total (%)	Total assets (£ m.)	Share of total (%)	Total assets (£ m.)	Share of total (%)	Total assets (£ m.)	Share of total (%)	Total assets (£ m.)	Share of total (%)	
1930	1,026	145	39.1	53	14.3	198	53.4	43	11.6	241	65.0	371
1940	952	287	38.0	93	12.3	380	50.3	79	10.4	459	60.7	756
1950	819	469	37.3	145	11.5	614	48.9	171	13.6	785	62.5	1,256
1960	726	1,435	45.3	366	11.6	1,801	56.9	371	11.7	2,172	68.6	3,166
1970	481	5,416	50.1	1,539	14.2	6,955	64.3	1,414	13.1	8,369	77.4	10,819
1975	382	12,797	52.9	3,701	15.3	16,498	68.2	3,432	14.2	19,930	82.3	24,204
1976	364	15,144	53.7	4,257	15.1	19,401	68.8	3,943	14.0	23,344	82.8	28,202
1977	339	18,391	53.6	5,324	15.5	23,715	69.2	4,856	14.2	28,571	83.3	34,288
1978	316	21,489	54.4	6,411	16.2	27,900	70.6	5,320	13.4	33,220	84.0	39,538

Note: All the figures in this table are taken from the balance sheet figures published in the *Building Societies Year Book*. Unfortunately, not all societies have the same balance sheet date; thus the Halifax Building Society makes up its balance sheet as at 31 January and the Woolwich Equitable and Leeds Permanent Building Societies make up their balance sheets on 30 September. Thus, the table is not comparing like with like but the error is consistent and thus the trends are a realistic reflection of what has been happening

Source: *Building Societies Association*, 1980.

Table 5.5 Share of total assets – end 1978

Societies in rank order by size	Total assets (£ m.)	Share of Total (%)	Cumulative Total assets (£ m.)	Share of total (%)
Largest 5	21,489	54.4	21,489	54.4
6–10	6,411	16.2	27,900	70.6
11–15	3,526	8.9	31,426	79.5
16–20	1,794	4.5	33,220	84.0
21–25	1,113	2.8	34,333	86.8
26–30	809	2.0	35,142	88.9
31–35	599	1.5	35,741	90.4
36–40	422	1.1	36,163	91.5
41–45	354	0.9	36,517	92.4
46–50	308	0.8	36,825	93.1
51–55	272	0.7	37,097	93.8
56–60	242	0.6	37,339	94.4

Source: *Building Societies Year Book* 1979.

rates of tax of a sample of building society deposit and shareholder account holders; this practice thus discriminates in favour of those investors with a marginal tax rate which is greater than the composite rate and against those with a lower marginal rate of tax. For instance, in 1979/80, the composite rate applied was 21 per cent, that is 70 per cent of the basic rate of 30 per cent. This tax advantage for investors in building societies not only distorts the savings market but is thought to have a regressive distributional effect (Foster 1974).

The item 'Government advances' has its origin in the House Purchase and Housing Act of 1959 wherein the government was empowered to advance money to the building societies for the purpose of making loans on pre-1919 property. Following restrictive economic measures in July 1961, lending under this scheme was terminated and as repayments of principal were made on outstanding balances, the total of government advances dwindled continuously until 1974, when as a result of loans arranged by the government to prevent unprecedented increases in the mortgage rate, the total went up from £32.2 m. to £339.2 m. As Table 5.6 reveals, repayments have reduced this sum to the relatively minor amount of £9.2 m. in 1978.

The other major items on the liability side are general reserves which account for 3.7 per cent of total liabilities. Taken as a percentage of total assets this measure is known as the reserve asset ratio. It experienced a steady decline during the period 1964 to 1975, rising abruptly in the years 1976 and 1977, and remaining high into 1978 (see Table 5.2).

General reserves represent the net worth of a building society and are

Table 5.6 Building Societies' consolidated balance sheet 1977–8

| | Liabilities (£m.) | | | Assets (£m.) | |
	1977	1978		1977	1978
Shares	31,109.7	37,012	Mortgage assets	26,426.5	31,758
Deposits	1,224.1		Investments (int'l. accrued interest)	5,945.6	5,840
Government advances	14.2	9	Cash in bank and at hand	1,463.8	1,971
Taxation and other liabilities	6,676.1	709	Office premises	396.3	623
General Reserves	1,264.3	1,462	Other assets	56.1	
	34,288.44	39,192		34,288.3	39,192

Source: *Report of the Chief Registrar of Friendly Societies*, 1977, 1978.

the result of accumulated surpluses each year. Table 5.6 illustrates how this net surplus is arrived at for 1977 and 1978.

Reserves occupy a central position in the activities of building societies. Societies view these reserves as a source of confidence to investors whose savings are used to finance relatively long-term lending as a 'cushion' to meet any losses on sale of investments and to cover for the inevitable time lag between increasing the rate paid to investors and the rate charged to borrowers. The National Board for Prices and Incomes reporting on mortgage rates of interest in 1966 took the view that, for many of the larger building societies, the majority of investors would pay little regard to the reserves which those societies maintained. In their view reserves held were in excess of those required to maintain confidence and represented an impediment to the promotion of mortgage loans. The role of the reserve asset ratio in building society activities is discussed later in this chapter.

The building societies' specialisation in housing finance is reflected in the asset side of the 1978 consolidated balance sheet (see Table 5.6) where 80 per cent of total assets are attributable to the outstanding value of mortgage loans. The equivalent figure for 1977 is a lower percentage in comparison with previous years and reflects an abnormally high liquidity ratio of 21.6 per cent. Liquid asset holdings of building societies (1978) largely consist of British government securities (43% of total), local authority debt (37% of total) and cash and balances with banks (13% of total). They are represented by the categories 'investments' and 'cash at bank and in hand' in the balance sheet of Table 5.6. During the period 1964–77 the liquid asset ratio fluctuated between a minimum of 14.5 per cent and a maximum of 21.6 per cent with an average of 17.7 per cent (see Table 5.2).

Both the liquid asset ratio and the reserve asset ratio serve as financial criteria for trustee status and membership of the Building Society Association. In both cases individual societies must satisfy the following financial requirements:

1. A 7.5 per cent minimum liquidity requirement.
2. General reserves should be at least 2.5 per cent of the first £100 m.; for societies with assets of more than £100 m., a reserve ratio requirement of 2 per cent must be maintained on the next £400 m. of assets, 1.5 per cent in respect of the next £500 m. of assets and 1.25 per cent against any assets exceeding £1,000 m.

In practice, both general reserves and liquid assets are maintained at levels well above these legal minima as inspection of Tables 5.2 and 5.6 confirms. The possible existence of economies of scale in reserve holdings is confirmed by Table 5.4, which suggests that a continuing trend towards increasing levels of concentration would lead, *ceteris paribus*, to a falling reserve asset ratio for the building society movement.

The most important aspect of the Building Societies Association's activities is that its council recommends the rates of interest relating to shares, deposits and mortgages. The BSA council is composed of executives from member societies and though its recommendations are non-binding, most societies comply with them. This leaves individual societies free to allocate the inflow of funds at the prevailing interest rate structure, subject to the legal constraints outlined above. What the determinants of this allocation are, and what implications there are for the housing market is the subject matter of the remaining sections of this chapter.

The macroeconomic analysis of building society behaviour

Past work in this area ranges from the *ad hoc* and institutional to the rigorous and general. This section provides a discussion of the major microeconomic analytical approaches which are the foundation of macroeconomic studies of building societies. It takes as its major concern, the problems of conceptualising the flows of funds to and from the mortgage market within the context of building societies' behaviour. Here the major concerns are whether interest rate movements equilibrate the market or whether rationing takes place in the mortgage market and, if so, why and how does it emerge? First the theoretical issues which have emerged in this area are examined and then the methodological problems facing applied work on mortgage markets is discussed.

Theoretical analyses

In the United Kingdom the seminal economic analysis undertaken with respect to building societies as financial intermediaries is that of Ghosh (1974). Ghosh analysed the determination of asset and liability composition within the conventional neoclassical theory of portfolio choice framework. By assuming societies to be well-informed profit maximisers Ghosh applied standard economic analysis to provide a useful reference point for initiating analysis of building society behaviour.

The essence of Ghosh's model is the hypothesis that the central concern of building societies is with their reserve asset ratio. This indicator is crucial to their ability to sustain growth in assets which is presumed to be a major source of motivation for building society decision takers. The basis for this hypothesis are the following formulae

$$g = \frac{s}{r_d - s} \qquad [1]$$

where g is the rate of growth of assets between two points in time, t and $t-1$, and s is the ratio of the surplus earned between those two dates and the level of total assets at t. If, as Ghosh argues, the maintenance of a certain desired reserve asset ratio r_d is considered by societies to be of paramount importance then, in order to maximise g, they must, for a given $r = r_d$, maximise s. This then is the rationale for the assumption that building societies maximise profits (surplus).

Ghosh formalises this objective by stipulating a specific utility function, for decision takers within societies, whose sole argument is planned rate of addition to general reserves π. Societies are assumed to maximise the expected value of this function. Using Ghosh's notation the utility function is specified as:

$$u = 1 - e^{-b'} \frac{\pi}{W_0} \qquad [2]$$

where W_0 are total reserves at the beginning of the decision period; π is profit or net surplus earned during the period and is defined as the excess of normal income, as generated by the return from assets, over normal expenditure, as incurred via payment of interest yield on liabilities (see Table 5.5)

Planned rate of addition to the general reserve ratio is given by π/W_0. If uncertainty exists with respect to future interest rates π will be stochastic. Societies are assumed to have well-behaved and defined subjective probability distributions defined over all possible outcomes and thus the decision problem is treated as a risk equivalent one. It can be shown that by taking expected values of [2], expected utility will be maximised if the objective function

$$R = \frac{\mu\pi - b'}{2W_0} \sigma_\pi^2 \qquad [3]$$

is itself maximised. Here $\mu\pi$ is the expected value of π and σ_π^2 is the variance of π around its expected value. The problem is transformed into one of constrained maximisation by the formulation of constraints which ensure that the balance sheet must balance and that the legal minimum liquid assets ratio be satisfied.

Using the Lagrangean multiplier method the marginal conditions which must be satisfied for a maximum can be derived. Using these conditions, individual building society demand and supply functions for the array of building society assets and liabilities can be deduced; these functions will be dependent upon the expected values, variance and covariance of the interest rate returns on building society assets and liabilities, as well as those of competing assets and liabilities. If all building societies possess identical subjective probability distributions with respect to interest rates, then the individual demand and supply equations can be aggregated to the industry level.

Although this is only a brief outline of the Ghosh model, there are two interesting features which emerge from the exposition:

1. The theory abstracts from factors which imply that building societies are not profit maximisers, that is, a wider range of managerial objectives is not considered.
2. The model utilises a comparative static framework within which there is instantaneous adjustment of actual to desired magnitudes. That is, adjustment costs are de-emphasised.

Other objectives

It has been indicated by Clayton *et al.* (1975) that there may not be sufficient grounds for claiming a direct line between reserves and the growth of assets in an *economic* sense. The net surplus ratio S, i.e. the rate of addition to general reserves, is an *ex post* magnitude in the sense that it is a residual which occurs at the end of a period. But if, at period t, the reserve ratio is below its desired level, r_d, then this need not necessarily adversely affect growth of assets during the period beginning at t 'because as it accepts the shares and deposits from the personal sector and relends these, . . . it will be adding to its reserves by virtue of the margin it adds to the shares and deposits rate'. This sequence implies a rather different view of the casual mechanism which can also be read into the formulae given in [1] by solving for S to give,

$$S = r\frac{g}{1+g} \qquad [4]$$

Thus, for a given constant reserve ratio, the higher is the rate of growth of assets, the higher will be the surplus ratio. This mechanism, it can be argued, is a more relevant representation of building society behaviour since it meets the stated objectives given by building societies themselves which stress rate of growth of assets. That is, growth rather than surplus is the prime concern of decision takers.

Other characteristics of observed building society behaviour also prompt a certain scepticism with respect to the view that they are profit maximisers. As Table 5.2 shows, mortgages as a percentage of total assets have remained relatively stable over the period 1962–78. This can be interpreted as *prima facie* evidence suggesting that building societies have the long-run aim of establishing a fixed division of the net inflow of funds between mortgages and other assets. The rationale for this appears to be that building societies behave in a prudent fashion and enter into mortgage commitments in period *t* for an amount which they know they can meet, this being dictated by the net inflow of funds during period *t* – 1 and the particular division being determined by building society experience with respect to the risk factors involved. It could therefore be expected that mortgage advances in period *t* depend upon the net inflow of funds in period *t* – 1. The diversity of operational targets for headquarters and local building society managers is discussed in more detail below.

Costs of adjustment

The idealised world of instantaneous adjustment presented in Ghosh's model may misrepresent the decision problems and processes facing managers. The building society movement is analogous in nature and behaviour to the economic model of collusive oligopoly within which the conventional Walrasian price adjustment equation no longer pertains. In particular the movement's inertia or stickiness' with respect to changes in their interest rates is well-documented. The roots of this inertia are derived from the following two factors:

1. In the British case a rise in mortgage rates is applied to all existing borrowers and not just new mortgages. As a result rises in mortgage rates activate political and social considerations on behalf of the building societies themselves. In general it has to be assumed that the rise in other interest rates is not likely to be temporary before raising rates. Government pressure and intervention are also of importance as for instance in 1957, 1965 and more recently in 1974. The present government have not, throughout 1979 and 1980, yielded to pressures to help restrain mortgage rate rises.
2. Changes in existing borrowing rates is a formidable administrative task whose costs are of such significance as to be a major factor in causing rate rigidity.

It can be argued, on *a priori* grounds, that this rigidity in the interest rate setting process will be a source of disequilibrium in the mortgage market in the short run at least. This can be conceptualised by making the following assumptions: (i) The flow of building society mortgage lending is a constant proportion of the inflow of funds into share and deposit accounts; (ii) This inflow of funds into share and deposit accounts varies positively with respect to its interest rate return r^d, negatively with respect to the interest rates offered on competing financial assets r^{oc} and positively with respect to income Y; (iii) The mortgage rate r^m is set on the basis of a fixed mark up λ on r^d; (iv) The demand for mortgage funds M^d by potential house purchasers is positively related to income and negatively related to the mortgage rate r^m and prevailing house prices P_h. These assumptions can be summarised in functional form as follows:

$$M^s = \theta D^s \qquad \text{where } \frac{dM^s}{dD^s} = \theta \text{ and } 0 < \theta \, 1 \qquad [5]$$

$$M^d = g(Y, r^m, P^h) \quad \text{where } \frac{\delta M^d}{\delta Y} > 0, \frac{\delta M^d}{\delta r^m} < 0, \frac{\delta M^d}{\delta p^h} < 0 \quad [6]$$

$$D^s = f(r^d, Y, r^{oc}) \quad \text{where } \frac{\delta D^s}{\delta r^d} > 0, \frac{\delta D^s}{\delta Y} > 0, \frac{\delta D^s}{\delta r^{oc}} < 0 \quad [7]$$

$$D^s = D^d \qquad [8]$$

$r^m = \lambda r^d$ where λ is a given constant in the short run. $\qquad [9]$

Suppose that at the outset the market in mortgage finance is in equilibrium so that at given values for Y, P^h and r^{oc}, the prevailing r^d is such, that the condition:

$$g(Y, \lambda r^d, P^h) = \theta\{f(r^d, Y, r^{oc})\} \qquad [10]$$

is satisfied. If rates of return on competing financial assets rise from r^{oc} to $r^{oc'}$, there will be a reduction in the inflow of funds into building societies. If it is assumed that r^d is fixed in the short run due to political and administrative considerations on the behalf of building societies, excess demand for mortgage finance will emerge and rationing will take place. This process is illustrated in Fig. 5.1. The inflow of funds schedule D^s in quadrant 2 shifts to the right with the rise r^{oc} to $r^{oc'}$ as savings are diverted from shares and deposits to the more attractive competing financial assets. In the absence of instantaneous adjustment with respect to r^d and thus r^m, contraction in mortgage lending inevitably results as a consequence of our specification in function [5] above, and the shortfall in supply is given by distance A−B in quadrant 4.

This is a rather naïve view of the short-run determination of building society mortgage finance in that choice of the composition of other assets and liabilities is ignored. An interesting additional question is whether or not rationing is a purely short-run or temporary phenom-

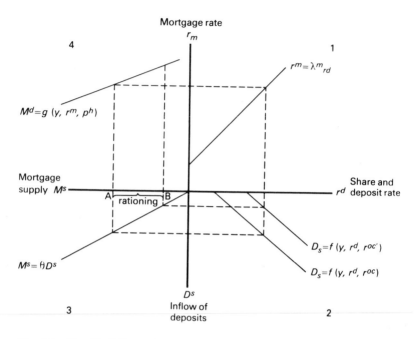

Fig. 5.1 Fixed building society interest rates, excess demand for mortgages and rationing

enon. In order to tackle this question it is necessary to specify the disequilibrium adjustment mechanism and here the determinants of building societies' interest rate changes must be considered. Hendry and Anderson (1976) approach this question by taking a more complicated view of building society behaviour than that taken so far in this chapter. They argue that disequilibrium is potentially present in the long run, owing to the attempt by building societies to optimise an objective function comprising several conflicting goals, using instruments whose variability inflicts costs upon the societies.

Multiple objectives and adjustment constraints

The conflict of objectives hypothesis has a certain plausibility about it, given that building societies are mutual organisations who do not have proprietors apart from those who hold shares. Consequently, it can be argued that since control has been concentrated in the hands of management, both at the national and local levels, the adoption of objectives functions commonly used in managerial theories of the firm may be appropriate. Sources of motivation commonly suggested by these managerial theories are prestige, power and promotion, status, professional excellence, security and elements of corporate 'conscience'. These would correspond to such building society objectives as the rate of growth of mortgages, minimising lending rates, maintaining a satisfactory reserve asset ratio, meeting the *ex ante* demand for mortgages, or an objective function comprising these arguments would lead to attempts by building societies to reconcile them via the use of instruments such as the liquidity ratio and borrowing and lending interest rates.

It is the costs incurred when varying these instruments combined with the conflicting nature of building society objectives which prevent the mortgage market clearing via the use of these instruments. Thus, although in a situation of excess demand, building societies would derive satisfaction from an upward revision of interest rates and a consequent increase in the inflow of funds and ability to meet demand. This is constrained by their unwillingness to increase lending rates to existing borrowers and the adjustment costs incurred. Therefore, only partial elimination of mortgage rationing can be expected due to the inherent nature of building societies' decision making process.

Hadjimatheou's study (1976) is an example of the adoption of an objective function in which there is a conflict between goals. The objective function has as its arguments, the maintenance of some desired liquidity ratio ℓ^* and meeting the demand for mortgages. This function is maximised subject to the building societies' 'strong dislike of changes in their interest rates which appears to be explained by their consideration of the interests of existing borrowers, political pressures and administrative expenses'. This latter point is of importance because without flexible adjustment of their interest rates, pursuit by building societies of these two objectives can produce conflict and a trade-off between them. Expressions [5] to [9] allow us to illustrate this hypothesis. Suppose the asset side of the building society balance sheet is comprised only of liquid assets and mortgage advances. It follows that θ in function [5] will be equal to $(1 - \ell)$ where ℓ is the liquid assets ratio. The condition which must be satisfied for equilibrium in the mortgage marked is now:

$$(1 - \ell)\{f(r^d, Y, r^{oc})\} = g(Y, \lambda r^d, P^h) \tag{11}$$

With r^d and λ considered fixed in the short run, it is unlikely that the flow of mortgage finance forthcoming at $\ell = \ell^*$ will be equal to M^d, assuming that the determinants of ℓ^* are related to security considerations which are independent of the extent of excess demand for mortgage finance. In Fig. 5.2 the possible relationships between ℓ and the level of excess demand for mortgage finances, with given values for r^d, Y, λ, P^h and r^{oc}, are illustrated. In cases 1 and 2 there is no conflict between the two objectives because at $\ell = \ell^*$ demand is equal to supply

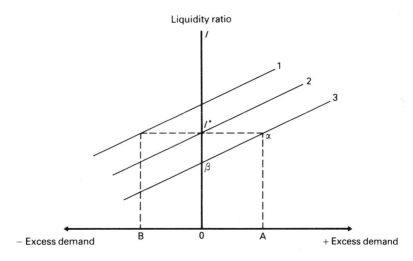

Fig. 5.2 The liquidity ratio and excess demand for mortgages

in case 2 while there is excess supply OB in case 1; thus the level of demand is being met in both cases and $\ell = \ell^*$ also pertains. However, in case 3, maintaining $\ell = \ell^*$ is incompatible with the objective of meeting *ex ante* demand as supply is insufficient and excess demand OA pertains. In such a situation Hadjimatheou argues that building societies will be prepared to allow ℓ to fall below ℓ^* in order to enhance their ability to satisfy the *ex ante* demand for mortgage finance; they will thus choose a point lying on or between α and β. Notice that the short-run burden of adjustment is placed upon ℓ.

This adjustment process can also be illustrated in terms of Fig. 5.1 where the effects of a rise in interest rates on competing assets was analysed. This is reproduced in Fig. 5.3 with θ replaced by $(1 - \ell^*)$. At the outset there is a situation corresponding to schedule 2 of Fig. 5.2, where at the desired liquidity ratio ℓ^*, the mortgage marked is in equilibrium. The increase in r^{oc} to $r^{oc'}$ will, *ceteris paribus*, induce rationing and result in a shift to a point corresponding to α on schedule 3 of Fig. 5.2; in the face of excess demand, building societies can be expected, given their assumed dual objectives, to reduce the liquidity ratio thus shifting the mortgage supply schedule in quadrant 3 of Fig. 5.3 to the left and reducing the extent of mortgage rationing from A−B to A−C. The responsiveness of ℓ to excess demand will presumably depend upon the willingness of building societies to trade loss of security against ability to satisfy the demand for mortgage finance.

Much of the analysis in this section is of relevance to applied work in this area; quite clearly, if the mortgage market has a chronic tendency

126

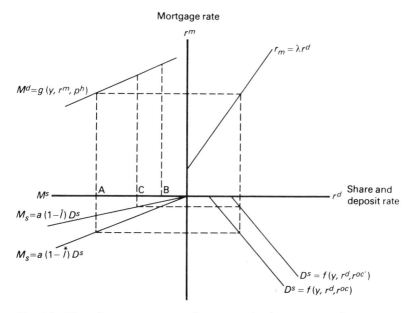

Fig. 5.3 The adjustment process when competing interest rates rise

to disequilibrium then there are going to be methodological problems in estimating functions such as the mortgage demand and supply schedules. These problems are now examined in more detail.

Econometric studies of UK building societies

Although they now represent a growing area of concern (Mayes 1979; Boddy 1980) empirical studies on UK building societies and the mortgage market are limited in number. Perhaps a reflection of the problems of estimation encountered when disequilibrium characterises the markets. As has been argued earlier, disequilibrium is most likely within the mortgage market and thus the methods underlying applied work in this area are worthy of study. It has to be stressed, however, that similar problems may pertain, but for different reasons, in North America.

The work of Ghosh and Duffy is an example of empirical studies which make no allowance for disequilibrium behaviour. Ghosh's estimating equations are based on the theoretical model outlined earlier and incorporate the conventional market clearing equation that *ex ante* demand equals *ex ante* supply. If this condition holds then observed quantity traded lies upon both *ex ante* demand and supply schedules and thus can be used in the estimation of both schedules. Figure 5.4

127

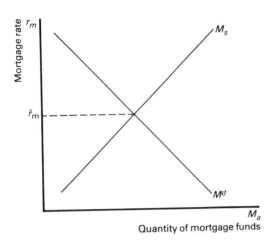

Fig. 5.4 Disequilibrium in the mortgage market

illustrates the main problem introduced by disequilibrium in the mortgage market. That is, in the absence of an equilibrium condition, the observed quantity traded may not satisfy both the demand and supply schedules. If, as seems reasonable in the case of the mortgage market, the observed quantity is equal to either the quantity demanded or the quantity supplied, it will be equal to the minimum of these two quantities.

$$M_t^q = min (M_t^d, M_t^s) \qquad\qquad [12]$$

where M_t^q = observed quantity traded in period t; M_t^d = *ex-ante* demand in period t; M_t^s = *ex ante* supply in period t.

In terms of Fig. 5.4 only the shorter portions of the two schedules can be directly observed. When the quoted mortgage rate is less than r_m, there is excess demand and equation [12] implies that supply will equal the observed quantity while demand will be unobserved. Conversely, when the quoted mortgage rate is greater than r_m there is excess supply, and demand will equal the observed quantity, while supply will be unobserved. If the hypothesis that, for the most part the UK mortgage market has been in excess demand during the *post*-Second World War period is accepted, then there are few direct observations on the demand schedule upon which to base estimation of the demand for mortgage funds schedule.

One of the first attempts to deal with this problem is the study of O'Herlihy and Spencer (1972). They estimate structural equations which are designed to explain the demand for mortgage advances, the net inflow of funds into building societies, the mortgage rate of interest and borrowing rate, repayment of mortgages and withdrawal of shares and deposits. Of particular relevance to the earlier discussion is their attempt to identify the *ex ante* demand schedule for mortgage advances. O'Herlihy and Spencer note that 'an outstanding characteristic of building societies is that they ration mortgage lending by "non-price" means and apparently make little use of changes in the mortgage rate as a way of influencing demand'. Thus they correctly assume that building societies operate a flexible policy with respect to mortgage contract terms. In particular, terms such as the loan to value ratio, loan to income ratio and term of loan are allowed to vary depending upon the state of the market for mortgage finance. Such factors as size of deposit can be expected to exert a negative influence on *ex ante* demand. This phenomenon was accounted for by the use of two dummy variables; $D(1)$, to indicate the presence of 'mild' rationing, and $D(2)$, to indicate 'strict' rationing. These variables were constructed from subjective assessment of qualitative comment made in issues of *Building Society Affairs* and the *Economist*. The estimating equation used is interpreted as a 'modified' demand equation and had the form

$$\frac{M_t^q}{P_t^h} = \beta_0 + \beta_1 \left.\frac{M^q}{P^h}\right|_{t-1} + \frac{\beta_2 Y_t}{P_t} + \beta_3 r_t^m + \beta_4 D_t(1) +$$

$$\beta_5 D_t(2) + \beta_6 S_t(1) + \beta_7 S_t(2) + \beta_8 S_t(3)$$

with P_t^h = price index of new houses, Y_t/P_t = real disposable income, $D(1)$ and $D(2)$ = 'rationing' dummies and $S(1)$, $S(2)$ and $S(3)$, seasonal dummies. The mortgage rate of interest proved to have no significant explanatory power.

The rationale behind this interpretation is illustrated in Figs. 5.5 and 5.6 where the prevailing mortgage rate is assumed to be r^m. At initial mortgage contract terms *ex ante* demand exceeds *ex ante* supply by A – B in Fig. 5.5 and C – D in Fig. 5.6. The assumption underlying O'Herlihy and Spencer's estimation procedure is, that in response to the emergence of any such disequilibrium, non-price contractual terms are immediately adjusted, inducing a shift in the *ex ante* demand schedule so that in fact the equilibrium clearing condition is satisfied, but not by the conventional means of instantaneous adjustment of price. The coefficients on the dummy variables (which implicitly proxy for the change in contractual terms) yield estimates of the extent of non-price rationing. O'Herlihy and Spencer's results imply that 'mild' rationing results in a reduction in *ex ante* demand of 9.7 per cent, whilst in periods of 'strict' rationing, the reduction amounted to 17 per cent.

The methodology used here relies heavily on the assumption that disequilibrium adjustment occurs via shifts in the *ex ante* demand schedule alone. If the Hadjimatheou and Hendry view of building society behaviour is correct, then adjustment to disequilibrium will also entail shift in the supply schedule induced by a willingness to meet prevailing demand. Criticism has also been levelled at the subjective nature of the rationing variables which are discrete, limited to three values and entered exogenously thus giving no 'explanation' of rationing.

In contrast, Law (1977) utilises the 'switching of regimes' method of identification; here the supply and demand equations are identified by separating his time series sample, from the third quarter of 1955 to the second quarter of 1970, into supply and demand regimes such that each schedule may be appropriately fitted against the observed quantity for the sample points falling within its regime. The basis for separation are

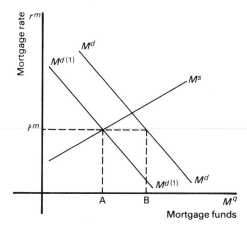

Fig. 5.5   Non-price adjustments by societies

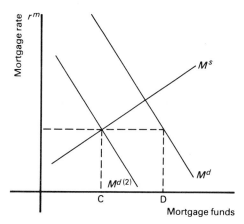

Fig. 5.6   Non-price adjustments by societies

O'Herlihy and Spencer's dummy variables, used here as indicators of the discrepancy between *ex ante* demand and supply. Hence, when $D(1)$ and $D(2)$ indicate rationing, there is assumed to be excess demand, and the supply function will be identified. This, of course, implies a contrary interpretation to that of O'Herlihy and Spencer, where $D(1)$ and $D(2)$ are proxies for the change in non-price contractual terms which bring *ex ante* demand equal to *ex ante* supply, thus allowing identification of the demand schedule. When $D(1)$ and $D(2)$ indicate no rationing, there may be equilibrium or excess supply and in either case the demand function will be identified. Thus, given that condition [12] holds, the dummies are presumed to provide accurate indication as to which of the shorter portions of the two schedules in Figs. 5.4 is being observed. Once again, however, rationing is exogenously imposed and thus not 'explained'.

In the context of the United States, Fair and Jaffee have suggested the use of price setting behaviour to alleviate estimation problems. In order to explain their suggestions, let us make the following assumptions about the mortgage market:

$$M_t^d = \alpha_0 X_t^d + \alpha_1 r_t^m + \mu_t^d \qquad [13]$$

and

$$M_t^s = \beta_0 X_t^s + \beta_1 r_t^m + \mu_t^s \qquad [14]$$

where X_t^d and X_t^s denote independent variables other than the mortgage rate r_t^m and the error terms μ_t^d and μ_t^s, that influence the demand and supply of mortgage funds M_t^d and M_t^s respectively. Conventionally, price setting behaviour is specified as a function of the prevailing level of excess demand such that $\triangle r^m$ can be used as an indicator of excess demand. Thus:

$$\triangle r_t^m = \delta(M_t^d - M_t^s) \qquad 0 \leq \delta \leq \infty \qquad [15]$$

The instance of δ equal to zero represents the polar case of no adjustment while δ equal to infinity is the polar case of perfect adjustment. Earlier comments in this chapter suggest that δ lies between these polar cases.

Solving for the level of excess demand gives

$$(M_t^d - M_t^s) = 1/\delta \, (\triangle r_m) \qquad [16]$$

From equation [16], it follows that a positive increase in r_t^m implies excess demand and $M_t^s = M_t^q$ if condition [12] holds. Thus:

$$M_t^q = M_t^s = \beta_0 X_t^s + \beta_1 r_t^m + \mu_t^s, \quad \triangle r_t^m \geq 0 \qquad [17]$$

and from [16]

$$M_t^q = M_t^s = M_t^d - 1/\delta \, (\triangle r_t^m) =$$
$$\alpha_0 X_t^d + \alpha_1 r_t^m - 1/\delta \cdot \triangle r_t^m + \mu r_t^d, \quad \triangle r_t^m \geq 0 \qquad [18]$$

131

Therefore, the parameters of the demand schedule can be estimated despite the prevailing excess demand and using observed quantity as the dependent variable, as long as change in mortgage rate is included as an implicit adjustment for the amount of rationing. The same principles apply with respect to a reduction in the mortgage rate. In this case, equation [16] implies excess supply and $M_t^q = M_t^d$, therefore:

$$M_t^q = M_t^d = \alpha_0 X_t^d + \alpha_1 r_t^m + \mu_t^d, \triangle r_t^m \le 0 \qquad [19]$$

and from equation [16]:

$$M_t^q = M_t^d = M_t^s + 1/\delta \cdot (\triangle r_t^m) = \beta_0 X_t^s + \beta_1 r_t^m$$
$$+ 1/\delta \cdot \triangle r_t^m + \mu_t^s, \triangle r_t^m \le 0 \qquad [20]$$

The system of equations [16]–[19] can be reduced to one demand schedule, which can be estimated over the entire sample period, if the appropriate adjustments are made as given by the direction of change of the mortgage rate.

$$M_t^q = M_t^d - 1/\delta \triangle r_t^m$$
$$= \alpha_0 X_t^d + \alpha_1 r_t^m - 1/\delta \left[\triangle r_t^m \right] + \mu_t^d \qquad [21]$$

$$\left[\triangle r_t^m \right] = \begin{cases} \triangle r_t^m & \text{if} & \triangle r_t^m > 0 \\ 0 & \text{if} & \triangle r_t^m < 0 \end{cases}$$

and

$$M_t^q = M_t^s + 1/\delta \triangle r_t^m$$
$$= \beta_0 X_t^s + \beta_1 r_t^m + 1/\delta \left(\triangle r_t^m \right) + \mu_t^s \qquad [22]$$

$$\left(\triangle r_t^m \right) = \begin{cases} r_t^m & \text{if} & \triangle r_t^m < 0 \\ 0 & \text{if} & \triangle r_t^m > 0 \end{cases}$$

Equation [21] is equivalent to [18] and [19], while equation [22] is equivalent to [17] and [20].

There are a number of weaknesses and problems associated with the application of this method. First, the specification implies symmetry of the disequilibrium adjustment process. That is, the rate of change of excess demand with respect to change in the mortgage rate is the same irrespective of whether the prevailing mortgage rate lies above or below its equilibrium level. This, it may be argued, is not plausible. Second, there is the technical problem of simultaneous equation bias due to the endogeneity of r_t^m and $\triangle r_t^m$. Third, equation [15] may be an incorrect specification, particularly in the UK context. The inflexibility of building society rate setting behaviour suggests that the mortgage rate may respond to some lagged value of excess demand rather than to the current value, thus leaving doubt as to the excess demand status of the market at switching points in the mortgage rate change series. A further important point is that rate rigidity in the UK is due to political considerations and cost factors (see pp 125). This would imply a far more complicated specification than that given in equation [15].

Riley (1974), Hadjimatheou (1976) and Mayes (1979) have, however, used a variant of this method, with the discrepancy between the actual liquidity ratio ℓ and the desired liquidity rate ℓ^* used as an indicator of excess demand. As noted earlier, Hadjimatheou's disequilibrium adjustment hypothesis is that building societies are assumed to vary their liquidity ratio directly with the degree of excess demand so that a compromise is struck between *ex ante* demand and optimum supply M^{as}, where the latter is defined as that flow of mortgage advances which maintains $\ell = \ell^*$. To deduce specification for M^d and M^{as} for estimation purposes, Hadjimatheou uses the equalities of the building society balance sheet. Assume that the asset side of the building society balance sheet is comprised of mortgage advances M, and liquidity assets, L, liabilities to constitute shares and deposits, S^d and general reserves, G^r, then:

(i) $A \equiv M + L$ (ii) $T \equiv S^d + G^r$ [23]

where A = total assets and T = total liabilities. Defining $\ell = \dfrac{L}{A}$, the liquid assets ratio and $\dfrac{G^r}{T} = g_r$, the reserve asset ratio and setting total assets equal to total liabilities gives:

$$\frac{M}{1-\ell} \quad \frac{S^d}{1-g_r} \text{ or } M(1-\ell)\ aS^d \text{ where } a = \frac{1}{1-g_r}$$ [24]

The actual flow supply of mortgages advances M^{as} will be:

$$M^{as} \equiv M^a_t - M^a_{t-1} \equiv a\left[S^d_t(1-\ell_t) - S^d_{t-1}(1-\ell_{t-1})\right]$$ [25]

Earlier the optimum flow supply of mortgage $M^{as'}$ was defined as being that amount which will maintain the liquidity ratio at the desired level ℓ^*. Substituting ℓ^* for ℓ_t in [25] yields:

$$M^s = a\left[S^d_t(1-\ell^*) - S^d_{t-1}(1-\ell_{t-1})\right]$$ [26]

If it is assumed that building societies pursue the dual objective of maintaining $\ell = \ell^*$ and meeting *ex ante* demand, then this can be specified as:

$$M^{as} = M^s + \theta(M^d - M^s) = \theta M^d + (1-\theta)M^s$$ [27]

where it is expected that in situations of excess demand, $0 < \theta < 1$, so that building societies are prepared to run down their liquidity ratio in order to enhance their ability to meet demand. When demand equals supply, $\theta = 0$ as both demand and liquidity ratio objectives can be attained, while in the case of excess supply, $\theta = 1$ as $M^{as} = M^d$ and building societies allow their liquidity ratio to rise above ℓ^*. Substituting [26] from [25] yields:

$$M^{as} - M^s = aS_t^d(\ell^* - \ell_t) \text{ or } M^{as} = M^{as} - aS_t^d(\ell^* - \ell_t) \qquad [28]$$

and substituting for M^{as} from [27] gives

$$M^s = M^d - aS_t^d(\ell^* - \ell_t) \qquad [29]$$

which upon using [28]:

$$M^s = M^d - \left[\frac{1-\theta}{\theta}\right] aS_t^d \left[\ell^* - \ell_t\right] \text{ where } \left\{\ell^* - \ell_t\right\}$$
$$= \begin{cases} (\ell^* - \ell_t) \text{ if } (\ell^* - \ell_t) > 0, \\ 0 \text{ otherwise} \end{cases} \qquad [30]$$

yields the basis of an estimating equation from which estimates of the demand parameters and θ can be derived.

More recently there has been a series of attempts in the UK to simultaneously model the housing and mortgage markets. A full discussion of macroeconometric models of this kind is beyond the scope of this book. But a brief comment is in order. In recent studies of house price appreciation at the national (Mayes 1979) and regional levels (MacAvinchey and Maclennan 1981) econometric models have simultaneously examined housing demand, supply and finance sectors. In the Mayes model a very full monetary model of the building society sector is allied to housing starts and demand equations to explain price trends for new housing and Mayes concludes that building societies have had an effect on the rate of house price appreciation. The regional model of Maclennan and MacAvinchey, which includes secondhand as well as new housing, has a much less extensive specification of the financial sector but concludes that expansion in funds available for lending has a rapid effect on house prices. However, the strength of this effect varied across regions and, at the urban or regional level, a much more detailed analysis of building society behaviour is required. That is, it becomes increasingly important to develop models of building society behaviour which are operationally useful at the local level. However, the microeconomics of lender behaviour, which is critical to an analysis of local housing markets, has not been systematically developed although there are now some strands of empirical research being developed.

The microeconomics of building society behaviour

The microeconomic models of building societies discussed above pertained to instances where a representative society was concerned with top-level decisions where variations in interest rates, liquidity or reserve ratios, *etc.* were under consideration. But here there is a more detailed concern with two questions. First, do all societies behave in the same way and are there any signs of allocative inefficiency arising from oligopoly practices. Second, at the individual branch level, where interest rates, liquidity ratios, *etc.* are taken as given, how do individual decision takers allocate funds for house purchase? In particular, do rationing policies have any well-defined spatial or sectoral effects within a local housing market?

Industry level analysis

In a recent study Hill and Gough (1980) were concerned that increasingly industrial concentration within the building society movement had resulted in market imperfections rather than economies of scale. Assuming that society managers would react in accordance with models of managerial utility maximisation, they hypothesised that allocative inefficiencies would be reflected in levels of advertising expenditures, executive salaries and management expenses.

On examining the ratio of management expenses per £100 of assets against society size Hill and Gough suggested that this ratio fell with society size but at a decreasing rate. Further, they maintained that this relationship was stronger for larger societies and had strengthened between 1976 and 1979. This finding implied that, whilst there were few efficiency gains from the growth or merger of middle-sized societies, increased managerial efficiency accompanied growth in large societies. In addition, larger societies appeared to be more efficient in relation to the number of branches required to conduct business. However, regarding salary levels, they were significantly higher per units of assets held in larger societies. Thus society growth and managerial salaries are positively correlated. The work undertaken by Hill and Gough is a useful first step to the development of an 'industrial economics' of the housing market but further detailed studies are required before there can be any conclusive statement as to whether societies are efficient or inefficient.

Branch-level analysis

In many respects the critical interaction between housing consumers, or at least intending purchasers, and the mortgage market is conducted at the individual branch level. At the branch level, in the short and medium term, the supply of funds available for lending and the interest rates prevailing for borrowers and lenders are exogenously fixed by higher level decisions. Even if the mortgage rate set were to clear the national mortgage market it is unlikely that a unique equilibrium of the demand for and the supply of mortgages will prevail in all local housing markets. Thus, in localised or general mortgage market disequilibrium a series of instruments are available to local managers to control or ration the effective demand for mortgages.

135

Society managers may vary the percentage loan they will make for house purchase, lowering it when severe excess demand exists and raising it when the potential number of customers is falling. Or the duration of the mortgage may be altered. A reduction in loan period will raise repayment flows and managers may also view shorter term loans as being less risky. Further the building society, nationally or locally, may have, in periods of excess demand, priorities for lending. In Britain, with a cavalier disregard for filtering arguments and the connectivity of housing submarkets, societies reportedly bias lending towards first-time purchasers and job-related housing moves. In such conditions of excess demand for mortgages, which have been prevalent throughout the 1970s in Britain, these policies may impose severe welfare losses on the non-priority groups.

Building societies, even in periods of mortgage market equilibrium, must also scrutinise, at the branch level, applications for mortgages and mortgage amounts in order to ensure the safety of lenders' investments. That is, the society has to ensure that the riskiness of lending is consistent with the mortgage rate and the desired supply of mortgages. Thus, in assessing mortgage applications a society may employ a variety of criteria.

1. Applicants' income level. The society must be satisfied that the level and likely stability of an applicant's income will allow the purchaser to repay the mortgage with minimal risk of default. However, it could be argued that, unless concerns for the welfare disbenefits of default to the borrower rather then lender interests are paramount, British societies are somewhat conservative in this regard. Insurance schemes and appreciating property values generally imply that societies will incur no loss to lenders if a property is resold following a mortgage default. Of course such defaults raise building society costs and may lead to a loss of managerial utility or, if they are persistent in a given branch, they may damage individual promotion or salary prospects. Such considerations probably result in loan offers and income multiples being somewhat lower than those which would prevail in a competitive mortgage market. It need not be the case that a near zero rate of default is the optimum default rate.

2. Society managers, particularly with resalability of a property and likely improvement costs in mind, adopt rules regarding property types suitable for lending. Historically in Britain, small, low amenity flats have not attracted particularly high levels of support from building societies. However, since 1975, it is apparent that British societies, either pursuing a new social objective or following the pattern of rehabilitation activity, have increased lending on older, inner-city properties.

3. It is often argued that regional or local branches of building societies pursue explicit spatially based lending policies. That is, particular

areas of a local housing market are mapped out and declared unsuitable for society lending. This is commonly called 'red-lining'. Such a strategy, if it does exist, may reflect several possible managerial decisions. The decision may reflect exactly the distribution of structurally unsound, high risk properties, or it may be entirely whimsical. Both these explanations are implausible and more probably if areas are red-lined it reflects a managerial perception of risky lending which, for administrative ease, is expressed in geographic terms. It is, of course, pertinent to question why particular areas or properties are viewed as being bad risks. The risk to the building society only exists if the borrower is unable to repay interest and principal. Such default is only likely to occur if property values fall from the initial purchase price level due to shifts in submarket demand (which is hardly a relevant concern in older, inner-city housing in Britain in the 1970s) or if the property develops structural difficulties. Since properties are surveyed prior to the granting of a loan this should imply that older areas *per se* are not riskier although the proportion of unsound houses may be greater. In this respect, of course, the society manager is heavily dependent upon the advice of property surveyors who may have area preferences and prejudices. Moreover, when excess demand for mortgages prevails, the society manager suffers no penalties from refusing to lend down market.

If red-lining exists, either as a whim or as a broad administrative convenience, then there will be area lending deficiencies with potentially serious spatial and social consequences within the local housing system. But does red-lining really occur?

Red-lining

Concern regarding the lending behaviour of urban housing market institutions first became significant in American cities in the 1960s. Political responses by neighbourhood and community groups resulted in a series of piecemeal studies which suggested that the price and availability of home loan finance differed between inner core and suburban areas. Progressive improvements in academic research produced first systematic descriptions of lending patterns and interest rates, then better statistical descriptions of the types of areas affected (using census tract data) and, finally, econometric tests to discover whether area lending patterns reflected consumer or institutional behaviour. The North American literature, which has induced substantial legislative change but has not generated definitive conclusions on the economic determinants of area lending patterns, is concisely summarised in Benston (1979).

Although the red-lining hypothesis has been transferred with considerable polemical vigour (Boddy 1976) to the British context, the subsequent research effort has been disappointing and economists have ignored the issue almost entirely. Instead the red-lining issue has been investigated in two major ways. First, using an analytical framework which stresses the role of urban managers or 'gatekeepers' sociologists have examined the 'attitudes' and role of building society managers. Results of such surveys (Ford 1975; Jones 1979b) generally imply that managers deny the existence of red-lined areas, are willing to explicitly discuss income or property type lending rules and defensively assert that low densities of society lending in inner areas reflect a lack of consumer demand for mortgages in such locations. Of course, geographical studies of lending patterns confirm such area deficiencies (Boddy 1976, 1980) but have been rather naïve in assuming that such patterns directly reflect red-lining decisions at the managerial level. A more convincing approach in this respect has been provided, if for a very small area, by Williams who describes a series of changes in lending behaviour over time as an inner area (Islington) was gentrified (Williams 1976).

A recent economic study (Maclennan and Jones 1980) attempted to explain lending patterns in the city of Glasgow for 1976. The pattern of finance, on an individual house basis, was established for each major society at a detailed spatial scale, and this pattern was related to the location, tenure structure, size and rateable value and price of houses in each small area (500 m²). The proportion of society transactions in sales in a given area was found to be low for smaller, older, lower value houses in the inner city. But a survey of building society managers in the local housing market indicated that only one society declared that it operated an area based lending policy. However, for the same time period, 524 house purchasers (first-time buyers) had been surveyed to establish the nature of their housing and loan finance search processes. Failures to acquire houses and loans had been established. It was then hypothesised that the failure to secure a loan could have a well-defined area pattern arising from

1. An explicit area based lending policy.
2. An income rule which would ration-out low income households who would, in all probability, be examining low price houses in the inner area.
3. A property type rationing rule which could, because of the spatial structure of the housing stock, result in area loan deficiencies.

A logit analysis indicated that the probability of a loan refused would increase for smaller houses, for low borrowing capacity houses and for inner area locations. Thus a series of lending rules produced an area effect. Two further conclusions were important. First, in the absence of detailed knowledge of structural defects of property the area effect could still reflect sensible building society lending policies in relation to 'risky' property. Second, the no-demand defence of building societies was confounded by the facts and, in addition, it may represent a theoretical mis-specification of the housing choice process involved. For, building societies are a prime source of advice to first-time purchasers and as such they participate in and influence area search and choice strategies for housing and they 'nudge' households away from Glasgow's inner core.

Conclusion

In the development of a microeconomics of local housing markets it is critical to have a well-modelled financial sector. Considerable theoretical progress, and indeed empirical testing, has occurred in relation to developing a 'microeconomic' basis for macroeconomic models. But at the urban focus of research monetary economics and urban economics have contributed negligibly to the development of housing models and research in this field has remained theoretically and empirically unconvincing, at least in Great Britain.

6 The political economy of housing policy: an overview

Housing policy analysis – diversity of approach

During the last four years there has been a sustained growth in the volume of informed publications concerned with housing policies in the United Kingdom (see, for instance, Murie, Niner and Watson 1976; Stafford 1978; Lansley 1979; Housing Policy Review, Technical Volumes 1–3, HMSO 1977; Duclaud-Williams 1978; Cullingworth 1979). Although housing policies for the United Kingdom are viewed by all these contributions as being, at least in certain respects, irrational and inefficient (with the exception of the more delusive sections of the Green Paper) the identification of inadequacies and prescriptions for remedies varies across all these contributions. For instance, in the essentially economics texts, Stafford (1978) calls for a reduction of the role of government in housing policy and for a reconstruction of policy according to 'liberal' Paretian criteria. On the other hand Lansley (1979) presents a vigorous defence of intervention in the housing system and he emphasises concerns for equity and problems of chronic market failures.

Disagreement on policy is not, of course, restricted to academic circles and inter-party political differences on policy are well known. But even within the same party or government successive ministers may adopt quite different approaches to housing policy. For instance, in calling for a review of housing finances in 1975 the late Anthony Crosland labelled the then existing system as being irrational and inadequate and that no 'sacred cows' of policy should survive the review. Between 1975 and 1977 the housing finance review was expanded in coverage to become the housing policy review and at the same time Peter Shore became the responsible minister. By the time the review was in its final stages of preparation and on subsequent publication it became apparent that most of the sacred cows were still grazing peacefully. The finance and subsidy systems remained largely unaltered though the government displayed a concern to take a broad and 'consensus' view of policy. Instead of radically revising policy the then Labour government were prepared to take account of new policy pressures by adding a new layer of *ad hoc* and restricted policy measures to enhance housing choices, to expand owner-occupation, to undertake limited and selective sales of council houses and to stimulate investment in private rental housing (Housing Policy, Cmnd. 6851, 1977).

But why does such a diversity of viewpoints on housing policy arise? At least three factors influence views on policy. First, individuals take different views on what constitutes housing policy. Second, different ethical positions are adopted and, all too frequently, value judgements of analysts are disguised beneath a patina of apparent technical sophistication. Third, in the absence of the results of applied research, individuals adopt different views or assumptions about how the housing system actually operates. For instance, the fierce parliamentary debate over the sale of council houses (January 1980) illustrates all these points but the absence of information on which to base policy is particularly evident. The diversity of individual viewpoints adopted for ethical, empirical or analytical reasons generally results in analysts finding some grounds for becoming dissatisfied with housing policy and labelling it 'irrational', 'non-comprehensive' or 'unsystematic'. Indeed, policy may be all these things when judged against theoretically derived counsels of perfection arising from either market based or socialist models. But is such a comparison fair and/or valid as such theoretical models often exclude discussion of the costs of and mechanisms for formulating policy?

The political economy approach

It is possible that many of the polar viewpoints and tensions which emerge in the discussion of housing policy amongst economists arise from a failure to undertake policy analysis from the standpoint of applied political economy. In the previous chapters of this volume it has been suggested that neoclassical microeconomic models were primarily utilised for their theoretical properties which allowed a deductive aggregation of market influences from microeconomic to macroeconomic levels (Weintraub 1979) and that these models are not always appropriate for the empirical analysis of housing markets. When these simple models are inappropriate for the analysis of housing markets then deductive, partial or general equilibrium models should not be used as a theoretical framework for evaluating the effects or efficiency of housing policies even if Paretian value judgements are a summary of society's welfare function.

Governments or society may, in addition, choose to pursue non-Paretian objectives. In Chapter 3 it was stressed that it is important to understand the variety of objectives facing households, to identify 'the models of the world' which individuals use to pursue these objectives and to trace the processes of adjustment to preferred solutions. By analogy, therefore, it is not enough to restrict the role of the political economist to accurately describing market behaviour for policy makers – although such action may be an improvement on proferring advice largely based on deductive reasoning and assumption. Instead, applied economic analysis of policy (or political economy) requires the analysis of a more detailed set of questions. For instance, the analyst must enquire as to what are the objectives of government, what role housing policy plays in attaining such objectives, who actually makes housing policy, what economic and political constraints restrict action, what advice and information exists and what model of the housing system is used by policy makers? These questions are not to be viewed as minor concerns for applied economists. Economists may deduce conditions for optimality or second best conditions for the design of housing policies *ad infinitum* but unless they understand how economic analysis and research is absorbed and transformed by the policy process they run the risk of having their work, at best, ignored or, at worst, misused.

In the North American context Grigsby (1978) has identified 'two worlds' of housing research. 'World 1' contains individuals pursuing the construction and, more occasionally, testing of precise deterministic models of the operation of the housing system. 'World 2' includes economists and others involved in the process of formulating policy. The existence of a range of skills and degrees of involvement in the policy-forming process is no bad thing for academic economists but when interests become so sharply and visibly fragmented miscommunication and misunderstanding are liable to grow. If theoretical or applied economic analysis is to have an important and useful role in housing policy formulation in the UK, and the preconditions for this involvement are now auspiciously satisfied (Maclennan 1979c), there must be an interaction of deductive and inductive approaches.

The demand for economic analysis of housing policy

A failure by economists to clarify ethical and technical assumptions has, perhaps, allowed policy makers to be swayed by disciplinary conceptions of policies and housing systems which are ideologically clear and acceptable to governments but which rarely contained an underlying theory or model of how the housing system actually operates. In particular economic analysis is often mistakenly presumed to be simply about competitive housing markets and this has resulted in so-called 'social' as opposed to 'economic' approaches to housing policy – an important and false dichotomy in the UK.

It can be argued that recent attempts to raise the economic input to housing policy analysis in Britain have not occurred as a result of new conceptual or academic developments linking social and economic approaches to housing problems because such approaches have not evolved. Rather a series of external events have dictated the demand for economic analysis of housing systems. First, the overall performance of the national economy has been so poor that not only are resources for policy constrained but recent governments have taken the view that the share of public expenditure in the economy is detrimental to growth. As a result all public policies have become subject to more detailed scrutiny both internally to government and also externally. Thus, 'economic' priorities begin to transcend 'social' requirements. The trend to reducing the rate of growth of public expenditure is important in the housing policy field as housing and environmental budgets are relatively prone to nominal or real cuts (OECD 1979). The emergent pressure on housing policy resources since the mid-1970s has now been accelerated by the return of a government with an avowed reliance on markets as being the desired allocative mechanism. This commitment to freeing the economy from government intervention makes not only ethical judgements but technical assumptions and the latter may be questionable in relation to the housing market. Of course, these are quite wrong reasons for according status to housing economics – under market or socialist systems of provision economics is always important in indicating resources available for pursuing individual or collective objectives.

Not only have broad economic and political changes pushed economic analysis of housing to the fore but there were already shifts within the housing policy field which required new approaches. Since the First World War a peculiar mixture of 'administration', 'geography' and 'physical planning' tended to be the principal conceptual influence on housing policy. This reflects the historical housing priorities of governments. For instance, initially there was a preoccupation with disease eradication and the provision of sanitation. Subsequently there was a concern to provide a given number of houses of a particular quality to remove 'homelessness' or an absolute housing shortage and these houses were principally allocated by administrative rules rather than markets. In both instances policy analysis was largely couched in terms which could be, or were perceived to be, physically measurable. Housing amenities were physically defined in relation to size and style of house. Housing attributes related to environmental conditions and access to employment or leisure locations were generally ignored. At the same time benefits of policies were evaluated particularly in relation to centrally or paternalistically decided views as to what constituted household housing requirement. With these policy concerns dominant housing policy could be evaluated by relating physical outputs to costs (although the distributional effects of subsidised public rents created more conceptual difficulties). Thus, the major thrust of postwar policy in Britain really failed to consider individual demands and preferences and paid little regard to the operation of private housing markets or public-private sector interactions. The removal of widespread absolute shortages of housing has meant that an increasing number of house-holds are now faced with choice decisions within public housing and rising real incomes have enabled the choice of housing alternatives outside of the public sector.

If housing policy is to impact effectively on the housing system it is clear that policy has to take account of public-private sector inter-actions, it must plan, more or less actively, for the private sector and it cannot afford to ignore public sector preferences. Economics, if it is sensibly applied, can help central and local policy makers to identify preferences and choices and, following such an identification, assist in the policy planning process. Central government, if somewhat belatedly, has recognised this planning requirement and the Green Paper of 1977 (Housing Policy, Cmnd. 6851 1977) not only called for the need for policy to take account of preferences but also imposed on local authorities a statutory obligation to prepare housing plans for their areas which would take account of both public and private sectors. In Britain local authorities have an important role in interpreting and implementing housing policies but prior to 1977 they often had a prin-cipal or sole focus on public housing. Now they are having to explicitly research, monitor, analyse and plan for private housing. Under such an approach to policy, if housing system analysis techniques are locally applied and information and policy co-ordinated between central and local governments, then there is an important role for housing econo-mists in the preparation and analysis of housing policies. But to develop this role we first have to outline British housing policy.

The importance of housing policy in Britain

What is housing policy?

It was stated in the introduction to this chapter that disagreements on housing policy may sometimes arise because of different interpreta-tions of what constitutes housing or policy. In this chapter the label 'policy' is applied not to specific instruments or intervention but to a broader strategic conception. Policy may be active or passive – that is, non-intervention, as long as it is a posture adopted after consideration of options, should be regarded as a purposive policy position. For the moment the question of 'whose' policy or for whom will be left aside until later. Policy is then the purposive selection of a strategy by a government or its agents.

But it is still difficult to select a simple and widely acceptable definition of housing policy. At the simplest level it is conceivable to think of the operation of a housing market system in which there is no direct public provision or public pricing of housing and with no income redistribution via housing subsidies. In such a context, housing policy can be readily identified with that set of policy instruments designed to remove market-frictions and imperfections − hence facilitating the 'freely' competitive operation of markets. Here, housing policy is viewed as interventionist only with regard to imperfections endogenous to the housing market. This policy approach can be distinguished as housing *market* policy and constitutes the set of policies which the market orientated economists understandably, but mistakenly, have equated with housing policy more broadly defined.

A broader conception of policy becomes essential because of the budgetary significance of housing costs, the complexity of the commodity and the externalities generated by good and bad housing. Extending the market imperfections motive for intervention, tax subsidy and legal interventions may be required to correct complex externalities. The complexity of housing as an asset and commodity also implies that housing conditions directly impinge on a related set of other policies. For instance housing policy is directly linked to tax policy, local government finance, urban policy, environmental policy, monetary policy, social and education policy in direct and important ways. If the government pursues non-market strategies in these other areas of policy then complementary or compensating distortions may be required in the housing system. Thus it is misleading to apply a partial equilibrium approach to policy analysis as if the housing sector and housing policy existed independently of other policy areas. The formalisation of this argument is well-established in welfare economics (Lancaster and Lipsey 1957).

This broader conception of policy is particularly important in relation to the distribution of income and wealth. For governments may not only decide that the existing distribution of income and its associated pattern of housing expenditures is sub-optimal but they may also view the housing system as being an important channel of income redistribution. The nature of such intervention is discussed more fully below. At this stage it is emphasised that the narrow market 'imperfections' approach to policy severely understates the contribution that economics may make to housing policy analysis and that a broader approach is required.

145

Expenditure on housing policies

Adopting a broader conception of housing policy makes it difficult to identify precisely, let alone evaluate comprehensively, housing policy in Britain. A first approach to this problem can be made by empirically identifying the quantitative importance of various strands of housing policy. (See Postscript for changes since 1980.)

In this section we concentrate on comparative expenditures on housing policy, across time periods and countries, but this is a less than perfect measurement of housing policy. For instance, in the UK, expenditure occurring under government's 'Housing' budget, excludes rent and mortgage payments made for households by the Supplementary Benefits Commission and this sum, as indicated below, is substantial. Even if all housing expenditures are accurately identified to indicate exchequer commitments to policy an aggregate figure of this kind would neither indicate the real opportunity costs of raising the fiscal revenue nor would they indicate potential benefits in any precise fashion. Moreover expenditure, even if a detailed analysis of real costs and benefits were available, would not indicate the extent or effectiveness of all active housing policies. For housing policy objectives or housing market effects may be obtained via special tax as well as subsidy treatment of housing. For instance, the UK tax system may discourage private rental of housing and its improvement by refusing to allow landlords to depreciate assets against tax liabilities or the demand for owner-occupation may be stimulated by the failure to tax imputed rents on housing, or to offset mortgage interest payments against income tax liability (at an estimated revenue loss or cost to the exchequer of £1,500 m. in 1978/9) or by exempting principal residence from capital gains taxation (with an exchequer revenue loss of £2,000 m. in 1978/9). Additional administrative and judicial control devices, particularly on the supply side of the system and in the private rental sectors, have critical housing policies effects not measured by expenditure figures.

Accepting the limitations made above, expenditure figures can indicate some important characteristics of housing policy in Britain. Table 6.2 indicates the broad comparative significance of policy expenditures in the UK and Table 6.1 indicates the more detailed pattern of recent developments. The Tables indicate the following points:

1. Until 1980 housing programmes absorbed a relatively large share of public expenditure and, in turn, public expenditure is a relatively large share of gross domestic product. In the UK, this implies that policy expenditure on housing (narrowly defined) utilises around 3.25 per cent of GDP and this figure rises to almost 5 per cent when tax treatment of owner-occupiers and social security housing payments are included. Thus, although comparative international figures indicate

Table 6.1 *Public expenditure on housing in Britain (capital plus current)*

£ m. (1978 prices)	1973/4	1978/9	Expansion factor
Central government: housing	1,176	2,411	2.05
Central government: all	39,552	45,038	1.14
Local government: housing	2,931	2,414	0.82
Local government: all	16,875	16,951	1.00
All public expenditure	58,830	65,199	1.11
All public/GDP (%)	39	42	–
Housing/All public (%)	7.29	7.67	–
Housing/GDP (%)	2.85	3.22	–

Table 6.2 *Housing policy expenditure share of programme by level of government*

Country	Year	Central	State	Local	Figure
UK	1973/4	28.7		71.3	All government expenditure
UK	1978/9	50		50	
Australia	1971/2	29	24	47	Final consumption expenditure
Canada	1971/2	12	66	22	Gross expenditure
Germany	1973	19	43	38	Current expenditure
Netherlands	1970	67	–	33	All expenditure
Switzerland	1974	6	42	52	All expenditure

that residential investment expenditure is a relatively low share of GDP in Britain (see Housing Policy, Cmnd. 6851 1977) housing is policy intensive – at least in a relative sense.

2. Despite economic difficulties between 1974 and 1979, housing policy expenditures have had an expansion factor since which has exceeded local government and GDP expansions. However in 1976, 1977 and 1978 there were real falls in housing expenditure, particularly for capital programmes.

3. Of particular interest, with respect to who controls and implements policies, has been an apparent tendency for central government housing policy expenditures to grow more rapidly than local authority commitments. However, as in most other developed economies, a substantial share of housing policy expenditure is either controlled or implemented by local governments (see Postscript).

The more detailed presentation in Table 6.3 indicates some further important characteristics of housing policy in Britain.

Table 6.3 *Changes in public expenditure on housing policy: United Kingdom 1973/4 to 1978/9*

Item	Expansion factor 1973–8	% of total public expenditure on housing 1978/9
Current central government subsidies to local authorities	1.87	23.9
Rate fund contributions to local authorities	1.38	49
Central government subsidy to New Towns and SSHA	1.47	3
Housing Association – revenue deficit grant	2.22	0.4
Total current general subsidy	1.73	32.14
Rent rebates from central government	0.96	6.1
Rent rebates from rate fund	1.70	1.9
Rent allowance from central government	1.77	1.8
Total income related subsidy	1.15	9.9
Organisation and administration	1.51	4.2
Total current	1.55	46.22
Local authorities	1.01	41.25
New Towns and SSHA	1.21	4.2
New Towns and local authority sales(–)	1.14	– 3.3
Improvement grants from local authorities	0.46	3.0
Gross local authority lending for home loans	0.36	3.6
Loans and grants to Housing Associations	2.72	11.14
Total capital expenditure	1	
Total capital plus current	1.17	–

4. Even under broad headings, and with the exclusion of tax and control policies, there are clearly a large number of important housing policies.

5. Current account subsidies were predominantly, and increasingly 'general' rather than income related subsidies. The rent rebate and allowance schemes in Table 6.3 are directly related to recipient incomes (as of course are additional supplementary benefit payments) but the general subsidies have no such precise relationship. The general subsidies demonstrate a markedly higher expansion factor than do income

subsidies (1.87 versus 1.15) for the period 1974−9. (For a recent contrast see the Postscript).

6. More than 50 per cent of public expenditure on housing, in a given year was on capital projects − the bulk of this expenditure being on new building as opposed to rehabilitation, though the latter programme had a high rate of expansion (expansion factor of 2.72) in the period 1974−9. This direct intervention by government on the supply side of the system implies that government in Britain does not restrict its interventions to a marginal cajoling of tastes and preferences but, rather, pursues a major interventionist role regarding the number, style, size and location of dwellings.

7. Even within an expenditure focused inventory of policies it is apparent that policy influences flow not only from central government but also from New Towns, Housing Corporation, *etc.* as well as local governments.

It is clear from this simple analysis that housing policy is important in the UK, its economic significance is increasing and policy consists of a complex of demand and supply side policies which are pursued by at least two levels of government. It is important now to consider, from an economic standpoint, why housing policy is so extensive and complex, because it is apparent from the figures presented above that housing policy in Britain ranges far beyond the correction of market imperfections.

Economic analysis and policy formulation

Cullingworth (1979) is correct to stress that housing policy analysis is often more concerned with 'getting the issues right' than becoming involved in detailed 'arithmetic', and in this respect economic theories and descriptions of the housing system may be valuable as long as they do not adopt a narrow view of policies. But economics can assist policy not only by clarifying the issues through research but also by indicating whether analytical assumptions are primarily technical (i.e. scientific) or ethical judgements. Further, when acting in an advisory capacity, the economist can accept government determined priorities or objectives as being the targets for optimisation and indicate the appropriate mix of policies to achieve the government's or society's objectives. This technical role for the economist can utilise market models as a framework for discussing the empirical outcomes of policies without presupposing that the results are to be ordered according to a Paretian welfare function. Economic models do indicate the market circumstances in which policy is likely to be required. The likely forms of policy may also be suggested by deductive argument. It is therefore important to assess how economists have developed justifications for or critiques of

149

housing policy. The minimal intervention or 'free market' school of thought has been pervasive in the analysis of housing policy.

The free market argument

It is useful to review the 'Free Market' arguments with respect to housing policy for at least three reasons.

1. The present government is making a greater commitment to free markets and price mechanism resource allocations than any of its postwar predecessors. Thus the arguments have a practical relevance.
2. Housing policy analysis is undertaken not only by economists but by contributors from other disciplines who may be unaware of the technical and ethical properties of market models and who, as a result, either accept or reject economic analysis of policy unthinkingly.
3. A restatement of the free market arguments is a useful starting point for economic analysis of policy as a clear statement indicates the technical and ethical properties of the model.

The confusion arises because two quite distinct schools of thought utilise the term 'free market' somewhat differently. The Paretian liberal conception of a 'free market' is concerned with markets which work without frictions, that is they are free from endogenous structural or operational limitations. This notion of a free market is consistent with the existence of policies to remove imperfections. Thus, if the Paretian liberal conception of 'free market' pertains then Lansley is quite incorrect in stating that the existence of policy reflects the fact that the free operation of the pricing mechanism would be unable to meet housing objectives (Lansley 1979). For policy may exist to 'free' the market.

However, a different conception of free market pervades *laissez faire* approaches to policy. The *laissez faire* school, to which many members of the present government appear to belong, combines a liberalist philosophy designed to minimise restrictions on individual freedom with a rejection of the notion of the state as an omniscient servant of the public good. This approach to policy implies non-intervention unless markets are exceptionally uncompetitive and even then intervention is likely to be judicial to shift the distribution and control of property rights in order to regenerate competition.

In the remainder of this book the term 'free market' applies to freedom from operational imperfections — that is endogenous fixities, structures or frictions which would prevent prices and profits acting as effective signals and preclude optimising adjustments. Thus, the term 'free market' or 'market' approach is here used to indicate the existence of a competitive market system for resource allocation by households and firms. The term does not imply that a market economy is 'freer' in some wider social or political sense, nor does it imply that the system is free from policy, nor does it imply that a social optimum has been achieved.

Economic optimality and Pareto optimality

The evaluation or welfare interpretation of market or policy outcomes has long posed a major, and so far insoluble, problem for economists. Economists conventionally assume that individual welfare consists of satisfactions derived from the consumption of goods and services and that social welfare is a simple sum of individual well-being. But welfare, utility or satisfaction are not cardinally measurable and it is therefore logically impossible to assess whether the welfare loss one individual suffers from a policy change is less than, equal to or greater than the gains of a beneficiary. Even if utility was measurable such comparisons would require the judgement that the welfare of all individuals in a society was equally important − perhaps not an unreasonable judgement but a judgement none the less.

To escape the problem of making doubtful scientific judgements regarding the marginal utility of income as encountered in Pigou (namely, the assertion that the marginal utility of income declines with income which implies that redistribution increases social welfare) or of making inherently ethical comparisons of gainers and losers from policies, many economists, at least until prior to the 1950s, made welfare evaluations based on whether or not policy changes satisfied the Pareto criterion. The Pareto principle stated that:

> If any change in the allocation of resources increases the income and leisure of everyone or at least of one person . . . without reducing those of any other, then the change should be considered to have increased social welfare (Nath 1969: 19).

This is the Pareto welfare criterion, a criterion which is in fact not applicable to many changes in housing policy which have gainers and losers and which involve actual as well as potential changes. However, the idea of Pareto optimality became deeply entrenched in welfare economic analysis because it could be demonstrated that a perfectly competitive market in equilibrium would produce a position of Pareto optimality. (Nath 1969; Rowley and Peacock, 1975). However, this fortunate coincidence of the 'micro' and 'welfare' paradigms was not to last unchallenged.

The equation of a welfare optimum with perfect competition in equilibrium is still an important idea in housing economics and many economists appear to be willing to adopt both the beliefs that the market is perfectly competitive and that Pareto criteria have social relevance − see for instance Stafford (1978). Leaving aside the problems associated with the prior ethical assumptions of the Pareto paradigm that the existing income distribution is acceptable, markets produce Pareto optimality in the following way. Self-interested, satisfaction optimising decisions of rational households result in a market demand schedule where willingness to pay the price reflects the marginal satisfaction an additional unit of a given good will yield to the household. Moreover, this rational choice by households is extended over all goods in the consumption set so that the ratio of marginal utility to prices is equalised over all goods. This Exchange Condition ensures that no reallocation of household budget would raise household satisfaction. In addition, it is assumed that households optimally allocate resources and time between consuming and producing goods and services. Finally, the Technical Efficiency Condition implies that firms have responded to all cost and price relationships so that: 'The ratio between the marginal physical products of any two factors must be the same in the production of all commodities' (Nath 1969: 14).

Clearly these conditions are satisfied in general competitive equilibrium where prices are equated with short-run marginal costs in the short run and long-run marginal costs when capacity is varied. But economists have to be careful in their labelling of the Pareto outcome in competitive markets. That is:

> Though this concept is often loosely referred to as an 'optimum allocation' or an 'economic optimum', the only name it can be given if the risk of misleading people is to be minimised is that of 'a Paretian' optimum because the allocation that the concept refers to is optimal only in the light of the Paretian set of value judgements, [that is approval of the initial distribution of income and resources and consumer sovereignty]. An allocation which is Paretian optimal might be non-optimal in the light of some other value judgements (Nath 1969: 19).

Moreover, this preoccupation with the technical statement of a deterministic, precise, optimum can often obscure the basic operational allocative principles which may exist outwith 'perfect' competition. That is, market allocation, even with less than perfect competition, assumes that offer prices accurately reflect subjective valuations of commodities. Thus in the housing market, if two individuals with equal incomes were bidding for the same house the household with a stronger preference for that house would pay more for it and would, as a consequence, become the owner or tenant. Under a price or market system, therefore, subject to income distribution constraints, goods are allocated to households which most desire them. At the same time as prices act as a rationing device, they also act as a critical signal to suppliers to alter their provision of housing – either by raising service levels, conversion or new building. Rising prices for current sales or existing stocks will encourage suppliers to transfer resources to the housing sector until normal profits are earned and a new equilibrium price attained.

The standard Paretian welfare model, to produce a single determined optimum – usually instantaneously, requires the assumption that supply is organised in perfectly competitive markets. By implication, the analysis shows that when barriers to free choice or supply side adjustment exist they should be removed. That is to say, events or endogenous characteristics of markets which preclude excess demands being reflected solely in prices (which then stimulate profit levels which trigger supply adjustments) should be removed or alleviated by policy. But this Paretian search for the 'ideal', whilst it is an illuminating exercise, is too strong or extreme a statement of the case for markets – indeed those economists who would prefer market to socialist systems of allocation may damage the credibility of their case by stating it in such extreme or 'perfect' terms. Few markets, if any, operate in the demanding, deterministic fashion, required by the neoclassical model – indeed, even perfect competition may not possess the informational characteristics required to produce an optimum resource allocation (G.B. Richardson 1959).

Certainly, the housing market, as indicated in Chapters 1 to 5, whilst having a dispersed set of transactions, has inherent imperfections from a Paretian standpoint. Thus even without perfect competition the choice between market and socialist systems of allocation still remains. The question is not whether a Paretian organisation of the housing market would be better than a pure socialist organisation (in fact, the results may be theoretically rather similar) but whether the housing market, or even part of it, is sufficiently competitive to make it preferable to an outcome designed by governments. There is, in the choice of allocative devices, an alternative between systems with economic imperfections and those where the imperfections are administrative/political. The latter type of intervention cannot be lightly dismissed by economists.

Whilst accepting that economists qua economists have no right to expect that their own or their discipline's judgements will be accorded priority there may be problems in accepting the role as technician to government in the pursuit of politically derived value judgements. What if the political system is unrepresentative or if major issues are jointly decided or if manifesto issues or promises are not translated into political action? In such circumstances should the economist accept that society's value judgements are accurately revealed? Abandoning a naïve assumption about the marginal utility of income should not force economists into equally naïve assertions about political systems. A mixed system may have the best, or worst, of both kinds of allocative system.

Thus the case for a free market in housing does not have to be argued in terms of perfect competition and the search for a Pareto optimum. For instance, when Adam Smith stressed the virtuous alliance of self-interest and competition (the Invisible Hand) he was not thinking of perfect competition but of some broader conception of competition. Even if this broader conception of competition is adopted and a non-Paretian social objective function exists there may be residual problems, or even major problems, in relying on prices as a rationing and allocative device in the housing market.

There are a variety of reasons why governments would wish to intervene in housing markets because the price system fails to allocate resources according to social criteria. Three main classes of intervention can be identified:

1. There may be a set of policies to establish efficient markets to remove frictions, imperfections and failures.
2. There may be a view that housing markets are inherently not amenable to 'corrective' or 'freeing' policies and that the price mechanism should be largely suspended.
3. There may be a view that, even if markets are allocatively efficient or amenable to efficiency policies, objectives (housing or non-housing) other than allocative concerns may dominate policy choices. For instance, concerns over income distribution or the dynamic growth aspects of housing policies.

These interventions represent a successively greater departure from reliance on the market as an allocative device and it is appropriate to examine such reasons for housing market intervention in more detail. Charles (1977) is probably correct to stress that there is no reason why there should be special rules for housing policy, even if the commodity is complex and an important share of household budgets. But this complexity combined with the varied and imperfect nature of the housing market does mean that multiple and important government interventions will take place.

Policies for improving market efficiency

Removing natural monopoly or monopoly

Under a competitive system of housing provision, in equilibrium, the price that the marginal consumer will be prepared to pay for the marginal unit of housing service will be equal to the marginal cost of providing that service. However, if there are monopoly elements, where producers have the economic or political power to fix service prices, then allocative inefficiencies may arise. In Fig. 6.1, AC and MC represent the cost curves facing producers of housing services. The market demand curve is AR_m and thus represents the average revenue curve facing a monopolistic firm. The schedule MR_m is the monopolist's marginal revenue schedule. If the monopolist is maximising short-run profits then the price P_m and output level H_m will prevail. This allocative configuration generated by the monopolist is

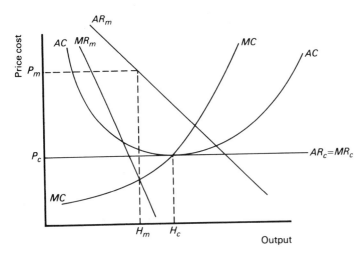

Fig. 6.1 The comparison of competitive and monopolistic firms' decisions

conventionally, and perhaps unfairly, compared with competitive output by assuming that price taking firms, with market equilibrium, will individually face a horizontal demand schedule, AR_c which cuts the AC curve at its lowest point. At such a position marginal costs of competitive production just equal the marginal valuation of additional housing services to consumers. The competitive price will be P_c and output H_c.

From the diagram it is apparent, and this is a general proposition, that monopoly price exceeds competitive price and monopoly output falls short of competitive output. As a result there is resource misallocation which favours the monopolist at the cost of consumer welfare. Of course this analysis is oversimplified. Monopolists may have access to internal scale economies or in a wider specification of the monopoly model non-profit motives may be pursued, cost curves may drift upwards, organisational or X inefficiencies may increase and advertising expenditures may become excessive. But do such monopolies exist in the housing system?

In general economists (see, for instance, Olsen 1969) assume that the housing market is atomistically competitive. In the British context assumptions of monopoly ownership have only been made by political commentators or Labour Party legislators in relation to private rental housing. Even in quite small areas of cities, the ownership of rented property is considerably dispersed and the development of new housing is also deconcentrated (see Ch. 8). Ironically, it is only really local public authorities which are monopolists in a market sense and their monopoly may be reflected not only in exploitative prices but also in poor practice, which, in some cases, may result in some tenants paying council rents in excess of probable market rentals (see Ch. 9).

As stressed in Chapter 4, the 'structure-conduct-performance' framework for the welfare analysis of markets or industries may not be appropriate in relation to the supply of new housing services. Aggregate numbers of housing producers and consumers in a particular housing system are not a good indicator of short-term but potentially recurrent monopolies within specific submarkets. The phrases 'sellers' and 'buyers' markets are commonplace in housing analysis, but here market power arises from lags or restrictions on adjustment to excess demands (scarcity rents) rather than in relation to ownership or producer concentration ratios (monopoly rents). For instance, monopoly as conventionally defined is seldom applicable to the structure of housing markets – but persistent excess demand arising from, say rent controls or lagged supply responses, increases the price-setting and discriminatory powers of landlords and sellers. The housing market may be particularly susceptible to such short-term generation of excess demands since demand responds more rapidly to changes in incomes, prices or mortgage availability than does supply. In consequence short-term excess demand may trigger off a variety of non-price adjustments, such as discouraged movement, reduced house-hold formation or increased occupational densities which may diffuse and reduce the clarity of price signals to suppliers. That is, housing is such a complex commodity that excess demand induces a variety of non-price adjustments which are difficult to monitor and this diffusion of price signals may hinder supply adjustments. If this then creates short-run monopolies a policy to increase awareness of housing market activity amongst 'extra-marginal' or 'marginal' suppliers may be appropriate – that is, 'indicative' information could emerge from local Housing Plans.

Further sources of housing market imperfections may arise as trans-acting in the housing market often requires households to deal with surveying, legal and financing agents. In the United Kingdom, for instance, housing finance is largely provided through building societies who, by approval, collude to fixed interest rates and who adopt generally similar policies on area lending or credit-worthiness of households (Hill and Gough 1980). The collusive behaviour of the building societies introduces a variety of distortions which affect particular groups of individuals or areas. For instance, restricting interest rate rises protects present borrowers and may disadvantage potential new entrants willing to pay higher rates of interest but not able to find funds for borrowing. Or area lending policies may result in households at the cheaper end of the housing market undergoing long and costly search processes for alternative finance or, worse still, force

156

households into a cash purchase and thereby deprive them of some of the fiscal benefits of home-ownership (Maclennan and Jones 1980). Or policies on advertising or costs may be criticised (Hill and Gough 1980).

In addition the ancillary services of surveying or conveyancing also require consideration. Repeat surveying with charges related to agreed scales is a doubtful practice in a competitive system. Even more questionable, at least in the UK and particularly in Scotland, is the system of charging for conveyancing fees which is, at best, only approximately related to solicitor cost or effort, and where an agreed scale is also operated. Expensive conveyancing in England and Wales has survived the recent Royal Commissions on legal services but the parallel Commission for Scotland has made more radical proposals which offer the hope that competitively priced conveyancing services will be available in the foreseeable future [Royal Commission, Cmnd. 7846. 1980].

Thus, natural monopoly tends only to be a characteristic of public housing although monopolistic elements exist in the services which are ancillary to housing transactions. Where market power exists in the housing market *per se* it generally arises from unadjusted excess demands which may reflect structural imperfections or policy interventions.

Externalities

It is possible in a market system that the pricing system does not extend over all the attributes of a commodity. That is, particular characteristics of a house such as its design, or its external finish may yield consumption satisfactions or dissatisfactions to individuals who are neither the owner nor renter of the property. Housing is a mixed private/public good. In instances where non-purchasing individuals cannot be excluded from enjoying attributes of the property (in the case of a beneficial externality), either because exclusion is technically not feasible or costly, then there may be under-provision of these facilities unless there is a tax-subsidy scheme, which taxes 'free-riders' and subsidises 'providers' of beneficial externalities. Similarly the producers of harmful housing externalities could, in principle, be taxed to reduce the output of external 'bads'.

In Fig. 6.2, let the horizontal axis represent increasing housing design services embedded in a single dwelling. Given the market demand curve, AR, and competitive supply conditions for housing services, MC, then the marginal individual will pay P_p for a house of quality H_p. But at some minimum level of housing quality, say H_0, individuals who do not reside in the dwelling will begin to enjoy (by assumption) the visual benefits of improved design. If these individuals are not able to form a club to bribe an owner to take account of their visual benefits then policy intervention may be required. Because, in this instance, social decision taking is concerned not just with the individual's demand curve but must also take account of the sum of the valuation of visual benefits across the benefiting parties. Let *AS* represent this valuation of externalities. Thus, *ceteris paribus*, the social demand for housing services is the vertical sum of *AR* and *AS* and this is represented by the schedule as '*ARS*'. In this instance individually chosen output, H_p, will fall short of the desired social output of housing services H_s. A subsidy scheme will generally be required to shift private output from H_p to H_s.

If benefit taxation schemes can be devised then public involvement may approximate to competitive market output. Alternatively, externalities may be controlled or regulated by policies other than taxation/subsidy. For instance, in the United Kingdom regulations or laws have generally been used to restrict disamenities arising from poor building and housing standards. This form of intervention, to prevent the spread of disease which would originate in low income housing but spread across a whole city, was an early and important component of British housing policy, with origins in the late nineteenth century. Thus a whole series of ethical decisions regarding the responsibility for producing or assuaging externalities may be taken which set the regulatory structure within which housing markets actually operate.

Information and uncertainty

Problems of information and search for consumers and producers are largely assumed away in neoclassical welfare economics because of

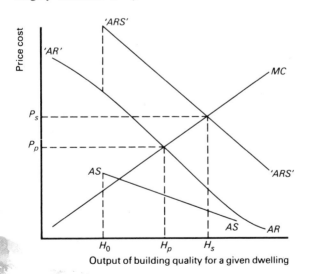

Fig. 6.2 Externalities and optimal housing output

assumptions about the nature of decision takers – namely that they possess perfect knowledge and complete rationality. If, as has been stressed earlier, housing purchases are infrequent and information made rapidly redundant, then policy should be designed to improve information services within the market and to ensure such services are competitively provided. For instance, in the UK would competitive legal service/financing/surveying provision combined with an open housing market, more akin to an auction market, result in better informed consumers operating in a more 'information-efficient' market? Is government wise to continue to allow gazumping or sealed bidding systems (in Scotland) as important influences within the market?

These three types of reason for housing market intervention, (removing monopolies, externalities and improving information) all are consistent with reliance on market systems of housing allocation and are intended to make markets freely competitive. But, using our broader conception of housing policy, governments may wish to pursue a range of policies through the housing system.

It should be stressed that the above policies are consistent with income redistribution, as long as income transfers occur through the direct tax system rather than via price distortions resulting from the system of housing subsidy.

When either monopoly or scarcity rents are likely to persist, or where policies to free resource allocation are impossible or expensive to devise then public provision may be required. For instance, rent controls were first introduced under wartime conditions in 1915 as there was no likely foreseeable supply adjustment. Second, in the postwar period, Bevan argued (and the subsequent MacMillan government apparently acquiesced in the view) that postwar reconstruction and slum clearance required public planning and redevelopment – though this is neither an argument for continued public ownership nor for direct works departments. In a more positive vein, the Scottish Special Housing Association has a particular remit to anticipate and ease housing problems associated with economic growth in local areas by responding to shortage, for instance in the areas of oil related on-shore development of north east Scotland. Or in dense urban areas, 'prisoners' dilemma' effects (Rothenberg 1967) and inelastic expectations regarding neighbourhood futures may require public action and expenditure to provide the focus and confidence for area revitalisation.

Policies when efficient markets cannot fulfil social objectives (non-Pareto welfare functions)

Consumer sovereignty and needs

The market approach assumes that individuals or households are the best judges of their own welfare. However, society can take a view that particular types of households will fail, even with general income redistribution, to consume adequate levels of housing. It is argued, for instance, that in a large family children or older persons may suffer as a result of not being involved in expenditure decisions. Or it may be argued that households are unaware of the consequences of their own actions (i.e. poor housing consumption generating bad health, *etc.*), or it may be that negative externalities are produced which cannot be internalised by developing bargains between the affected parties. For instance, if higher income groups have a concern for lower income groups in the arguments of their choice function, then interdependent utility functions require income redistribution to reach Pareto solutions (see Hochman and Rodgers 1964). Thus 'merit' wants are a poorly defined category of reasons for intervention as they can be justified on conceptually distinct grounds, e.g. externalities, optimal income redistribution, information failure, *etc.*, but they all imply that subsidised housing be provided directly to specific groups. Again such intervention may be consistent with Pareto optimal income redistribution or it may reflect an alternative political judgement about housing 'merits' or 'needs'. Both arguments have probably been important in Britain.

Redistribution of income

In Britain, housing market intervention, such as rent controls or public housing subsidy, are frequently defended on the grounds that they redistribute income. But, in general, housing economists have tended to argue that direct income transfer and market pricing principles should provide the basis for housing policy as they preserve consumer sovereignty and do not induce allocative distortions (Stafford 1978; Hepworth, Grey and Odling-Smee 1979). In terms of Paretian welfare functions 'general' rather than 'price-reduction/consumption tied' redistributions are more 'efficient'. This argument is illustrated in Fig. 6.3, which represents the choice between housing services, h, and other goods, x, subject to a budget constraint, BB. Given initial market prices of housing and other goods, P_h and P_x, respectively, the household can, with a given fixed income level, purchase h_m of housing, x_m of other goods or some combination of h and x lying along BB. But if the state wishes, for the reasons outlined above, to increase average housing consumption from the market determined level h_m to the societally desired level h_s, then it must alter the price or income of the household. If the price is subsidised then the budget line moves out to BS. The household now selects h_s and consumes the desired level of housing. This move from h_m to h_s consists of two discernible parts — the substitution effect of the price change which influences the household's choice between housing and other goods and between subsidised and unsubsidised housing and the income effect, that is the real income increase which accrues to the household as the result of the price change. Conventional Hicksian demand analysis by the use of the compensating variation technique, $CV - CV$, shows that the subsidy to housing increases housing consumption by a substitution effect with a move from h_m to h_1, and then by an income effect from h_1 to h_s. It is possible to indicate that if this income effect had occurred at the initial set of relative prices, then with consumer sovereignty, less housing would have been consumed than at h_s, but more than at h_m, and that, with most values of the price and income elasticity of demand for housing, the individual would have been on a higher indifference curve.

The point is too easily forgotten, however, that government intervention is often proposed in the housing system not solely to effectuate income redistribution but to ensure minimum consumption levels for externality or distributionally related concerns specifically to housing conditions. In essence, consumer sovereignty for one group of society is suspended in order to pursue politically determined housing objectives which embody both redistributional concerns and housing consumption targets.

First, government may not be faced with a consensus on distribution of income and therefore it is constrained to attempt a disguised redistribution via service provision rather than taxation. In the UK, for instance, many households pay taxes (which are income related in the main) to receive back substantial subsidies related to consumption rather than income levels. As a result, choices are distorted and income

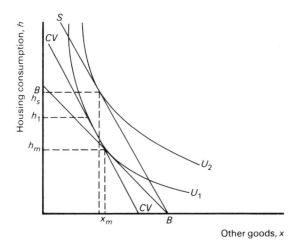

Fig. 6.3   Price and income related housing subsidies

161

redistribution has a largely unknown effect or incidence within the housing system. Second, and this argument was used by the 1917 Royal Commission on Housing in Scotland though its validity is now suspect, the costs of administering a redistribution policy separately of the housing system were prohibitive. Finally, important redistribution housing policies such as public sector rent structures in the UK may be implemented by local authorities who, as they do not have explicit sovereignty over instruments of income redistribution, may redistribute indirectly via service provision.

Other macroeconomic concerns

Governments may decide to use the housing system, apart from redistributing income, as an instrument rather than objective of policy. For instance, it has been commonplace in many countries, e.g. Sweden, to use house building as a device to stimulate or restrict aggregate demand. In the 1970s, in the United Kingdom, counter-inflation policies resulted in restricted rises in public and private sector rents and in government action to ameliorate or delay rises in mortgage interest rates.

Thus when the reasons for intervention in housing markets are examined it is not appropriate to take a narrow, static, allocative, neoclassical view, of housing policy.

Of course the arguments for the selection of a mixed housing policy can be turned around and instead of asking 'why intervene in a market economy' one can query 'in the socialist housing system when can market forces or pricing mechanisms be introduced?' Private housing provision actually occurs in many socialist economies – for instance the Soviet Union, Hungary and Poland. Freedom of choice, in particular for second or country homes, is allowed to exist mainly for higher income or political status groups. Additionally, in such systems it has been argued that price signals would help to determine the level and form of residential investment and a diversity of construction arrangements would speed up production and differentiate output. Indeed, where income distributions have already been socialised it may be advantageous to utilise the technical or signalling properties of markets.

Housing policies in Britain – a realistic view?

The objectives of policy

The above discussion has indicated that a variety of objectives may exist for housing policies ranging from policies to 'free' markets through to policies for general income redistribution via the housing system. Both may coexist and, of course, the greater the variety of objectives and instruments used for policy the more difficult it becomes to produce a rational, coherent policy which best uses resources to meet the goals of society. Housing policy may be irrational in economic terms, not because it contains non-market objectives, but because objectives are inconsistent and instruments inefficient. It is therefore misleading to discuss the efficiency or rationality of housing policy unless the overall objectives of policy are understood. But it is difficult to do this from an external analytical standpoint for a number of reasons.

The broad goals of policy, let alone the intentions of specific instruments, are seldom politically defined in operational terms — they are stated in terms of broad principles rather than specific targets. For instance, in the Green Paper of 1977, policy objectives were expressed in the following fashion:

> The Government believe that the objectives of housing policy must be rooted in the traditions and reasonable expectations of the nation, but must also reflect present realities. In the light of the conclusions on the present housing situation, the Government propose that policy for housing over the next decade should be directed towards the following objectives:
>
> (i) The traditional aim of a decent home for all families at a price within their means must remain our primary objective . . .
>
> (ii) We must try to secure a better balance between investment in new houses and the improvement and repair of older houses, with regard to the needs of the individual and the community, as well as to cost.
>
> (iii) Housing costs should be a reasonably stable element in family finances . . . They should not have to face sharp and disruptive increases in costs totally disproportionate to changes in their ability to pay.
>
> (iv) We must ensure that the housing needs of groups such as frail elderly people, the disabled and handicapped are met . . .
>
> (v) We must secure a reasonable degree of priority in access to public rented sector housing and home ownership for people in housing need who in the past have found themselves at the end of the queue . . .
>
> (vi) We must increase the scope for mobility in housing . . .
>
> (vii) We must make it easier for people to obtain the tenure they want . . .
>
> (viii) We must safeguard the independence of tenants . . . (Housing Policy, Cmnd. 6851 1977).

Even if such objectives were acceptable to the individual or society it would be difficult for an economist to make a concrete evaluation of them. This generality is in fact important. For instance the Green Paper on Housing Policy in Scotland (Scottish Housing, Cmnd. 6852 1977) expressed a commitment to increasing owner-occupation in Scotland. But since the extent of the desired shift, the location of intended changes and the rate of change were not indicated it was impossible to assess whether the policy and its instruments were consistent (Maclennan and Wood 1978).

Previously existing policies

The policy mix observed as in Table 6.3, is not, in all probability, the set of instruments or policies which would appear if the system was being designed *de novo*. There are several reasons for this. Policy tends to develop its own superstructure of expertise, interested parties and vested interests. In the case of housing policy, intergroup redistributions may be perceived to take on a well-defined pattern and gainers and losers from policy changes may be identified. In Britain when such divergences are serious and likely to have a cost in terms of votes, apparent fairness tends to be restored not by reducing the favoured party to the subsidy levels of the unfavoured group but by expanding subsidies to the latter. As a result, the level of commitment to policy expenditure may become extensive over time with households paying out large tax sums to central and local government which are, at least in part, returned in the form of housing subsidies. The distributional impact of subsidies in Britain is not known and it is therefore difficult to assess the net impact of policy on housing consumption.

The difficulties of evaluating existing policy are exacerbated because party policy differences may be stronger in rhetoric than in reality. In this respect, the views of Cullingworth are more convincing than those of Duclaud-Williams (Cullingworth 1979; Duclaud-Williams 1978). The major, broad (blunt?) instruments of British housing policy, which are examined in detail in the following three chapters, have evolved gradually since 1915 and successive governments have absorbed or progressively amended the legislation of predecessors rather than radically re-orienting policies. The Green Paper argued for such stability in policy as households had previously made rather long-term housing decisions on the basis of the then existing housing policy regime. But this is really a specious argument in favour of the *status quo* of advantage and disadvantage.

Who makes housing policy

Housing analysts often discuss policy as if the policy making agent was the sole policy decision taker in the field. Government is mistakenly treated as being a unitary whole with individual decision takers having uniform models, objectives and ideologies. But the very complexity of housing frustrates the achievement of such top-level co-ordination in government. Even within central government different departments have powers and policies to influence the housing system. This can be demonstrated at a point in time or over time. For instance (following Cullingworth 1979) housing policy was the responsibility of the Department of Health until 1952 (reflecting the health/sanitation priorities of housing policies), then the Ministry of Planning, the Ministry of Housing and Local Government, and then, reflecting a new wider environmental and urban concern, the Department of the Environment.

At the same time other government departments (other DOE ministries, the Treasury, Department of Industry, DHSS) have operated policies with housing market effects and impacts. For instance, Donnison (1979b) has recently drawn attention to the vast flow of social security payments, via supplementary benefits, which are made as housing payments. Further, the Treasury may pursue macro-economic policies which may frustrate or hamper housing sector policies. In the early 1970s general inflation, interest and tax policies may have contributed to a growing demand for owner-occupation. However, since 1979 a macroeconomic policy which entails, at least in the short term , high interest rates as a means of reducing inflation accompanied with tax cuts (thus reducing tax liabilities against which mortgage interest repayments may be offset) seems to run counter to a major housing commitment to expand owner-occupation and to sell council houses.

Despite attempts at inter-departmental co-operation (and this does not always occur) a totally co-ordinated policy is unlikely to emerge when a number of departments pursue a large set of goals for public policy. In addition important, discretionary decisions regarding housing policy may be administratively decentralised to regional offices of government departments. For instance Wales, Northern Ireland and Scotland all have decentralised administrative responsibilities in relation to housing and these are all important regions for housing problems and policies. The effects of decentralisation are difficult to pinpoint but these regions have been distinctive in the tone of circulars, the selection of research priorities and the development of planning systems which influence housing policy. For instance, a separate Green Paper was prepared for Scotland in 1977, Housing Plans and recent changes in the form of central government housing grants to local authorities have tended to precede changes in the rest of the UK by at least one year.

The complexity of decision taking within government is formidable but there are additional and important public policy influences which arise outside of government departments. The judiciary may influence the operation of policy, for instance the breakdown of the traditional definition of furnished and unfurnished tenancies reflected legal difficulties (see Farrand 1975). Similarly, although they are largely financed by central government, agencies such as the Scottish Special Housing Association, or the Housing Corporation, or even Rent Assessment Committees, have certain freedoms from central government. Such local flexibility may be appropriate for policy if objectives and principles are well defined nationally but a serious problem of policy control loss may occur if local objectives and ideologies are implemented.

Similar concerns over central-local relations may arise in connection with the activities of local governments. Local governments, and there are now almost four hundred local housing authorities in the UK, have an important role to play in relation to housing planning and policy. In general, public housing in Britain (32% of the stock) is locally built, allocated and improved. Central government may influence local decisions by varying the mix and level of housing subsidies for the public sector, by refusing loan sanctions on major capital projects, by advisory circular or by moral suasion or by imposing statutory obligations on local governments.

In the last decade, not only has central government increased scrutiny and control over local expenditure, but there has been a series of bills or actions by central government to enforce local housing changes. Housing Plans, the Homeless Persons Act and the Housing Act of 1980 have all increased central control over policy objectives. For instance, the Tenants Rights Act (Tenants Rights, HMSO 1980) is partly designed to counter the failure of circulars and advice from central government to persuade Scottish local authorities to sell council houses. By legislating to provide council tenants with the 'right to buy' central government circumvents and erodes local authority control over public housing. Local authorities have considerable control over the level of new house building, allocation priorities, the structure of rents in relation to housing quality, *etc.*

In a mixed housing system governments have, for too long, failed to take account of public-private sector interactions and it is often possible for central/local policies to become unco-ordinated, even if there is a coincidence of central/local public objectives. For instance, by a mixture of pricing and allocation policies local governments could upset central government policies to counter inflation (by raising rents or by not raising rents respectively for the Callaghan and Thatcher governments), for income redistribution (by restricting rent subsidies or by varying the proportion of housing revenue account financed from the rate fund contribution) or for regional labour mobility (by residence qualifications for waiting list or by the house related and non-transferable element of public housing subsidy). But central governments

166

must assume, not unreasonably given the urban/regional variations in the characteristics of housing systems, that local political choice is more informed on local policy requirements. Of course households, as in the Tiebout model (Tiebout 1956) may be able to move to select their most preferred local housing policy/rates bill combination. But this is not true of all households. A variety of rented tenures is uncommon outside central cities and public tenants have restricted mobility.

The variety of government intervention raises important co-ordination problems, particularly where the local housing planning system is not well developed. Within any local government area it is pertinent to reflect on the locus of control for policy in the four major tenure sectors, recognising that consumer choice and mobility may link them functionally. First, in the owner-occupied sector, although there will be local planning controls over building standards and planning permission, the major influences on demand will be either influences exogenous to policy (age structure of the population, economic growth, *etc.*) or they will be factors such as the price and availability of housing finance, the rate of inflation, tax rates, *etc.* These are variables which are more directly influenced by the Treasury than by any central or local government housing department or agency. Second, in the private rental sector, again local legislative standards may apply, but the main instruments of policy are rent control criteria and security of tenure legislation which is centrally determined but, because of its unclear specification, subject to variable local interpretation. Third, in public rented housing there will be a mix of central and local controls and subsidies. Finally, in the housing association sector, activity will reflect an interaction of central and local governments on a third party, the Housing Corporation.

This complex organisational model for housing policy in Britain would not necessarily be inadequate if some centrally determined operational principles for policy existed such as market pricing or income/wealth related subsidy systems. But where policy, as in Britain, lacks a central organising principle then the distribution of subsidy reflects neither house type nor household characteristics but is an outcome of chance, history and, in particular, tenure selected. Thus, whilst it has been argued that housing market intervention may be rational and required, it is difficult to believe that the present system could not be improved or it may even be that the imperfect market system that the policy is designed to circumvent would perform more effectively as an agent of allocation and redistribution. However, it is probably not possible to answer this question in the UK because, as in most fields of policy in the country, there is often more concern with the level than the quality of public expenditure.

Research and planning to improve policy

The previous section has been concerned to indicate that the political, administrative structure for housing policy in the United Kingdom is unlikely to be able to allow a co-ordinated and economic, or cost-effective fulfilment of housing policy objectives. But the rational pursuit of policy objectives may be forsaken much earlier in the process of policy formation. In the conventional economic textbook analysis of policy it is assumed that decisions are taken by evaluating alternative (market or non-market) policy outcomes. There is often an implicit assumption that this analysis is undertaken by analytical experts who, using well-developed theories and techniques, are able to research relevant empirical data and state market or housing system effects in reasonably precise terms. But is this a reasonable view to take of a country where even aggregate price and income elasticities of housing demand have not yet been satisfactorily measured, where housing research expenditures, within central or local government, are minimal and where central statistics are inadequate or uncollected (for instance the 1976 census!)?

Housing research for policy, from the economic standpoint, may be classified into macroeconomic research on well-defined statistical series, which is of limited use for understanding allocative or distributional research issues, or into locally oriented and intensive analyses, usually survey based. Even when the latter studies are undertaken (and it has been stressed throughout this book that the housing system is a complex and difficult system to research and comprehend) researchers, particularly academics but also within government, must ensure that their research findings are not so simplified as they proceed up the administrative ladder that they become increasingly trivialised and compromised. It must be of some concern within central government that many officials responsible for policy have no initial familiarity with housing and that, within the British Civil Service, transfer often follows mature acquisition of insight. Similar comments must apply within local authorities and the lack of formal training within public housing management is now the cause of some concern, particularly within Scotland with its proportionately large public sector.

In this context for policy formulation there are two alternatives, at least, to produce information for formulating strategies. First, ministers, as is the avowed intention of the present Secretary of State for the Environment, will listen to the arguments of pressure groups and interested parties. Power, in this case, not to the people, but to the groups with organisation and capital to present the most convincing (not the best) case. Alternatively, ministers with an inner circle of policy advisors may form a view as to what is an appropriate policy. These views may be based either simply on ideologies or on a limited or even partially researched view of the housing system.

If the reader thinks that the tone of this section is somewhat sour he may care to reflect on the background and evaluation of recent and important housing legislation in the UK. For instance the sale of council houses as proposed in the Tenants' Rights Bill is not a policy or a strategy based on a long-run evaluation of the outcome of sales – it is an ideological commitment, in this instance so strong that not even market prices will be charged for sales. For some, with a *laissez faire* commitment consistent with nineteenth-century Conservatism, the creation of a new 'yeoman' class may be a major short-term objective of public expenditure. But Labour governments have also been staunch in their ideological commitments – for instance the inadequately researched and badly designed Rent Act of 1974 was an ideological commitment to further reduce private rental supply (Maclennan 1978) and in the end may have greatly harmed the intended beneficiaries. Even where ideological commitments are de-emphasised, as in the 1977 Green Paper, policy may be badly designed as the result of inadequate research. There, it was assumed that the growth in owner-occupation reflected growing preferences for the tenure and policy was adjusted accordingly. But this view, as is indicated in Chapter 7, was only partially correct.

In this context for the formulation of policy the economist, or indeed social scientist, has an important role to play. That is, to adopt the stance of articulate and informed critic of government policy. This is a somewhat difficult posture when government, directly or indirectly funds the bulk of housing research. Indeed, rather than ethical predilections *per se*, it may be that disappointing contact with the actual process of policy formulation in the UK tends to move economists towards a preference for markets as the principal mechanism for the allocation of resources. But this is too extreme a viewpoint. Policy intervention, for the reasons outlined earlier, will always be required in the housing system but economists must present government with usable models, methods and material which can improve the quality of public policy.

Conclusion

In this chapter it has been suggested that the conventional, deductively based analysis of housing policy is only a starting and not a finishing point for housing policy evaluation. Traditional welfare economics does indicate some justifications for housing market intervention given Paretian value judgements. But the analysis of policy has to be broadened in several directions. Paretian and non-Paretian welfare functions have to be considered. The nature of the housing market must also be realistically described in order to optimise policy expenditures to achieve any selected objective function. Since housing is an important and complex commodity partial equilibrium or non-equilibrium analyses restricted to the housing sector will understate the impacts and significance of housing policy.

It has also been suggested that policy is not designed and implemented by a single, omniscient government department. Rather, policy analysis is poorly informed, has a limited conceptual base and is spread disjointedly across and within levels of government. Economic analysis and economics education have a substantial role to play in improving the process and outcomes of policy formulation.

7 The economics of policy for the owner-occupied sector

The structure and content of this chapter, and indeed the subsequent chapters, is a response to the generally negative evaluation of the existing applications of housing economic theory to policy which has been presented above. Here, the objectives of government housing policies are taken as given and policy instruments actually utilised are evaluated against ideas and information which have been organised according to the theoretical framework indicated in earlier chapters. Thus each chapter contains the outline of a particular housing trend or problem of interest to government, the microeconomics of the issue are then examined and, where possible, empirical evidence assembled. Then existing and new policies are considered in relation to the applied economic analysis.

The selection of issues

In a volume of this kind the treatment of housing policy is inevitably abbreviated and a selection of issues examined. Here the detailed discussion of policy is centred upon the three major tenure subdivisions of the housing system in the United Kingdom. This approach is justifiable for the following reasons:

1. Housing policy in the United Kingdom, since it has been piecemeal, has largely consisted of legislative or economic measures which have been organised by tenure subdivisions. Policy is both tenure oriented and tenure organised.
2. Partly as a result of (1), the economic pricing and investment mechanisms for housing in the UK differ across tenure groups. For instance, in the owner-occupied market the 'price-search-quantity adjustment' models outlined earlier have an obvious relevance. But, in the absence of market pricing systems in private and public rental,

non-price adjustments and allocative devices have considerable importance but the methods and dimensions of adjustment are influenced by tenure structures. This does not mean, as has been implied by several commentators, that economic analysis is inappropriate for the analysis of non-market or distorted market systems of housing allocation and investment. Rather, it requires a subtle approach in examining housing systems.

A tenure by tenure analysis of policy does not necessarily imply a piecemeal approach to policy analysis but issues such as the general fairness or allocative efficiency of subsidy systems must be borne in mind. However, in this book three major strands of policy are examined. These are the economic aspects of policy for owner-occupation, rent controls and public housing subsidy and management.

The expansion of owner occupation

At the beginning of the twentieth century the majority of houses in Britain were let by private landlords with private renting providing more than 90 per cent of households with their housing (Housing Policy, Technical Volume 1977). However, since that time there have been two major and different processes contributing to tenure change (see Tables 7.1 and 7.2). Public sector housing, at first in the interwar period, and then between 1950–70, was developed so extensively that public housing became the dominant housing tenure in the 1950s. But at

Table 7.1 Distribution of housing stock by tenure 1914–78. United Kingdom (%).

	Owner-occupier	Rented from local authority or New Town Corporation	Private rental and others
1914	10	–	90
1950	29	26	53
1960	42	26	32
1965	46	28	26
1970	50	30	20
1975	53	31	16
1976	53	32	15
1977	54	32	14
1978	54	32	14

Sources: Social Trends. *Housing and Construction Statistics.*

Table 7.2 Components of change of housing stock by tenure: England and Wales 1914–75 (m.)

	Owner-occupied	Local authorities and New Towns	Private landlords and miscellaneous	Total
1914–38				
New building	+ 1.8	+ 1.1	+ 0.9	+ 3.8
Purchases (+) or sales (−)	+ 1.1	neg	− 1.1	0
Demolitions and changes of use	neg	neg	− 0.3	− 0.3
Net	+ 2.9	+ 1.1	− 0.5	+ 3.5
1938–60				
New building	+ 1.3	+ 2.3	+ 0.1	+ 3.7
Purchases (+) or sales (−)	+ 1.5	+ 0.2†	− 1.7	0
Demolitions and changes of use‡	− 0.1	neg	− 0.4	− 0.5
Net	+ 2.7	+ 2.5	− 2.0	+ 3.2
1960–75				
New building*	+ 2.6	+ 1.6	+ 0.3	+ 4.5
Purchases (+) or sales (−)	+ 1.1	+ 0.1	− 1.2	0
Demolitions and changes of use	− 0.2	− 0.1§	− 0.8	− 1.1
Net	+ 3.5	+ 1.6	− 1.7	+ 3.4

Neg means negligible.
* Includes conversions.
† Mainly requisitioned during the war and subsequently purchased.
‡ Includes 0.2 million destroyed by air attack.
§ Mainly 'pre-fabs'.
Source: HMSO, 1977: Housing Policy, *Technical Volume* 1, 1977: 39.

the same time owner-occupation grew rapidly and steadily both by new building and by the sale of previously rented flats to owner-occupiers. Private 'owned' housing developments expanded both in the interwar and postwar periods (at least after the removal of wartime controls on supplies to builders after 1954) so that by the 1960s owner-occupation had become the majority tenure in the United Kingdom.

The growth of owner-occupation is therefore a dominant and long-standing feature of the housing system in Britain. However, it is only really in the 1970s that there has been a conscious government policy for expanding the sector. Indeed, following the Green Paper of 1977 it could be argued that expanding owner-occupation is one of the areas of political consensus on housing policy in Britain. This apparent agreement of governments may be somewhat illusory, however, not only because of intra-party differences in attitudes to owner-occupation, but also because the instruments and objectives for expanding owner-occupation differ substantially across the parties. For instance, the Green Paper, whilst making a commitment to further expanding the sector, was vague on the extent and time horizon of expansion and, as will be indicated below, made a minor expenditure commitment to change. The present government, by adding a vigorous legislative and 'advertising' programme for selling council houses to the previous system of fiscal and monetary incentives clearly wish to attain even more rapid growth.

The encouragement of owner-occupation

But why should governments wish to encourage growing owner-occupation? The previous Labour administration, if their views are fairly reflected in the Green Paper, clearly believed that the switch to owner-occupation, which had occurred despite real rises in house prices, was the reflection of either a shift in preference or a long-held housing aspiration level which could now be satisfied by growing real incomes. The subsequent, and minor, commitment to raising the rate of growth of home-ownership embodied in the scheme to assist first-time buyers was avowedly consistent with the overall intention to increase the 'preference' element in housing choices. In assessing policy it would have been useful to ascertain whether further expansion would have occurred without increased subsidy. In addition the hypothesis that policies regarding the price, quality and availability of public and private renting have been the real cause of the shift to owner-occupation deserves some scrutiny. Further, if shifting incomes and preferences were responsible for much of the tenure shift did these changes occur for all groups or households? And if price/quality/availability constraints were critical in other sectors should an 'expansion' of owner-occupation have been encouraged or policies and resources for other sectors revised? Thus, this chapter focuses on two broad questions regarding owner-occupation in the United Kingdom. First is the broad direction and structure of policy appropriate and, second, are the instruments chosen to pursue policy effective and fair?

Patterns of owner-occupation

The continued expansion of the absolute size and relative share of the owner-occupied sector in Britain is indicated in Tables 7.1 and 7.2. Starting from a post-First World War base of around 10 per cent, the owned share trebled by 1950 (in fact almost all this expansion took place in the period 1920–39), and in the period 1950–80 the sector has doubled in relative significance. Indeed, in the postwar period, expansion had taken place largely in the period 1954–64, and since then the annual rate of growth of the owner-occupied share has been relatively low. That is, the major expansion of owner-occupation took place during periods of Labour and Conservative rule and prior to the development of an explicit owner-occupied policy.

It is not clear from published material whether slow-down in the growth of the sector is attributable to supply, demand or financial sector factors. Throughout the postwar period, the supply of owner-occupied properties has not solely depended on new building but has also entailed inter-tenure sales of property from landlords to owner-occupiers (see Table 7.2). For instance, in the period 1968–71, although public housing completions exceeded private housing completions, tenure structure moved gradually in favour of owner-occupation due to sales of secondhand housing from rental to owned tenures. However, by the end of the 1970s this flow may have seriously diminished not only as the stock of residual private lets has fallen below 11 per cent but because Housing Associations, particularly since the 1974 Housing Act, may be competing to buy this lower quality stock. At the same time, there is now a new initiative to transfer public rental housing into owner-occupation.

Inter-tenure transfers, however, reflect the demand for, as well as the supply of, owner-occupied dwellings. For instance, in the period up to 1970, a considerable growth in the owner-occupied share occurred as a result of purchases by sitting tenants or by public and private rental sector tenants switching to owner-occupation. But throughout the 1970s, an increasing proportion of first-time buyers have become new households (33% in 1971, 46% in 1979). In addition, as is indicated below, a large proportion of first-time buyers emerging from private rental housing (16% of all purchasers in 1978) are in fact recent households with a short 'setting-up' stay in furnished rental housing (Maclennan and Wood 1980a). However, the Building Societies' Association and the 1977 Green Paper (BSA 1978) have indicated that changing demographic structure, reinforced by social trends generating small and single person households, are likely to result in a rising number of new households into the mid-1980s. Thus there are likely to be strong pressures to expand owner-occupation from these new households.

The 'strong' policy to sell council houses presently being undertaken may increase tenure 'switches' on the part of mature, continuing households. At present, with the current patterns of incentives, it is clear that the existing set of households have been largely absorbed into their particular tenure sectors. In 1971 for instance, Table 7.3 indicates that there was a substantial flow of older private tenants and public tenants switching to owner-occupation. A more detailed series of studies (Pennance and Gray 1968; Ineichen 1975) and more recently (BMRB 1977; Maclennan and Wood 1980a), have indicated that there is a relatively small flow of council tenants with children into owner-

Table 7.3 Estimated number of households entering and leaving owner-occupation in 1971: Great Britain (thousands)

Households entering owner-occupation	
Married couple new households:	
First marriage for either or both parties	145
Remarriages	20
Other new households	13
Total new households	*178*
Former tenants of local authorities and new towns	72
Former tenants of private landlords, employers, etc:	
Under 30	80
30–44	66
45 or over	41
Total households moving from other tenures	*259*
Households from outside Great Britain	15
Successor households from divorce	9
All households entering owner-occupation	*461*
Households leaving owner-occupation	
Moves to accommodation rented from employers	14
Moves to accommodation rented from private landlords, etc.	25
Moves to local authority tenancies:	
Due to demolition or closure	14
Moves by elderly people for other reasons	7
Miscellaneous	12
Total moves to other tenures	*72*
Households dissolved:	
Elderly (death or ceasing to live independently)	108
Divorce or separation	18
Remarriage	14
Total dissolutions of households	*140*
Households emigrating	27
Total households leaving owner occupation	*239*

Notes:

The estimates in this table are approximate only, and several are subject to wide margins of error. They should not be taken as exact to the nearest thousand.

The definitions count as a 'new household' all households where the housewife was not a housewife previously.

Source: HMSO, *Technical Volume* 2, 1977: 39.

occupation. Moreover, there is a small but positive flow of households from owner-occupation into public renting. These issues are examined in more detail below as they represent, at least in part, the inter- and intra-tenure effects of existing housing subsidies.

International and regional comparisons

With a moderately successful policy of council sales, combined with growing new household formation it is possible that the UK could have a tenure mix including 60 per cent owner-occupation by the mid-1980s. This would represent a level of owner-occupation similar to those now being experienced in North America and Australasia. Although levels of owner-occupation in Britain are lower than in these relatively high income countries tenure comparisons with European countries show no consistent pattern. Problems of statistical comparability do arise in such exercises. But it is apparent that Britain has a moderately high level of home-ownership by European standards and that there is no clear relationship between economic growth rates or income levels. High levels of owner-occupation are neither an indicator of economic growth nor, perhaps, even of the quality of life.

Housing tenure preferences may vary across as well as within countries and it may be that housing in Britain may perform an asset or social status function which it does not in other advanced economies such as France, Sweden or West Germany. For instance, because of party political and social class distinctions, owning may satisfy pre-formed social tastes (or prejudices), or fiscal and monetary policies may not be asset neutral in all countries nor to the same extent. The relationship between economic growth and housing tenure undoubtedly requires more study. In the United Kingdom commentators tend to stress (see Ch. 9), the output reducing effects of deterred labour mobility arising from public tenancies, but a much more important set of questions relates to the role of housing in an inflationary economy. There must at least be some concern, unless one adopts a monetarist view of a 'well-adjusted' macroeconomy, that increasing levels of owner-occupation with rising real prices of housing for secondhand housing (thus indicating the rising share of 'rent' to existing owners or landowners) will divert investment from the income generating sectors of the economy. Of course, since housing is immobile and non-tradeable, then there is a high probability of sustained price inflation and absorption of investible funds into the housing sector. It is perhaps with this concern in mind that the Wilson committee on financial institutions have criticised the historically protected ability of building societies to raise housing finance (Wilson Report 1980). It could be argued that the relatively long-run fixed house price/income relationship observed (or created?) by building societies in Britain (see Fig. 7.1), would cast doubt on this argument. But, with growing numbers of owner-occupiers, one would have to know the investment costs of public versus private housing and, in addition, it is not clear why a constant price/income ratio should pertain with rising real incomes. Thus international comparisons of housing tenure are fraught with interpretive difficulties.

Similar reservations may also be expressed regarding the use of UK level statistics as in the first section of this chapter. For it is generally true that there are greater variations in housing tenure across British regions than between Britain and other countries. A comparison between Scotland and London is revealing (see Table 7.4), and it is fair to question whether national policies should be geared to indiscriminately raising levels of owner-occupation or whether areas such as Scotland or the Northern region should have been accorded particular priority. As is the case in many other sectors of public policy in Britain, Scotland did receive particular analytical attention in 1977, with its own Green Paper and a suggestion that national target average figures should be reached but no time period was specified. Of course, although subsequent policies were not specifically intended to assist the growth of owner-occupation in Scotland, it is true that the new Tenants' Rights (Scotland) Act will have particular impacts on expanding owner-occupation by council sales (see Ch. 9).

Even at regional level tenure structure statistics may be misleading and the difficulties and consequences of tenure change masked. In the United Kingdom, tenure change has usually been associated with the spatial growth and restructuring of urban areas. Indeed, it is only in the

Table 7.4 The geographical pattern of owner-occupation 1966–1975

	Proportion of dwellings owner-occupied (%)			*Proportion of new dwellings completed for private owners 1967–75*
	End-1966	*End-1975*	*Increase*	
Northern	38.4	44.6	+ 6.2	46
Yorkshire and Humberside	46.0	52.7	+ 6.7	57
North West	51.5	57.3	+ 5.8	52
East Midlands	47.2	55.3	+ 8.1	65
West Midlands	47.7	54.5	+ 6.8	52
East Anglia	47.8	55.4	+ 7.6	67
Greater London	44.5	46.0	+ 1.5	27
Rest of South East	54.8	60.5	+ 5.7	64
South West	54.4	61.4	+ 7.0	72
England	48.9	54.7	+ 5.8	56
Wales	52.4	58.3	+ 5.9	58
Scotland	28.9	33.1	+ 4.2	27
Great Britain	47.1	52.8	+ 5.7	53

The percentage of new dwellings completed for private owners is rounded to the nearest whole number due to the change in regional boundaries. The boundary changes are considered unlikely to affect the comparison of proportions of the stock of dwellings owner-occupied.
Source: HMSO, *Technical Volume 2*, 1977: 69.

older housing areas or inner-city wards that there is a local scale mixture of public and private renting, Housing Associations and owner-occupation. In the owner-occupied sector resident preferences and institutional views have acted as spatially segregating tenure influences. In the public housing sector, scale economies of development have resulted in large-scale and tenure uniform housing developments both in inner-area renewal schemes and on peripheral estates. As an extreme example, the tenure structure of the city of Glasgow is such that on the outskirts of the city there are consolidated areas of more than 10 sq. miles (or containing up to 40,000 people) where there are no private houses at all. Spatial segregation of tenure, at the regional or intra-urban level, does of course contribute to demands for tenure change which might not arise in a system with an evenly distributed tenure mix. Before examining such influences in more detail, it is appropriate to match this disaggregated view of tenure structure with a disaggregated description of owner-occupiers and the houses they purchase.

Owner-occupiers and their homes

Not only is a national aggregate or average view of tenure change slightly misleading but stereotypes of purchasers and houses purchased, which appear to underlie the broad thrust of policy, may also be unhelpful in formulating well designed housing policies. There is a view, and it is statistically correct at the average, that increasingly first-time buyers are relatively new households, generally below the age of thirty, with no families or small families, with professional or skilled occupations and, for a given age range, with above average incomes. But these averages conceal a great deal of overlap between owned and rented sectors, particularly in relation to incomes. And this overlap on socioeconomic terms exists not just because some higher income or professional groups (see Table 7.5) reside in the public and private rental sectors but also because there are some low-income and unskilled manual workers who enter owner occupation. This reflects the fact that owner-occupation is in fact a very diverse tenure group with a wide spread of house type, house purchaser and house price involved. It is a major error to interpret all purchases as reflecting a 'preferred' shift by the stereotyped 'first-time purchaser' onto an 'escalator' of social class and housing consumption (Karn 1979; Maclennan and Wood 1980a).

Surveys of mortgages and census statistics, though the latter are now somewhat out of date, indicate that owner-occupiers have tended to reside in relatively high quality houses in terms of amenities and space standards, at least vis-à-vis private renting, and there has been a bias towards post-1919 housing and non-flatted dwellings. However, in the last five years the proportion of pre-1919 and flatted dwellings has increased, especially for first-time buyers. By 1979, less than 4 per cent of purchases financed by building societies were less than £7,000 and

Table 7.5 Distribution of household income by tenure. All households
Percentage of to's

| | All households | | | |
| | Local authority dwellings | Privately rented unfurnished dwellings | Owner-occupied dwellings | |
			Owned with mortgage	Owned outright
Under £1000	2	3	–	3
1000–1499	13	16	1	11
1500–2099	13	16	1	13
2100–2599	7	7	1	8
2600–3099	6	6	2	7
3100–3599	6	8	3	8
3600–4199	7	8	5	8
4200–4999	10	7	11	6
5000–5999	11	13	17	10
6000–6999	8	6	15	7
7000–7999	5	3	13	5
8000 and over	11	7	31	15
All incomes	100	100	100	100
Sample base (no. of households)	2,272	522	2,121	1,438
Mean	4,372	3,704	7,193	4,712
Medium	3,846	3,174	6,585	3,673

Source: *Housing and Construction Statistics* 1979.

only 20 per cent were less than £12,000. Building society survey statistics also allow a comparison of first- and second-time (plus) buyers. Again the importance of 'trading-up' may be more limited in some housing markets (see Jones 1978), but in general former owner-occupiers repurchasing are older, have higher incomes and sustain larger mortgages to purchase newer and detached houses. But again there are broad overlaps between first-time purchasers and other purchasers (see Table 7.6).

A reliance on building society statistics to indicate the characteristics of the owner-occupied housing market may lead to certain important omissions. First, there is a share of the upper end of the house price spectrum which is not financed by societies and, with much more significance, there is a larger 'cheaper end' of the housing market in which societies do not always participate. It is difficult to generalise about the segments of the market in which society funds are not utilised, but here the analysis of local authority home loans schemes and survey data (Karn 1979; Strathclyde Regional Council 1978; Dawson *et al.* 1980), indicates that there is an extensive 'cheaper end' of older, lower quality

Table 7.6 Building society funded purchases; comparisons between first-time and other buyers (end-1978)

	First-time buyers	Other buyers
Share of all mortgages (no.)	47.3	52.7
Dwelling price	12,023	18,792
Average loan	9,602	10,611
Loan/price (%)	78.7	56.5
Average income	5,283	6,161
Loan/income (%)	1.82	1.72
% pre-1919 houses	31	18
% under 25	37	6

Source: *Building Societies Associations.*

properties which house lower income and non-professional groups (see Table 7.7). As we shall indicate below, the existence of this group has significance for both the broad thrust and the specific design of policies aimed at expanding owner-occupation.

The existence of a sector, or perhaps several sectors of the housing market which are not financed by building societies draws attention to movers making cash purchases. Such purchases, which amounted to less than 25 per cent of purchases in the UK in 1976 but which had local significance may arise from several processes. For instance they may result from older, higher income households trading down market when families are 'launched' (see Jones 1978). They may also occur at the cheaper end of the private housing market when individuals are refused loans, either because the house is 'too cheap' to attract finance or where high transitory incomes are not evaluated by lenders as constituting 'permanent' credit-worthiness. In these instances, new purchasers do not have a mortgage and the appropriate grouping within the owner-occupied sector for the evaluation of major policy impacts is not between first-time buyers and others, but between households with a mortgage vis-à-vis those without a mortgage. Recently, and with some validity, Lomas (1978) has suggested that, for policy analysis, the most important distinction is between households with a mortgage and those who have no mortgage (either because of cash purchase or because they have repaid interest and principal to lenders). Either because non-holding of a mortgage is associated with refusal (for lower income, 'riskier' households) or with past repayment by now older households (with low non-property incomes), Lomas utilises tabulations of Family Expenditure Survey data to indicate that the probability of outright ownership increased rapidly below incomes of £3,200 per year (1976 data). In addition, Lomas indicates this may be an important consideration in that almost half the population of owner-occupiers have no mortgage. Apart from having lower incomes than mortgage holders, outright owners had a lower occupational status, were less well-

Table 7.7 Source of finance for Glasgow purchases by house price decile

Decile	Source of finance	1972	1973	1974	1975	1976	1977
1	BS	0.3	0.8	0.3	1.6	1.8	2.2
	LA	0.6	0.2	0.9	0.6	0.7	
	P	66.4	58.3	72.0	72.1	65 8	54.3
2	BS	1.8	2.2	2.7	5.1	3.3	4.4
	LA	2.5	1.7	7.4	10.6	3.7	
	P	65.8	57.8	62.5	56.3	48.8	33.5
3	BS	4.1	4.4	7.0	12.0	12.1	23.4
	LA	22.6	15.0	25.0	32.9	19.8	
	P	54.3	53.8	44.7	39.3	34.0	28.1
4	BS	7.8	9.0	12.0	15.3	23.3	43.5
	LA	49.2	29.4	43.3	48.7	30.5	
	P	33.9	40.5	37.0	32.3	30.4	23.3
5	BS	12.5	14.8	13.5	17.6	29.6	59.5
	LA	49.2	38.0	55.4	53.2	37.2	
	P	33.9	38.4	28.2	26.6	26.1	26.3
6	BS	27.5	31.1	30.7	39.5	56.0	65.7
	LA	36.9	34.0	39.2	31.2	13.7	
	P	33.5	29.9	28.0	27.8	26.5	27.2
7	BS	60.6	49.3	64.8	70.3	65.7	72.5
	LA	11.4	18.2	9.5	3.2	0.6	
	P	26.6	29.6	22.8	25.8	32.6	26.3
8	BS	73.8	71.7	72.5	72.4	69.9	77.4
	LA	2.9	1.7	0.8	0.6	0.0	
	P	21.6	25.3	26.1	26.5	29.6	21.4
9	BS	75.6	71.5	63.2	69.5	67.4	67.9
	LA	0.3	0.8	0.8	0.1	0.0	
	P	23.0	26.0	34.3	29.2	31.8	30.5
10	BS	68.8	59.5	58.8	68.0	66.3	65.3
	LA	0.4	0.0	0.5	0.0	0.0	
	P	27.5	36.0	36.7	29.5	32.8	32.7

BS = Building society mortgage; LA = Local authority mortgage; P = Other sources of finance.
Each cell gives the percentage of houses in that decile financed by a particular source during the year. Totals will be less than 100% if some houses in the decile were sold to institutions rather than individuals.
Source: *Glasgow Housing Market Study.*

educated and more than two-thirds of them were more than sixty years old (Lomas 1978).

The implications of this overview of the characteristics of owner-occupiers and their houses, in conjunction with the previous data on regional and intra-urban variations, is that owner-occupation covers a range of household, house types and effective subsidy arrangements which have grown rapidly in some areas and not in others. In developing an applied economic analysis of owner-occupation it is therefore critical to identify what is generic to owner-occupation *per se*, or to identify what mix of characteristics of the tenure may result in owner-occupied choices. Following this approach it becomes clear that a variety of motives may exist for becoming an owner-occupier and that an applied analysis has to be undertaken at the local/regional housing market level.

The economics of tenure choice

In this section there is an attempt to clarify the concept of tenure choice and to identify some likely influences on such choices. It may then be possible to develop a series of hypotheses as to what have been important influences on tenure change in Britain and these hypotheses may be examined, in the next section, against a series of 'micro' and 'macro' studies of tenure choice.

The concept of tenure essentially relates to the legal arrangements existing between properties and their owners and inhabitants. Thus tenure differences are essentially variations in the property rights and obligations of property owners and inhabitants. That is, tenure may influence the ways in which households acquire, use, alter and then ultimately dispose of housing. Tenure *per se* can therefore influence housing satisfactions and there are clear economic reasons why a variety of tenure forms could exist and why they are sustained by market forces. But housing tenure may also correlate with other influences on housing choice – for instance, house type or location, asset characteristics, or degree and form of support from government policy. To identify the influences of tenure *per se* on housing choices an initial series of assumptions are made for pedagogic purposes. These are:

1. Tenure choice is made in a context where housing and capital markets are in equilibrium. This implies that all markets are just cleared and that stable real prices and interest rates prevail. Shortages and price appreciation are assumed away and, in addition, entry to each tenure sector is smooth and well-informed.
2. The supply side of the housing system is in long-run equilibrium, so that there is a mixture of tenures and of other housing attributes such as house size or type at each location and within all neighbourhood types.

3. Government intervention is limited to the legal support of property rights or, less restrictively, housing subsidy is tenure neutral.

These assumptions are of course quite inconsistent with the analysis of theory and policy previously presented, but they permit an analytical view of the tenure issue and they are subsequently relaxed.

In this simplified context several important influences on tenure choice can be identified.

Ownership as a source of satisfaction

It is important to distinguish satisfactions which arise from the consumption of a given house and psychic benefits which flow from ownership *per se*. Politicians, perhaps in a bid to deflect attention from other unintended influences on tenure choice, often stress the deep-rooted 'aspiration for ownership' (see Pawley 1978). This implies that there is some basic territorial or protective urge (imperative) which is satisfied by ownership *per se*. It is plausible to argue that such an imperative is likely to be income elastic, that is it would occupy a lower level in a hierarchy of housing wants than would demand for shelter, neighbourhood, location, etc. It would be difficult to disentangle this motive for ownership from two other considerations. First, consumers may perceive that social status, which is assumed to be positively valued by households, is assessed by their peer groups in relation to housing tenure and this social status motive for ownership is also likely to be income elastic. Second, individuals in rented property may have severely curtailed property rights in relation to owners and landlords which may reduce home related activities and security of tenure. For instance, prior to the 1974 Rent Act, limited security of tenure pertained in the furnished rental sector, and eviction has obvious emotional and economic costs. Housing ownership can then be viewed as a device to reduce the probability of a forced move. It is reasonable to argue that all these motives could influence tenure choice with increasing income or with household and family formation. Hence it is likely that tenure choices will be related to income and family-cycle stage.

These, and similar, influences on tenure choice can be illustrated diagrammatically. In Fig. 7.1, let the family of indifference curves $B_1 . . . B_3$ represent the relationship between other goods and housing services when the latter are provided in owner-occupied properties. Then $R_1 . . . R_3$ are the equivalent, but different, indifference curves when the services are provided in rental units. Here it is assumed that the household has an intrinsic preference for owning and hence, for a given level of housing services, will require more 'other goods' to leave them at the same utility level when services are provided in rental rather than owned properties — that is, R_1, the equivalent of B_1, lies above B_1. For a 'rental lover' the ordering would be reversed and it should be

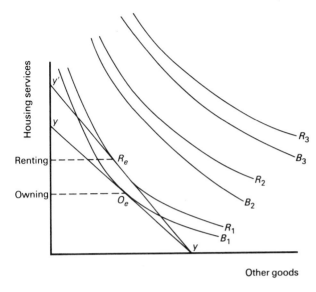

Fig. 7.1 The choice of owning and renting

noted that the R schedules do not have to run parallel to the B family, nor are both schedules necessarily of the same degree of homogeneity. Fig. 7.1 indicates for 'owning lovers' that with fixed relative prices for housing and other goods, and with rental and owner prices per unit of service equal, then ownership will always be chosen as the preferred tenure. Equally the result can be reversed by assuming that there is an intrinsic preference for renting if, for instance, individuals are ideologically opposed to ownership or if they are averse to the responsibilities associated with ownership.

Entry and movement costs

A more interesting and realistic case is where there are ownership preferences but that the fulfilment of these motives is costly. That is, the effective post entry price per unit of housing service is higher for owned rather than rented tenures. In a competitive housing market such a price difference could arise as a result of surveyors' and solicitors' bills or the provision of necessary and house specific fixtures and furnishings. Assuming tenant and owner will remain in the property for an equal length of time then the effective price of owning lies above renting as it is assumed that the landlord will discount purchase costs over a much longer time period. In these instances it is apparent that higher entry costs and shorter stay periods will move the relative position and slope of rental and budget lines so that rental becomes a more likely outcome. In Fig. 7.1, for example, lower entry

185

costs may shift the rental budget line to YY' and result in rental tenure choice R_e.

Savings and consumption preferences
The influences of savings and asset preferences are more important and complex when urban housing and capital markets are not in equilibrium. But they have some relevance in equilibrium because households may have a preference for a particular lifetime pattern of housing payments. For instance, they may choose to rent a particular house and pay a constant rent over their lifetime, or if they are concerned that they may face a life-cycle related fall in labour market earnings they may choose to minimise long-term commitments by purchasing a house earlier in the life cycle.

This simple equilibrium model of tenure choice suggests that with a given representative set of preferences, the probability of becoming an owner-occupier and the amount of owner-occupied housing purchased will rise with income. Rising income not only generates a demand for savings but also because 'security', 'status' and 'territorial' motives are likely to be income elastic tenure attributes. This hypothesis has *prima facie* empirical support in both the United Kingdom (Maclennan and Wood 1980) and the United States (Struyk 1976). In other housing systems where status is not expressed in relation to residential property or where rental sector property rights are closer to owner rights then, *ceteris paribus*, there may be a lower and less income elastic demand for owner-occupation. For instance Kemeny (1978) in discussing owner-occupation and renting in Sweden stresses the looser relationship between social class and housing tenure than in the UK. At the same time, in Sweden, owner-occupation demands for an individual rise with family formation and fall with expected population subgroup mobility rates. Life-cycle position in relation to occupational and family status could then be expected to affect tenure demands. The empirical validity of the basis of these 'ownership' demands is examined in more detail in a subsequent section, but first it is equally important to consider influences on tenure choice which arise from disequilibrium properties of housing and capital markets and the actions of government.

The simplifying assumptions relaxed

Housing market imperfections
It was stressed earlier that owner-occupied housing choices are made in relation to both new and secondhand housing. Thus private housing has particular, neighbourhood, locational and structural characteristics, which are distinctively different from those provided in administratively controlled public housing. That is, the earlier assumption that all tenures were available for all types at all locations is inaccurate in a

British context. Indeed the extent and form of public housing may make this concern particularly acute in the UK where distinctive public housing, in design and layout, covers extensive geographic areas. That is, as a result of housing policy large areas of cities are pre-empted by public housing. Within this public tenure class the level of housing services available may be limited or not amenable to income related bidding. Thus, if a public tenant wished to raise their consumption of housing services this higher level of services may only be available in private housing. Further, within the private sector in the UK rent controls have discouraged new house building for rent and the residual urban rental sector is almost entirely in low quality, inner-city flats or terraced houses.

These policy induced supply restrictions or administrative rules will result in higher income households with positive income elasticities of demand for housing, expanding housing consumption by making a tenure switch. For instance, in Fig. 7.2 it is assumed that the prices of owning and renting a given amount of housing services are identical and that there is no inherent desire for tenure *per se*. Here the household is making a choice between housing services and other goods. But above levels of housing service or quality indicated by H_1, only owned properties can supply such housing service levels and service levels below H_1 only exist in rental housing. With initial income levels, in this example, housing services H_F are consumed along with X_1 of other goods. A rise in income shifts the budget line outwards to B_2B_2 indicating housing service consumption H_p, which requires a switch from owning to renting. This is a simplified example. Tenure preferences *per se* can be introduced into the analysis along with owner/rental

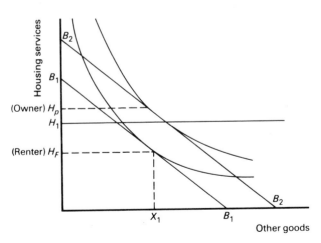

Fig. 7.2   Income and tenure choices

price differences but the analysis adds nothing to the comments of the previous section.

It is also important to stress that market imperfections as well as policy interventions may influence the spatial or structural characteristics associated with particular tenures. For instance, either because of land clearance costs, information problems or a market leading role, private developers have rarely (until the last three years) provided newer housing for owner-occupation in the inner city. Thus, inner-city residents with strong locational preferences may be restricted to renting rather than buying a house. Area lending policies or risk averse attitudes or building societies and related institutions (see Ch. 5) may also limit the possibilites of owner-occupation tenures existing in core urban areas and choice of tenure may be distorted.

Capital market imperfections

The asset characteristic of housing, as a durable good, was considered in Chapter 2. There it was stressed that in the owner-occupied sector housing expenditure decisions (that is the purchase of an individual stock of housing) reflected a joint demand for housing consumption services and housing assets. The asset properties of housing arise insofar as housing is a durable good for which the market price may rise (or fall) at a rate greater than the general price level. Thus the demand for owned housing will depend partly on the monetary and inflationary experiences of an economy but also on the role of housing in that inflationary process. Thus, if there is an inelastic short-run supply of housing, as normally prevails in the housing market, coexisting with a housing demand schedule which may respond rapidly to rises in nominal incomes then it could be expected that the asset demand for housing will be increased and sustained by the following factors:

1. The rise in recent past house prices relative to the general price level. That is, if expectations of future asset values are assumed to be based on recent price histories, then house price rises may ration individuals down a given housing demand curve but, and at the same time, shift the curve outwards. It is therefore difficult to deduce, *a priori*, the net effect of a price change on owner-occupied housing demand.

2. The lower the nominal interest rate rises to compensate for inflation. Most house purchases, as has been noted earlier, are financed from borrowing, i.e. mortgages. Thus if the real interest rate is upwardly sluggish for either the general interest rate structure or building societies in particular, then real income is transferred from lenders to borrowers over time. This redistribution occurs because the owner-occupier is repaying a fixed nominal sum of money over a period of years. Thus, *ceteris paribus*, a rising general price level erodes the real value of debt repaid and outstanding. A rise in the nominal interest,

in line with inflation, would reduce this redistribution from lenders to borrowers. However, it has been generally the case in Britain since the 1960s that the rate of house price inflation has exceeded the growth in the general price level and that the mortgage rate has lain below the general price inflator (see Table 7.8). Recent analysis of this effect, which is most important when governments restrain mortgage rate rises in periods of inflation, and the associated 'composite' tax arrangements for lenders to building societies (see Foster 1974) indicate that these arrangements may have a regressive effect on the long-term distribution of income and wealth. (See Postscript.)

The Nationwide Building Society have recently published an illuminating analysis of the effects of inflation on housing debt of households and its monthly burden, i.e. repayments in relation to income

Table 7.8 The cost of mortgage

Year	Average annual mortgage rate (%)	Net mortgage rate after tax relief at the basic rate (%)	Annual rate of inflation as measured by the Retail Price Index (%)	Mortgage rate after allowing for the effects of tax relief and inflation (as measured by the Retail Price Index) (%)
1960	5.8	4.1	1.8	2.3
1961	6.3	4.4	4.4	0.0
1962	6.5	4.5	2.6	1.9
1963	6.0	4.2	1.9	2.3
1964	6.0	4.2	4.8	− 0.6
1965	6.7	4.6	4.5	0.1
1966	7.0	4.7	3.7	1.0
1967	7.1	4.8	2.4	2.4
1968	7.5	5.1	6.0	− 0.9
1969	8.3	5.6	4.7	0.9
1970	8.5	5.8	7.9	− 2.1
1971	8.4	5.8	9.0	− 3.2
1972	8.2	5.8	7.7	− 1.9
1973	9.8	6.9	10.6	− 3.7
1974	11.0	7.5	19.1	−11.6
1975	11.0	7.2	24.9	−17.7
1976	11.0	7.1	15.1	− 8.0
1977	11.0	7.2	12.1	− 4.9
1978	9.4	6.3	8.4	− 2.1
1979	11.8	8.1	18.0	− 9.9
Jan 1980	15.0	10.5	18.0	− 7.5

Source: *Nationwide Building Society Bulletin*, 1980.

(Nationwide 1980). Consider a first-time buyer entering the housing market in 1973. Figure 7.3 indicates that during the period for which nominal repayments vary only slightly with small changes in the borrowers' interest rate, nominal and real incomes expand for the household. As a result, since housing costs are largely historically based, the household's share of housing expenditure to income falls rapidly. A renting household would expect rents to be revalued to market levels at less infrequent intervals. Of course, when the purchaser moves, and the Nationwide suggests that average mortgage duration is now less than six years, a new market valuation for the new property will exist initially. But, in time, rising money incomes and a negative real rate of interest reduces this burden again. At the same time this purchaser will be gradually reducing mortgage debt and increasing the value of equity in the home, assuming house prices are rising. Figures 7.3 and 7.4 indicate the average position for a first-time buyer in 1973. Thus house price rises, increasing nominal incomes (even without fiscal effects or real income growth) with negative real interest rates on borrowing combine to allow the household to reduce debt, increase equity, and decrease real expenditure on housing at the same time. This combination of macro-economic circumstances, characteristic of Britain in the 1970s, not only raises the asset demand for owner-occupation by new entrants but should raise trading up or turnover rates for existing borrowers as they adjust gearing on housing assets. There is evidence that both effects have occurred in the UK until 1980.

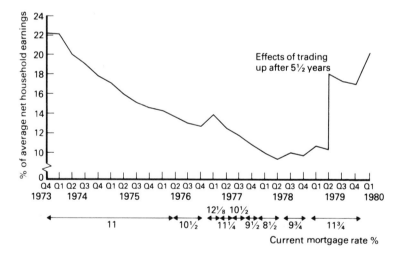

Fig. 7.3 Proportion of average earnings committed to mortgage repayments.

Source: *Nationwide Building Society Bulletin*, 1980

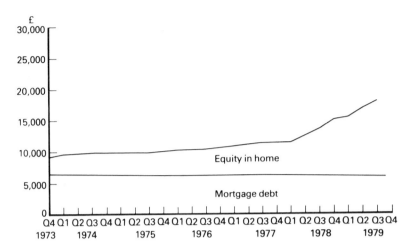

Fig. 7.4 Growth in first-time buyer's equity

It is rather difficult to represent the housing asset choice of house-holds diagrammatically when the house price inflation rate exceeds other asset price appreciation and where the real rate of interest is low or negative. For in such instances, which would not exist in a well-ordered, competitive capital market, the household should borrow as much as possible. When housing and capital markets are not in equilibrium then the possibility exists that long-term or permanent house-hold wealth will depend upon housing consumption. This raises a difficult conceptual problem in relation to the use of the permanent income hypothesis in housing demand models. Borrowing, in theory, could be backed by the collateral of rising real wealth – due to house price inflation. But several factors limit this extensive gearing-up. First, housing asset holding is not without risks so as overall asset holdings increase there may be a tendency, at least for higher income risk averse households, to diversify portfolio structure even towards assets with lower rates of return. Second, holding a stock of housing assets also implies that the consumer has an associated flow of consumption services. There may be limits to the extent to which the flow of services from stock may be reduced and as a result actual housing consumption may exceed desired housing consumption. For instance, smaller, wealthier households may feel insecure in a very large dwelling or they derive disbenefits by feeling 'ostentatious' etc. That is, at high levels of housing asset holding and consumption, asset and consumption influences on demand may cease to be complementary to each other and to become 'antagonistic' towards each other. That is a trade-off between housing consumption and asset choices may develop at high levels of housing consumption. However, capital market imperfections

191

may preclude households reaching this trade-off position. First, most house purchase loan institutions will not allow lending to be secured entirely against expected house price appreciation and past appreciation requires costly movement and sale before it can be used as a supplement to or collateral for a larger housing loan. Second, and following from the previous point, lending institutions may ration loans against some concept of permanent income which excludes housing wealth and rather relies on a labour market conception of income and wealth.

It is, of course, correct to query the extent to which house price rises in excess of the general price level may be regarded as 'capital gains'. Indeed, it may be that rising prices stimulate short-term demand not because of intrinsically asset properties of housing but because the household perceives that the price of a desired lifetime path of housing consumption is rising. But capital gains are made in the sector. Clearly if a household has a life-cycle of housing demands then in the earlier trading up phases if holding gains on the previous house are all reinvested in a subsequent house which had appreciated at historically the same rate then a gain in real income has not occurred in relation to the household's consumption pattern. But if the household trades down market or extracts part of the previous holding gain for non-housing expenditures by trading up with an increased mortgage then real wealth has increased for the household. Thus house price inflation, in aggregate, may systematically transfer wealth from new entrants or those moving up-market to those moving down or out of the market. There is no reason to believe that capital gain effects balance out for the individual or the economy over time. In addition, the existence of submarkets with short-term changes in prices or price differentials may result in capital gains for 'early' movers who 'spot' or even 'set' trends.

Thus, in addition to the sources of demand for owner-occupation which can be conceptualised in terms of a simple equilibrium model of tenure choice (Maclennan and Wood 1980a; Struyk 1976) there are a series of likely disequilibrium characteristics of housing and capital markets which influence tenure choices. Further rising income by raising desired levels of consumable housing services or by stimulating asset demands, will probably generate rising demand for owner-occupation because of the low quality of existing rental housing in Britain and the expropriation of capital gains in rental housing by landlords rather than occupiers. Thus, the slow growing real incomes, high inflation rates, negative real interest rates and high rates of household formation which characterised Britain in the 1970s have all contributed to a growing demand for owner-occupation. It is therefore highly probable, even in the absence of policy intervention to deliberately stimulate owner-occupation, that the sector may have expanded.

Before examining past and present policies for the owner-occupied sector it is pertinent to survey the studies of motives for entering or preference towards owner-occupation. This may indicate whether or not which, if any, of the above hypotheses are important in the recent British context. It would not be expected that these surveys would produce results which are comparable in magnitude over space and time. The owner-occupied sector may have a differently perceived role in different countries or indeed in different regions of the same national economy.

Evidence from choice, 'preferences' and aspiration studies

The difficulties of making a precise economic interpretation of 'preference' studies, whether they relate to tenure or spatial choices, have been discussed in Chapter 2. But a broad statement of the 'aspirations' or 'preferences' of households can be used to indicate whether the broad direction or thrust of policies is in the interest of the consumer. For instance, if government, for some prior reason, wishes to increase owner-occupation, a preference or aspiration study may indicate that a policy to support expansion would be appropriate although the design and precise specification of the policy requires more detailed information on parameters of consumer behaviour.

A series of housing tenure aspiration studies have been undertaken in the UK since the late 1960s. The three major studies of tenure preferences noted above have indicated two broad conclusions of some relevance. First, among existing households, there is a very strong aspiration or desire to become or remain owner-occupiers amongst younger age groups. Some 60 to 70 per cent of households below the age of forty-five aspire to owner-occupation. An aspiration for council tenancies was positively correlated with age and present residence in the public or private rental sectors. When tenure aspirations were cross-tabulated with existing tenure the surveys indicated that more than 95 per cent of households in owner-occupation intend to remain in the sector, and more than 40 per cent of private and public tenants 'aspire' or intend to change into the owner-occupied sector. A survey of the Durham area indicated a lower intention to shift from renting to owning of the order of 25 per cent. A survey of private renting in Glasgow, at least for the private furnished rental sector, indicated that not only did more than 50 per cent of tenants in the sector intend to make the tenure switch within the next two years but there was a current latent and effective demand for owner-occupation (in income and price terms) amongst more than 20 per cent of tenants (Maclennan and Wood 1980a). In the latter context there was not only an aspiration but an excess demand for owner-occupation. These surveys all indicate that the broad direction of policy for owner-occupation was in line with consumer preference but they do not indicate why this preference exists.

Two recent and detailed studies have tried to identify the mix of motives for entering owner-occupation. The 1975 BMRB study indicated, that moves into ownership were prompted by an inherent aspiration for ownership, a desire for security and independence, financial and savings motives and problems of property tailoring and neighbourhood quality in public housing. The Glasgow study was of 524 first-time buyers, or a 1 in 4 sample of first-time buyers in Glasgow in the period November 1976 to May 1977. The variety of motives for entering owner-occupation suggested by the BMRB study were confirmed in Glasgow – an important conclusion since the city has the lowest home-ownership rate of any British city. But the survey, apart from identifying a genuine excess demand for owner-occupation, also indicated that first-time purchasers above the mean sample income level never actively considered tenure alternatives to owner-occupation. Their entry decision could not be viewed as being an informed marginal choice. In addition, reflecting the variety of subgroups and property types constituting the owner-occupied sector, some 15–20 per cent of purchasers were reluctant buyers in the sense that their preferred and intended long-term alternative really lay in public housing but problems of waiting time for quality property in public housing had forced them into the cheaper end of the private housing market.

This evidence suggests that although a preference or excess demand for owner-occupation may now exist in most parts of the UK, the motives for entry do not always reflect desire for tenure or property rights *per se* but may reflect housing and capital market disequilibrium and government housing policies for other tenure sectors. Further, not all entrants prefer owning housing options and policy must be sensitive to the existence of such groups and not make the error of equating choice and preference. At this point it is important to assess housing policies to encourage owner-occupation.

Policies for owner-occupation

In a previous section the reasons why individuals may wish to become owner-occupiers have been outlined. But why should governments wish to encourage a particular tenure form? It is, of course, quite consistent that governments may wish to assist owner-occupied tenures in the belief that they are helping individuals to attain their housing aspirations. But other reasons may exist. Assistance to owner-occupiers may reflect an attempt by government to maintain distributional justice or political balance across tenure sectors. Or, Marxians would argue, the creation of a property owning class is in the interests of long-term 'social control' by capitalist government. More prosaically, there are other reputed advantages of owner-occupation such as that owner-occupiers develop an interest in maintaining their property and reduce long-term public and private maintenance expenditures. And some critics believe that owner-occupation assists labour mobility although empirical evidence on this point is limited. In addition, it has been argued that increasing owner-occupation will decrease public expenditure commitments to housing policy. But, as indicated in Table 6.2, even this argument is open to doubt. Despite the lack of evidence to support any of the above contentions policy intervention may well be justified solely in terms of consumer/voter preferences.

The selection of a particular housing tenure depends not only on the 'price' of that tenure but also upon the price, availability and entry costs for other tenure options. Thus, the selection of owner-occupation depends not only on deliberate policies to encourage owner-occupation but on the effects of housing policies in other sectors and, in addition, the unintended effects of non-housing policies which impact upon housing choices. For the sake of brevity this chapter focuses only upon deliberate housing policies and the discussion is divided into the broad sets of considerations:

1. The tax and interest policies which have stimulated owner-occupation throughout the post-war period.
2. A variety of less systematic and generally smaller scale policies which have postdated, in the main, the Green Paper of 1977. Council sales are also considered here.

In the following discussion the chapter is concerned with describing the main constituents of assistance to owner-occupiers and in suggesting likely intra-tenure effects of these policies in relation to income distribution. But there is no definitive evidence on the incidence of subsidy for the UK and there are additional problems of assessing the inter-tenure fairness of the housing subsidy system in the UK (see the Green Paper, Technical Volume II, 1977; Whitehead 1977; Lansley 1979). Problems arise in comparing the 'subsidy' effects of assistance in different sectors even if the incidence of subsidy was precisely known. In particular, houses are not all priced at market rents and it is therefore impossible to assess to what extent subsidy reduces market rents or if, in some cases, it reduces administered rents to market levels. For instance (see Ch. 9) it is quite possible for administered rents to exceed market rents in poor quality public housing and it is therefore wrong to label assistance or rent reductions accruing to such households as consisting of subsidy. In the private rental sector, intervention by controls redistributes income from landlords to tenants and there again administered rents may lie below market rents. But is this transfer from landlord to tenant to be classed as subsidy? Additionally, even if owner-occupier and council tenant receive identical levels of state assistance are the benefits of subsidy comparable with, in all probability, the tenant being

195

effectively subsidised to consume but (given the prevailing macroeconomic context) with the owner being subsidised to save and purchase a rapidly inflating asset. Thus the issue of fairness in housing subsidy across tenures cannot be pursued with any degree of precise empirical support in the UK and there are more objections to simplistic comparisons than those outlined above (Whitehead, 1977).

Longstanding policies to sustain owner-occupation

Until the last two years British governments have had a policy of limited direct intervention in the owner-occupied housing market. In general the structure and extent of assistance to owner-occupiers grew by default because of the general characteristics and principles of the British tax system. Preferential taxation of owner-occupation vis-à-vis other housing sectors or other assets has been particularly important as a demand side stimulus since the 1960s. Housing supply policies have had minimal use in the private sector. A major exception to this generalisation was in the interwar period (Cullingworth 1979) when 0.46 m. houses from a total of 3 m. private sector completions, were subsidised under the 1919 and 1923 Housing Acts. However, the necessity for this subsidy was removed by the falling wage rates, building costs, *etc.* of the 1930s. Throughout the postwar period, supply side policies have consisted of controls and restrictions rather than subsidies. These controls on the building industry have operated at both the central and local government levels. After 1939, postwar building licensing controls which were designed to restrict private housing output to 20 per cent of residential construction output (Cullingworth 1979) were only finally removed in 1954. Since then local planning controls on developments and the imposition of standards, which may be necessary to reduce adverse externalities of totally self-interested development, have reportedly resulted in delays and higher housing costs.

Since 1926, and with growing importance in the postwar period, the principal policy stimulus to owner-occupation has been its tax treatment. Under the principles of taxation, established in 1799 and revised in 1803, the British tax system seeks the widest possible base for income taxation. Thus, realising that capital is often necessary to produce or raise a given level of income, the system is designed to offer tax relief on interest paid on loans utilised to purchase assets. In turn the income or yield flowing from the acquired asset is taxed. But the returns to an asset may occur in cash or kind. For instance, in the agricultural sector, land may produce crops which are sold and taxed or it may be used to grow for domestic consumption. Unless the domestically consumed crops are valued, that is a price 'imputed' to them, then the tax system will produce a bias towards the production of subsistence rather than cash crops. Similarly in the housing sector, a landlord who purchased a house (prior to 1969) would claim tax relief on interest to acquire the property but would be taxed on the rental income.

The principle requires the owner-occupier to have a schizophrenic view of the tax system. Tax relief on the interest of the loan is granted to him as owner, but as owner and occupier tax should be paid on the value of income from the housing asset. In a competitive housing market this would be the opportunity cost of inhabiting the house (at least). That is an 'imputed' rent has to be agreed and taxed. Insofar as owner-occupied housing is treated differently from other housing sectors or other assets then it may have a net advantage or attractiveness in fiscal terms. The semantic handstands performed by the BSA in this respect in their response to the Green Paper (see BSA 1978) did not do the building society movement in Britain great credit. But equally, it is unfair to claim that both interest relief on loans and the absence of a tax on imputed rents (since 1961) constitute a net advantage to owner-occupation. Either one instrument or the other constitutes the element of advantage. Of course, even in a competitive housing market it would require careful setting of tax rates to ensure tax neutrality in the owner-occupied sector. The different elements of the tax system impinging directly on the housing market now require an explanation.

The absence of a tax on imputed income for owner-occupied housing
A tax on the rent or imputed rental of owner-occupied houses was charged, under Schedule A taxation, in Britain until 1961. At that time it was decided, for essentially political reasons, to make the tax redundant and it was claimed that only a small fiscal revenue was lost (of the order of £200 m. per year). But in fact, the essential reason for scrapping the tax was that the 1961 imputed rents were based on rate-able value assessments for 1957 which, as will be explained in the subsequent section, were still largely related to 1938 property values. The tax base was, as a result, severely undervalued. If it had been revalued to 1961 rental values based on market rates then with rates of tax similar to other sources of income, there would have been a very marked rise in 'imputed' tax bills. In general, they would have probably doubled or perhaps trebled. Such a rise may have resulted in a drop in residential investment and would have, inevitably, preferred the rental tenure sectors.

Cullingworth is thus probably too dismissive of the effects of non-taxation of imputed rents in arguing that the removal of the tax did little to stimulate the growth in owner-occupation (Cullingworth 1979). Even if this was true in 1961, the required revaluation of the tax, to preserve overall tax fairness, would probably have hindered the growth in owner-occupation and with subsequent house price inflation and the growth in real property values the non-existence of the tax is probably now a major stimulus to owner-occupation. It has been estimated that the non-collection of the tax cost the exchequer over £2,000 in 1980 and there are clear 'fiscal fairness' grounds for its reintroduction. In addition, Welham (1978) has clearly indicated that the tax was generally progressive with higher value houses being owned by higher income individuals with higher marginal tax rates. Thus, in a period when government is anxious to widen the tax base in order to reduce taxes which are presently a disincentive to effort, the revenue from a tax on imputed income from housing assets deserves detailed reconsideration (Atkinson and King 1980).

Tax relief on mortgage interest
In the absence of an imputed tax on owner-occupiers tax relief on mortgage interest constitutes a major fiscal advantage to owner-occupiers. Since 1925/26 householders purchasing with a mortgage have been allowed to set interest payments made against tax liabilities but the criteria for eligibility for this tax exemption have become more restrictive in the last twelve years. First, the tax concession was limited to principal residence only in 1969 and, second, since 1974, a limit of £25,000 has been placed on the size of mortgage which can attract such tax relief. Since 1974, with continued inflation in house prices and nominal incomes this limit is becoming binding for an increasing number of families.

The extent to which tax arrangements encourage owner-occupation is an example of the poor design of housing support systems in the UK. Higher income individuals generally have not only higher incomes and larger housing expenditures and loans but, with higher marginal tax rates, have higher tax liabilites. Although the bulk of tax relief may accrue to middle income/house price households, Welham (1978) has clearly indicated that the system is regressive with high income groups receiving absolutely and proportionately larger tax reliefs. The option mortgage scheme was introduced, in the 1967 Housing Subsidies Act, to introduce a low interest rate mortgage for households who were not earning sufficient income, or who had other tax allowances, so that they were not paying standard rates of tax. However, the estimated half of owner-occupiers who did not hold a mortgage, either because of past repayment or initial payment in cash (and it is stressed that cash sales are generally found amongst lower income groups) did not receive any subsidy or advantage under this scheme. Thus the patchy incidence of the interest rate relief amongst owner-occupiers combined with its known regressive incidence make the scheme an unfair and inefficient means of housing support.

The estimated value of tax reliefs arising in this way has grown rapidly since the early 1970s (see Table 6.2) but the real value could decrease over time. Reductions of average and marginal tax rates planned by the present government may reduce tax liabilities even if policy raises interest rates and interest payments. At the same time the real value and limit effects of the £25,000 limit are becoming increasingly binding, though this may redistribute the relief towards relatively lower income groups without reducing total relief levels.

Capital gains tax treatment and stamp duty

Capital gains on a house, if it is the principal residence of the owner, are not subject to taxation and thus constitute a major bias in favour of holding wealth in holding assets. The non-taxation of such gains are based on the assumption that these gains are holding gains and that it would be unfair to tax gains on a household when the household has to purchase another house which has also appreciated in value. But this approach may be oversimplistic. Even if a substantial proportion of such gains are taxed when a house becomes part of an inheritance, there is some evidence to suggest that not all proceeds from a sale are reinvested in the subsequent house – that is, some holding gains are realised. For instance, some households trade down market. And even for those trading up, survey evidence (see Housing Policy, Technical Volume 2, 1977; Ball and Kirwan 1977) indicates that as much as a third of past gains are spent on assets or commodities other than housing.

Stamp duty is a form of transaction cost incurred by a house seller, it is levied at a variable rate starting at a minimum of £15,000 and rising to 2 per cent on transactions of above £100,000. In essence the tax is now, in the short run, a tax on mobility or ownership change. It may now discourage moves, particularly since the majority of housing market moves are over short distances and related to small changes in property size and quality. As a result the tax may encourage structural extension or conversion of houses presently owned. In addition the tax probably biases housing choices for young, mobile single or childless households towards the rental sector.

Except for stamp duty, the tax treatment of owner-occupation generally favours the potential purchaser and assistance can be viewed as being substantial and regressive. At the present time there are calls for the reintroduction of a tax on imputed rents and a reform and neutralisation of tax advantages for owner-occupiers, but political circumstances are unlikely to condone such changes even though no clear case is presented as to why such allowances should exist or why they should be so expensive.

Monetary policy effects

The general conduct of monetary policy in the economy has a critical influence on the cost and availability of house purchase finance. At various points in this book it has been indicated that mortgage rationing has been important in the UK, particularly when general interest rates and the price level are rising. Thus policies to restrain rises in the nominal interest rate have partly been a cause of the negative real rates stimulating borrowing for house purchase. On occasion, for instance 1976 and 1979, governments have been unwilling to stem general rate rises but have given specific loans to building societies to restrain rises in the mortgage rate – either for electoral reasons or to reduce pressure on incomes policies.

In 1979, and particularly at the present time, a shift towards monetarist policies, trying to control the real growth of the monetary supply is being attempted. The housing market effects of such a policy are likely to be dominated by the income and unemployment consequences in the short term (which may last for a very long time). But in the housing sector, restricted monetary growth is being pursued at the same time as there is an attempt to increase levels of owner-occupation. Unless real house prices fall, this implies an increasing share of a decreasing real money supply must be diverted to the housing sector. The output effects of such a policy have already been alluded to, but it is apparent that for the scheme to be successful the real mortgage rate must rise. In 1980, even with record nominal interest rates, inflows to societies were decreasing and there was an apparent excess demand for loans with waiting periods of up to six months commonly being reported. A further rise in mortgage rate in 1981 perhaps did clear the housing/mortgage market. In general, however, the past conduct of and institutional structure for monetary policy in Britain has been a stimulus to owner-occupation – perhaps at the cost of other sectors in the economy. (See Postscript.)

Other policy influences

Apart from these major fiscal and monetary instruments, governments (both Labour and Conservative) have adopted a range of policies to encourage owner-occupation by directing assistance towards older housing (which is generally cheaper and is perceived to form the first stage of an ownership career) and first-time buyers. There have been several measures of this type. For instance in the 1960s, local authorities were permitted and encouraged to lend on older and cheaper properties. Although the local authority share of transactions or new mortgages has declined since the early 1970s, this source of finance has particular significance in inner-city areas (see Karn 1979; Maclennan and Jones 1980) where local authority loans may fund up to 50 per cent of transactions in inner-area neighbourhoods. In Glasgow, in 1977, more than one third of first-time buyers used a local authority home loan for purchase. A squeeze on public expenditure which may reduce such lending or a diversion of local authority's loanable funds towards the financing of council sales may have severe and long-term effects on such older areas where local authority lending, improvement grants and rehabilitation programmes have done much to restore area confidence.

To supplement such lending by local authorities, central government has, particularly but not exclusively since 1977, used 'moral suasion' and guarantee schemes to persuade building societies to lend at the cheaper end of the housing market. For instance, the provisions of the Housing and House Purchase Scheme of 1959, or the Support Lending Scheme of 1977 were all intended to reduce society perceptions of riskiness of lending on older, cheaper property. The naïveté of the theoretical model underpinning these ideas has been examined in Chapter 5. But it is unlikely that minimal guarantees or persuasion will shift lending patterns when there is excess demand for society funds (which can all be allocated to perceive low risk properties) and where area lending patterns emerge not from well-defined spatial rules but from a complex series of beliefs and advice which pass between society employees and less than perfectly informed home buyers. Increased lending down market, which has occurred throughout the 1970s and particularly in periods of plentiful funds, is most likely to be achieved where rehabilitation and improvement policies convince managers of funds that areas are relatively stable or appreciating in terms of property values and where mortgage and deposit rates are allowed to rise to clear the mortgage market.

More recent policy initiatives

The first-time purchaser subsidy scheme proposed by the previous Labour administration was introduced in 1980. This scheme provides for first-time buyers who have saved, with a building society, a minimum of £600 over two years, to receive a matching low interest loan and a maximum savings bonus of £110 from central government. But this scheme, which it is estimated will cost £90 m. per year, is neither fair nor efficient. First, fairness is questionable as only purchasers who have saved with a society are supported vis-à-vis those who have saved elsewhere or who have not saved at all. Second, the subsidy has a marginal positive value to households and indeed may have a negative value to some. It is quite conceivable that house price inflation in the two year saving period will more than wipe out any bonus gains from protracted saving. In addition the duration of the scheme fails to recognise that most first-time buyers are newly married couples who may meet for the first time and progress to forming a household in much less than the required savings period. Further, the tenure preference and aspirational studies reported above indicate that house purchase is not really a marginal choice. For instance, the failure to consider alternatives for purchasers who enter owned housing above the median price range would confirm this view. In such cases the scheme may not influence purchase decisions at all, other than to raise price bids (a likely outcome given the inelastic supply of older, cheaper properties). First-time purchasers may be assisted more effectively by general housing supply and finance policies which clear housing markets or by making competitive the provision of legal and surveying services which constitute an important cost to all purchasers but to first-time buyers in particular. If the first time purchaser scheme is to continue it may be fruitful, in both allocative and distributional senses, to limit its applicability to the bottom third (or so), by income, of entrants with a reduction in savings period.

Thus it seems likely, although the recent Labour government had made a particular commitment to expanding owner-occupation, that the associated policy measures would have had little incremental impact. The present government have taken, despite their avowedly free market and non-interventionist stance, major steps to attempt to increase owner-occupation not only by continuing to assist newly or recently formed households but by encouraging tenure switch *in situ* of older continuing households in the public sector. The policy, which arises from the Housing Act and Tenants Rights Act of 1980 consists of a new legal right for council tenants to buy their own home matched with a subsidy policy which discounts the assessed purchase price by a factor related to the potential purchasers period of residence in the dwelling. This initial lump sum subsidy is, of course, in addition to the normal fiscal incentives. The overall merits of this policy are assessed in the final chapter but the repercussions for the owner-occupied sector are noted here. Three considerations are of particular importance.

1. The new policy will not stop the flow of council tenants into the existing owner-occupied sector who leave public housing because it is environmentally or locationally unsuitable.
2. The policy is, however, likely to appeal to long-term tenants in moderate to good quality public housing (poor quality housing being precluded by financing and reselling difficulties) because the discounts available, combined with a likely substantial inflation rate, at least for the foreseeable future, may make purchasing the house less expensive than renting (let alone acquiring possession of the asset).
3. Financing council sales, and here the government have been quite unrealistic in their assessment of likely building society involvement, will require a net addition of funds for house purchase. A diversion of funds will have the adverse effects on existing markets which were noted above. This financing may require either a rise in building society interest rates or an increase in public expenditure — at least in the short run.

Conclusion

The economic significance of the owner-occupied sector in Britain is continuing to grow. Whilst policies to further expand the sector have acted in the correct direction and generally been in line with consumer preferences they are not sensitively or efficiently designed. In the last two decades overall economic policy and events may have contributed more to sector expansion than housing policy *per se*. The effects of economic change on tenure choice are now becoming clearly recognised. But, and importantly, there has been no long-run concern with the effects of growing owner-occupation on the economy. From the tentative arguments expressed here it is clear that this latter concern deserves substantially more analysis as overcommitment of savings and income to home-ownership may harm overall consumption and investment levels in the long run.

8 Rent controls and rental sector policy

Introduction

This chapter has an overall structure similar to Chapter 7 and, indeed, tends to confirm some of the views of the UK housing policy process derived from a study of owner-occupation. But, of course, the subject matter is somewhat different in several important respects. The private rental sector, unlike the other tenure groupings, has been declining in aggregrate size and significance.

There is no real consensus view on policy for the sector at least in the principles of policy laid down by the main political parties. In rhetoric, Conservatives express a desire for an expanded private rental sector which they believe would operate competitively and well. The Labour party are committed to reducing the role of the private rental sector which they frequently assert to be monopolistically owned and operated. In practice, policies have been less extreme than policy statements with, for instance, the most recent Labour Administration considering possible stimulus to institutional investment for private lets, and, on the other hand, Conservative governments (1970 to 1974 and since 1979 to present) retaining the main provisions of the 1965 Rent Act introduced by a Labour Government.

Unlike owner-occupation and council sector policies, rent controls are a form of policy intervention which require minor public expenditure commitments (a total of nearly £10M,) was required to operate the system in 1978-9). In addition, rent controls in Britain were, unlike fiscal and monetary incentives for owner-occupation, explicitly introduced for housing policy purposes and they have had a longstanding significance in British housing policy. The principal concern of the chapter is to assess the impact of these controls on the private rental market, particularly in the last decade.

The present structure of private rental housing in Britain

For reasons discussed below, including both rent controls and non-policy events or trends, private rental housing in Britain now only houses 13 per cent of the population. This share has fallen from 89 per cent in 1914. But, as in the owner-occupied sector, a description in aggregate terms masks the significance of private letting either in specific intra-urban areas or in relation to the housing demands and requirements of particular client groups. Although, as explained below on p.211, the division between furnished and unfurnished sectors had no legal status since 1974 it is an important functional and historical subdivision in explaining property types and tenant characteristics in private renting. Tables 8.1, 8.2 and 8.3 indicate some of the characteristics of private rental housing. In general, all private rental housing is relatively small, contains a high proportion of pre-1919 housing, consists largely of flats and converted terraces and has low space and amenity standards. It is not uncommon for more than 40 per cent of dwellings in inner area wards (DOE 1975; SDD 1976) to be leased as private lets. Rents in furnished rental houses are not generally below those of local authority houses whereas the distribution of unfurnished rents is well below that of public housing.

Within the sector there are important subgroups of tenants. The unfurnished let sector is dominated by relatively low income, occupationally unskilled or older households who have lived in the sector, indeed even at their present address, for more than ten years. The Tables cited do, of course, indicate considerable spread around these mean values. The furnished rental sector contains tenants with a substantially different socioeconomic profile and two broad groups can be identified. First, and where a variety or provision is used such as lodgings, bedsits, shared flats, *etc.*, there is a substantial group of young, mobile, single person households often in further or higher education or in occupations with a relatively high permanent income. The sector combines this role of 'first step' on the housing life-cycle for many households with, perhaps less appropriately, a 'last refuge' role for a substantial sized group of older, larger families with low or discontinuous incomes who have been denied, or do not wish, access to local authority housing or owner-occupation. For instance, it is likely that a large proportion of the households evicted from council housing are forced into furnished lets. This diversity of tenants in private letting, as indicated below, is a critical factor in devising efficient policies for the sector and it has been too readily dis   ded in the past. These patterns of private rental provision and consumption have not emerged solely from a long-term market process but they reflect the interaction of social and eonomic change and the policies of central and local governments. It is therefore important to understand not only the longstanding nature of rent controls in Britain but also to indicate the detailed characteristics of these controls before selecting appropriate theoretical models with which to specify the economic effects of such legislation.

Table 8.1 Type of building by tenure of household: England and Wales 1971 (%)

	Detached house	Semi-detached house	Terrace house	Purpose built flat	Other flat or rooms	With business premises or other	Total	Households ('000)
Owner-occupied: with mortgage	24.7	46.1	24.7	1.7	2.0	0.8	100.0	4,528
Owner-occupied: owned outright	30.9	29.8	31.2	2.0	3.2	2.9	100.0	3,700
Rented from local authority, or new town	1.1	39.4	35.0	23.0	1.4	–	100.0	4,628
Rented unfurnished from private landlord	6.0	13.9	45.4	14.6	19.5	0.5	100.0	2,246
Rented furnished from private landlord	5	6	12	7	70	1	100.0	550
Rented with job or business	22	28	16	8	7	20	100.0	750
All tenures	16.4	34.4	31.0	9.8	6.5	1.9	100.0	16,434

Percentages do not always add to 100 because of rounding.
First decimal place not shown where sample number in the tenure is under 500.
Total of households in all tenures includes 32,000 households of unstated tenure.
Source: HMSO, *Technical Volume* 1, 1977: 3.

Table 8.2 Unfitness and lack of amenities: England and Wales 1976 thousands‡ (percentages in brackets)

	Owner-occupied	Rented from local authority	Other tenures(*)	Vacant†	All tenures
Unfit dwellings	310(3)	49(1)	384(16)	151(30)	894(5)
No fixed bath in bathroom	302(3)	47(1)	426(17)	126(25)	901(5)
No inside WC	407(4)	161(3)	471(19)	129(26)	1,638(9)
Lacking one or more basic amenities	547(5)	280(6)	640(26)	166(33)	1,633(9)
All dwellings	10,125(100)	5,067(100)	2,444(100)	497(100)	18,133(100)

* Mainly privately rented, but includes accommodation rented with job or business, and miscellaneous tenures.
† England only.
‡ Numbers are shown to nearest thousand for arithmetical convenience, but are not as accurate as that due to sampling variation.
Source: *Technical Volume 1*: 56.

Table 8.3 Size of household spaces by number of rooms: England and Wales 1971 (%)

Number of rooms	Owner-occupied	Rented from local authority or New Town	Rented unfurnished from private landlord	Rented furnished from private landlord	All tenures
One or two	0.6	6.4	7.8	50.4	5.8
Three or four	22.2	39.4	41.0	29.7	30.6
Five or six	63.2	52.4	44.1	16.0	54.7
Seven to nine	12.6	1.7	6.2	3.4	8.0
Ten or more	1.4	0.0	0.8	0.5	0.8
All sizes	100.0	100.0	100.0	100.0	100.0
Total ('000)	8,288	4,628	2,792	754	16,434

Accommodation occupied with job or business is included under 'rented unfurnished from private landlord' or 'rented furnished from private landlord' as the case may be.
Source: *Technical Volume 1*: 54.

Rental sector policy in Britain – a brief overview

Rent controlling legislation in the UK has had not only a long but also a complex history. Since 1915 there has been a succession of at least a dozen major pieces of legislation. Not only have most of these packages of legislation been individually complex but there has been a tendency to proceed by marginal or textual changes in existing law (Farrand 1975). As a result the Rent Acts, as now consolidated, are difficult to comprehend, not only for lawyers and scholars but, and more importantly, for tenants and landlords.

Each 'control' may differ in a number of ways. The control may be presented as an empirical rule, such as rents may not be allowed to exceed a given multiple of gross annual value. Or they may be stated as a principle, for instance rents are to reflect conditions prevailing in a competitive and balanced rental market. In addition the stated justification for the control may vary over time. Wartime scarcities and difficulties of postwar reconstruction, fears of monopoly ownership and exploitation and, more recently, concerns over income and wealth distribution or an ideological commitment to remove or expand rental housing have all underlain rent controls in Britain.

In addition to specifying rent controls such legislation also necessarily makes provision for two qualitative aspects of rental housing provision. First, housing service provision levels may also be specified and controlled (at least to some extent) by an Act so that landlords, with controlled rents, are not able to reduce service provision. Second, legislation may alter the balance of landlord and tenant property rights either to prevent evictions following the introduction of controls or because a judgement is made regarding the distribution of property rights *per se*. Indeed in the UK, attitudes to tenure rights rather than the desirability of rent controls may now be the major cause of policy disagreement between the principal political parties. In general, in the UK, there has been increasing control over service provision levels and an upward, if fluctuating, shift in the distribution of property rights towards tenants and away from landlords.

Legislation, at any given time, may also differ in its designed and operational coverage. For instance, since 1965 rental sector legislation has increasingly tended to be designed for specific subsections of rented housing thus creating a diversity of controls existing at any one time. The post-1965 distinction between unfurnished or furnished lettings is the principal example of such changes. Unintended differentiation in the operation of controls, which are of course the creation of central government, may arise from different interpretation of the law or administrative rules. In recent times, under the 1965 Act, security of tenure provisions for furnished rental tenants in Scotland were effectively legally more substantive than in England and Wales because Scots law is based on different principles. Regarding administrative rules, it is now believed that rent officers and rent assessment committees, who have considerable discretion in interpreting Fair Rent legislation since 1965, vary considerably in the operation across different cities and regions in Britain.

These points regarding the complexity of legislation over time and its interpretation at a point in time are emphasised here. This is to dissuade economists, particularly those involved in local housing market research, from assuming that a simple deductively based model of rent controls will yield definitive results or predictions.

The supply of and demand for private rental housing depend not only on rent controls. Obviously policies for the other tenure sectors will influence rental demand, for instance the measures to stimulate owner-occupation cited in the previous chapter may reduce rental demand and also reduce rental supply with net sales of existing rental units to owner-occupation. In addition, housing demolition programmes in the inner city have had a particular impact on rental provision and more recently rehabilitation via Housing Corporation measures may encourage landlord sales to housing associations.

Within the broad heading of 'Housing Policy', local authority controls, for instance, to reduce or remove multiple occupation of property generally have rental sector impacts (Maclennan and MacVean 1978) and the tax policies of central government may discourage investment in private renting. For instance, at the present time, tax relief on interest is limited to a landlord's own residence, income is taxed and capital gains on rented housing are taxed. Thus the landlord and owner-occupier have a substantially different tax position for similar houses. At the same time, landlords are not treated akin to business in other sectors. They are not allowed to write-off depreciation on capital assets against tax liabilites. Thus private landlords have a distinctive tax treatment in the UK.

More recently, at least in the 1970s, rent levels have also been intermittently controlled by general as well as specific rent controls. For instance, counter-inflation measures in 1972, 1973 and 1974 all required a freeze on rent levels (Jones 1980; Maclennan 1980). Thus, when economic effects of rent controls in the UK are examined it is critical to bear in mind this background of other policy shifts which have, in general, acted in the same direction as Rent Acts. Before examining the history of change in the private rental sector, it is important to provide a general overview of relevant legislation.

Legislation and the rental sector

Before the First World War more than 90 per cent of the population of the UK lived in the private rental housing stock, then comprising almost nine million dwellings. At that time no rent controls existed and tenants had no rights of tenure or security. However, the private rental system did not then appear to be a major source of discontent and there were a large number of private landlords in most local housing markets. The onset of war severely destabilised prices in the housing sector. A rise in interest rates, taxation and building costs all induced landlords to raise rents and evictions for default grew alarmingly. The situation was also exacerbated by a redistribution of population for wartime production purposes. Thus, with rising rents, evictions and civil unrest the government introduced, in 1915, the Mortgage and Rent Restrictions Act (rents were to be controlled at 1914 levels).

At that time the measures were intended as temporary, emergency measures and it was stated that 'We do not put forward legislation which can be defended on logical and economic grounds' (Nevitt 1970). Some perceptive commentators realised, however, that it would subsequently be difficult to reverse this legislation in a democracy. The number of voter/tenants would always outnumber voter/landlords. In the early period of postwar reconstruction, and with a commitment to providing 'Homes for Heroes', rent legislation was continued although control was limited to houses built before 1919. A period of creeping de-control then ensued, in the Acts of 1923, 1925 and 1927, with previously controlled tenancies becoming 'decontrolled' when they fell vacant. With changing economic and political conditions full control on lower value properties was introduced. In 1938 and 1939 there was a move back to full control of all rented properties with 1939 rents set at a maximum value of 1914 rents plus 40 per cent.

Following the Second World War, rents remained fully controlled until 1957, although the 1954 Act increased landlords' allowances to combat the growing problem of under-maintenance (Carr 1954). The period 1945–54 saw the first major economic analyses of rent controls in the UK, and Harrod (1947) and Paish (1950) argued strongly for the removal of controls although they proposed different remedies for returning to a market based system of provision. Insofar as pre-1945 legislation had been pragmatically justified for wartime purposes, post-1945 formulation and discussion of rental sector policy became, and has remained, strongly ideologically based.

The 1957 Act, in response to free market arguments, was a major attempt to remove rent controls. Higher valued property was completely decontrolled, other properties had the 1939 limits revalued upwards (to double the 1914 rental values) and even these lower valued properties were to be progressively decontrolled and security of tenure status was reduced to four weeks' notice to quit. The Act of 1957 led to a disastrous deterioration in landlord/tenant relationships and failed to provide a suitable mechanism for decontrolling property which would avoid acute social distress. Thus the Labour Party, then stressing the exploitive, monopolistic power of landlords, became committed to recontrol on assuming office. Rent control had become a central ideological issue in British politics.

The legislation introduced in 1965 was complex and economically sophisticated in comparison to previous controls and it still forms the basis of present legislation. In modified form it has now survived three Labour and two Conservative governments. The 1965 Act, which was consolidated in 1968, made a major distinction between properties let with furniture and those let unfurnished. The furnished rental sector was largely uncontrolled although Rent Tribunals were empowered to limit rents and to provide limited extensions of security of tenure. The unfurnished sector, where properties were not already controlled by the 1957 Act, was to be subject to full security of tenure for tenants and the determination of rents according to 'Fair Rent' criteria.

The 'Fair Rent' was to reflect the rent which would prevail in a free market without scarcity. The rest, which would be the long-run equilibrium rent emerging in a competitive market was to be set by rent officers (generally with no professional background in the housing sector) or by rent assessment committees when landlord or tenant objected to the level set by the rent officer. The rent officer/committee fixed rents for a period of three years and service provision levels were assessed and were to be maintained. The 1972 Housing Finance Act, a Conservative Act, only marginally altered this legal arrangement by beginning to switch 'controlled' (under the 1956 Act) to 'Fair Rent' tenancies and at the same time introducing an income-related Rent Allowance Scheme.

Subsequent Labour legislation in 1974 and 1975 stopped progressive conversion of 'controlled' to 'Fair Rents' and discontinued the distinction of furnished and unfurnished tenancies. The 1974 Rent Act and its consequences are examined below and here only the legislative changes are noted. The 1974 Act made 'furnished' rental housing subject to full security of tenure and 'Fair Rent' provisions and created the new legal category of 'resident' landlord. The 'resident' landlord was not, along with other exceptions, subject to the provisions of the Act but was now covered by the Rent Tribunal system. After 1974 'resident' landlords became the relatively uncontrolled sector. The 'shorthold' tenancy provision of the 1980 Housing Act is designed to remove the full security tenure contract with some landlords although rent controls are not being relaxed.

Over the period of the implementation of this legislation the size of the principal rental sector in Scotland has progressively declined and this has led many commentators to stress legislative change as the cause of decline. But this is too simplistic an approach and before supporting or rejecting this view on the causes of rental sector decline it is best to indicate some theoretically based hypotheses about the effects of rent controls.

A theoretical framework for analysis

Most theoretical analysis of rent controls is framed in the context of either perfectly competitive markets with representative firms (landlords) or in relation to well-behaved markets with theoretically deducible supply and demand curves. The deductive identification of an industry supply curve implies that the market is assumed to be in competitive equilibrium. But what is known about the structure and competitiveness of the rental housing 'industry'? This is an important issue as opposing political parties, in the absence of empirical research, have tended to make divergent assumptions about market structures and competitiveness in the sector. Labour literature and statements in the 1950s and 1960s (see Duclaud-Williams 1979) have implied that problems of monopoly structures or monopoly rents exist in the sector. On the other hand, market oriented parties have stressed the competitiveness and dispersed structure of ownership. The latter imply that controls are unnecessary or, more occasionally, temporary controls are required to deal with 'scarcity rents', that is, rents accruing in periods of excess demand and disequilibrium. Thus an examination of the ownership structure of rental housing may provide an indication as to which set of assumptions about the market is reasonable.

The British government, despite its long-term commitment to rent controls, does not have a clear and informed view of the number and nature of 'firms' (i.e. landlords) providing rental housing. The evidence that does exist has come from a series of detailed but localised studies of rental housing which have spread out over almost a twenty year period. Studies of ownership structures in Lancaster (Cullingworth 1963), London (Francis Report, 1971), Edinburgh (Elliott and McCrone 1975), and Glasgow (Maclennan 1978; Strathclyde Regional Council 1978) have indicated some comparable results. In each study a variety of size of holding was identified, and size of holding is also associated with landlord type (private individual, property company, trust, *etc.*). In addition there were a large number of landlords in each location and although the majority of landlords held less than five properties the concentration ratio of property numbers was still low for the residual landlords. The most recent study available, which post-dates the 1974 Act, indicates the ownership structure for Glasgow (see Table 8.4). Whilst this evidence might suggest that structural measures indicate that the market is likely to be competitive several caveats are important. First, when the figures are examined on a local spatial basis – say political wards – concentration ratios can become much higher. For instance, in one significant ward for unfurnished rental provision in the city of Glasgow, a single company owned more than 90 per cent of the relevant stock. Second, ownership structures varied by sector with furnished rental housing being substantially more oriented to small-scale, locally based landlords. Third, the figures observed are not the outcome of a market process and thus it may not be possible to accurately adduce market structure from existing arrangements. Despite these qualifications, however, it is probably the case that the system is sufficiently decentralised for owners to compete with each other though, of course, supply shortages induced by rent controls may result in scarcity rents reducing competition insofar as they can be expressed in quantity rather than price terms.

To permit a more compressed discussion of rent controls, it is assumed here that the supply side of the system responds to price changes and for simplicity of exposition a supply curve is drawn as a single line. In reality, given the possible complexity of firm objectives, a less precise relationship may pertain and the supply curve can only be deducible *ex post* and it may be unstable. Leaving these difficulties aside, what can be predicted about the effect of rent controls on private rental supply?

The simple case

Assume that the rental housing market is initially in a position of long- and short-run equilibrium, providing $0Q_1$ units of housing at a price RE_1 (Fig. 8.1). The demand curve is represented by D_1D_1, and the short- and long-run supply curves by S_lS_l and S_ES_E respectively. It is assumed that the short-run supply curve for rental properties is relatively inelastic. If demand for rented housing now increases by shift of the demand curve outward from D_1D_1 to D_2D_2, a new short-run equilibrium price and output position is attained at R_s and Q_s. As a result of the demand shift prices have risen, output of rental housing has increased and super-normal profits are now being earned by all marginal and infra-marginal producers at the initial price RE_1. There is, therefore, a redistribution of income from tenants to landlords in the short-run. And, of course, there may also be a long-run redistribution if the long-run supply curve is positively sloped.

Either because the new long-run equilibrium price and output position is viewed as being undesirable or because it is believed that the market will not attain long-run equilibrium within an acceptable time period, government may impose a maximum price per housing unit. Assume initially that housing services per unit remain fixed and that there is no change in security of tenure provisions. Then the long-run

Table 8.4 Ownership and location of rental stock in Glasgow, 1976.

Wards with > 10 to renting

Total dwellings	% in private rented	Ward
5,972	15.8	Tollcross
4,793	18.0	Parkhead
5,646	10.8	Carntyne
3,459	31.5	Camlachie
3,426	18.7	City
3,279	37.3	Calton
3,931	24.0	Dalmarnock
3,001	43.6	Cowlairs
5,747	24.0	Dennistoun
4,658	16.6	Wyndford
3,167	37.7	Botanic Gardens
3,585	30.8	Park
3,959	39.9	Kelvin
3,207	39.6	Woodside
4,106	38.2	Partick East
4,395	38.7	Anderston
4,152	15.0	Anniesland
3,699	17.5	Kelvinside
6,231	13.9	Partick West
6,062	23.9	Scotstoun
6,148	32.0	Gorbals
5,244	34.4	Crosshill
3,995	16.0	Drumoyne
5,576	22.3	Fairfield
6,137	12.2	Ibrok
2,464	50.6	Kingston
4,058	13.5	Cardonald
4,988	13.8	Pollokshields
3,912	31.1	Strathbungo
4,128	27.6	Camphill
3,973	27.1	Mount Florida
4,205	34.3	King's Park

Ward No.	Number of properties owned by type of landlord*									Total
	1	2	3	4	5	6	7	8	9	
1	53	104	318	59	348	1	0	120	10	1,013
2	70	151	185	9	329	147	0	62	5	958
3	27	159	171	8	224	1	9	149	4	752
4	39	236	191	3	600	6	1	122	2	1,200
11	108	143	147	12	346	2	34	116	16	924
13	87	268	276	17	510	1	0	282	6	1,447

	Number of properties owned by type of landlord*									
Ward No.	1	2	3	4	5	6	7	8	9	Total
14	40	319	78	3	464	5	12	100	2	1,023
17	97	267	310	10	576	11	23	179	1	1,474
20	55	494	370	34	412	2	3	18	17	1,405
22	89	120	237	8	305	13	14	41	6	833
27	238	182	312	8	574	19	56	200	17	1,606
28	547	178	336	14	549	1	66	130	41	1,862
29	164	234	584	4	610	4	24	157	4	1,785
30	181	220	435	13	496	37	1	179	6	1,568
31	179	343	427	3	639	85	38	108	10	1,832
32	283	256	509	18	852	2	33	170	15	2,138
33	57	238	87	3	257	14	87	81	19	843
34	311	145	58	12	292	117	44	12	19	1,010
35	54	158	239	4	451	4	0	181	27	1,118
36	122	311	374	2	634	5	3	268	12	1,731
43	120	385	535	5	857	57	38	197	4	2,198
45	226	408	562	3	750	27	49	8	14	2,047
47	29	53	46	7	491	25	21	17	5	694
48	55	275	398	4	409	88	0	2,308	0	3,537
49	90	158	208	11	306	5	0	623	5	1,406
50	51	202	250	40	698	2	5	333	9	1,590
53	11	10	1	4	520	0	66	46	5	663
55	119	112	134	72	215	153	33	66	24	928
56	151	357	356	77	382	27	1	16	5	1,372
57	112	172	190	10	577	153	1	31	17	1,253
62	108	165	233	6	623	4	8	2	9	1,158
63	10	4	424	0	999	0	0	6	7	1,450
Totals	3,885	6,827	8,981	483	16,295	1,018	670	6,328	343	44,828
%	8.66	15.22	20.03	1.07	36.35	2.27	1.49	14.13	0.76	

* Key to landlord type
1. Individuals;
2. Individuals operating through factors;
3. Trusteeships (usually through a factor);
4. Private companies;
5. Property companies and private companies operating through a factor;
6. Housing Associations (excluding SSHA);
7. Nationalised industries and public authorities;
8. Local authority departments, other than housing
   (a) recorded occupied properties;
   (b) recorded vacant properties;
9. Miscellaneous.
Source: *Housing Policy Studies*, Regional Report Section, Strathclyde Regional Council, 1977.

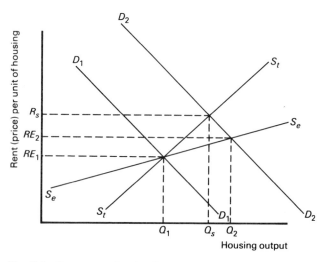

Fig. 8.1 Rent controls: simple case

effects of the control will depend on the level of rent set in relation to the long-run equilibrium rent. If, for instance (Robinson 1979; Stafford 1978), the rent is set at a level, R_c' between R_s and RE_2 the long-run supply of housing will be greater than or equal to the long-run equilibrium supply (Fig. 8.2). Eventually RE_2 will pertain and the difference between R_c and RE_2 will mainly affect the rate of adjustment to the new equilibrium. However, if rent is set at some level R_c'' between RE_2 and RE_1, then excess demand will exist and the rental market will not be cleared but there will still be an expansion in rental supply. An actual reduction in rental supply requires the controlled rent, R_c''', to be imposed at a level less than RE_1. Thus, to show that rent controls lead to market disequilibrium it is necessary to show that $R_c \neq RE_1$ or RE_2 and for supply to be reduced R_c''' must be less than RE_1. Further, to absorb increased demand for rental housing in the long run without an increase in price, without excess demand and without a shift in income distribution the long-run supply curve would have to be perfectly elastic.

Whilst this analysis is informative it is however very limited. Because 'other things' don't remain constant when rents are controlled nor is the form of the control always simply or clearly expressed. Many important aspects of rental legislation can be introduced by expanding the above analysis (Cooper and Stafford 1975).

Variations in service provision and maintenance
Since a house is a complex commodity which produces a variety of services, in conjunction with other inputs of capital, labour and management, the price paid reflects a number of services provided at a

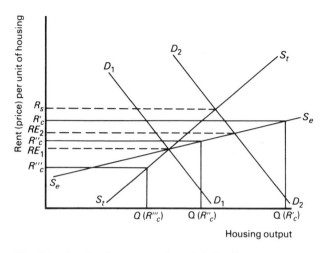

Fig. 8.2   Levels of rent controls and their effects

given level. Thus, policy has to aim to influence or control price or rent per unit of housing service. Indeed, in the Fair Rent legislation of 1965, rent officers are required to assess and record levels of furnishing, other services, *etc.* and make an allowance for them in settling rents. Land-lords are obliged, in principle to maintain such services. But where monitoring of quality is non-existent or limited to specific items (as in the British case) landlords may have some leeway to reduce variable factor inputs at the controlled rent. This issue has been analysed at length by Frankena (1975) and Moorhouse (1972). The theoretical analysis presented by Frankena suggests that landlords may view rent controls as a revenue rather than a price constraint. For instance, using an explicit competitive model of the landlord as a firm, Frankena indicates the quality adjustments landlords may make when rent control is expressed as a total rent (revenue) constraint for a given dwelling. When the landlord is free to vary factor inputs which raise or lower the level of housing services flowing from a given dwelling unit, then the price per unit and output of housing services may be varied. This is shown diagrammatically in Fig. 8.3. The relevant cost curves for short run average variable cost, short run average cost, long-run average cost and short-run marginal costs are indicated by *AVC*, *SRAC*, *LRAC*, and *SRMC* respectively. The line $\overline{R}\overline{R}$ indicates the rectangular hyperbola generated by varying price and output of housing service units per dwelling in order to meet the revenue or total rent constraint. That is $Pq = \overline{R}$. Frankena continues:

> Consequently, in the presence of the revenue constraint, the short-run supply curve of the firm will consist of the segment of the *SRMC* curve

217

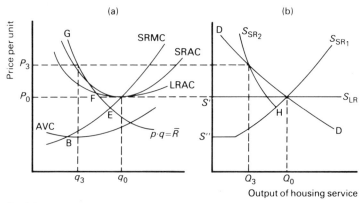

Fig. (a) Model of firm supplying rental housing services with application to rent control as a revenue constraint.

Fig. (b) Model of market for rental housing services with application to rent control as a revenue constraint.

Fig. 8.3 Rent controls as a revenue constraint.

Source: Frankena 1975: 306

> between the *AVC* curve and the rectangular hyperbola, and the segment of the rectangular hyperbola above the *SRMC* curve, i.e. the line *BEFG*. The long-run supply curve of the firm will be the segment of the rectangular hyperbola above the *LRAC* curve, i.e. the line *FG* (Frankena, 1975: 306).

Thus the firm, instead of maintaining output of housing services and incurring losses at or near P_0, q_0 (the competitive market price and output level), will contract output at least to the position P_3, q_3 where normal profits will be earned.

With this form of control landlords may avoid losses, raise price per unit of housing service and excess demand will be removed by reducing the quality of housing services. In principle the British system of controls which fixes both rent levels and housing services should avoid quality adjustments. However, problems of identifying and measuring such service inputs imply that this argument is important and probably has relevance in the UK case both with respect to pre- and post-1965 legislation. In addition, it has been suggested that all controls, particularly where there are minimal maintenance allowances, have discouraged private landlords from maintaining or improving property and led to a low uptake of private improvement grants.

There may, however, be instances where controls increase levels of service provision if rent controls are not equally applied throughout the rental sector. For instance, after the 1965 Act, landlords could avoid rent controls (to a large extent) if they provided furnishings. This can be indicated as follows in Fig. 8.4. Let the demand curves $D_u D_u$ and $D_F D_F$ relate respectively to unfurnished and furnished rental housing. Assume that $D_u D_u$ and $D_F D_F$ are independent. In the same way $S_u S_u$ and $S_F S_F$ relate to the competitive supply functions. It is assumed for simplicity that $S_F S_F$ lies above $S_u S_u$ by a constant amount. Now let the unfurnished rental sector be controlled at a rent R_c. Consider now the marginal landlord at rent R_c, at output Q_c. By adding the appropriate level of furnishings he can move onto the supply curve $S_F S_F$ and be equally profitable with controlled renting as long as rents are greater than or equal to R_N. But in fact the furnished sector is uncontrolled and he will earn a rent R_F, which exceeds the marginal rent required to attract him into the sector. In the same way, following the 1974 Act, landlords were exempted from controls if they provided a cooked breakfast for tenants. The 'Fried egg adjustment mechanism' could then come into play as landlords avoided control by increasing service provision. In this way, however, with continuing excess demand for rental property, British legislation has now produced a context in which landlords compete against the law rather than versus each other (Maclennan 1978).

Problems in setting rent levels by an administered process

It has been suggested above that supply reductions take place only if the controlled rent is set below the prevailing long-run equilibrium rent. Even though it is subject to a variety of interpretations and in detail may be economically nonsensical, the British Fair Rent legislation,

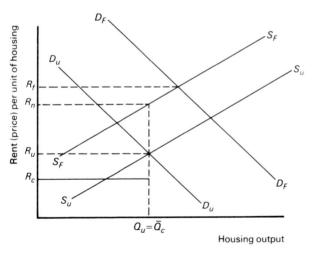

Fig. 8.4 Rent controls and sector shifts

which now permits rents to be increased as well as decreased, is broadly intended to establish long-run equilibrium rents. But the administrative rules for achieving this objective are inadequate.

The previous practice of setting comparable rents based on similar properties, which were already controlled has tended to be replaced by comparing capital values of equivalent houses. Assuming aside for the moment problems of general and house price inflation, there are still some difficulties. First, committees or rent officers agree on a reasonable or fair rate of return to landlords from letting the property. This is usually set in the range 6 to 8 per cent, somewhat below the range government itself is allowed to earn from most nationalised industries. This rate of return is assessed pre-tax and is not inflation adjusted. But then a 'scarcity factor' is introduced and the size of this factor is decided, on criteria that are unclear and unstated, at the local or regional assessment committee level. It is argued that capital values formed in the owner-occupied sector also reflect scarcity (excess demand) and that, to comply with 'Fair Rent' principles, they should be discounted by this 'scarcity factor' before being used for assessment of Fair Rents. For example, in 1977, the scarcity factor in Aberdeen was reputed to be 50 per cent and in Glasgow 30 per cent. Thus, controlled Aberdeen rents would offer a nominal pre-tax return of 3 to 4 per cent to landlords.

The 'scarcity factor' is counter-intuitive and probably prevents the rental sector from ever adjusting to equilibrium. If the scarcity factor reduces returns and stops the landlord letting, then tenants may seek to enter owner-occupation adding to 'scarcity' in that sector (unless there are appropriate supply side adjustments), thus increasing the 'scarcity factor', thus reducing rents etc. The 'scarcity factor' as currently operated in the rental sector is an economic nonsense and it is indeed unfortunate that the 1980 Housing Act does little to amend the system.

It is quite conceivable, therefore, that controlled rents, even Fair Rents, are set below likely existing equilibrium market levels and, as a result, supply reductions may take place.

Problems of inflation

The difficulties of setting Fair Rents are in some respects compounded by general or specific shifts in the costs of inputs for the provision of rental housing. A general upward movement in the price level not only reduces landlords' revenue in real terms but it also raises real and nominal cost expenditure. The historical system of control in Britain, taking controlled rents as a fixed multiple of a historically assessed and fixed capital and rental valuation, was particularly poorly structured to cope with inflation although it is true that periods of price depreciation (in the 1920s and 1930s) and low inflation (1950s and 1960s) characterised such periods.

Under the post 1965 Fair Rent system, rents are assessed for a three year period and rent officers/committees can make an allowance for expected inflation in setting rents. However, official inflation estimates usually lie well below out-turn figures and an accurate assessment of such price changes is not likely to be made. In addition, in the furnished rental sector, or where there are predominantly transient tenants, it may not have been in the interest of tenants to seek a registered rent which may be adjusted upwards to allow for three years of anticipated inflation. After 1974, however, Government restricted or phased private sector rent increases over a fixed period. Provisions to discontinue such phasing in rent assessment were incorporated in the 1980 Housing Act.

Inflation in property prices may, however, have had a stimulating effect on private rental provision in some locations and for certain types of landlord. Long-term, large, letting companies with a continuing interest in letting private property may not gain from house price inflation in that replacement costs of housing assets will rise with house price inflation. There is no evidence, unlike the North American context, to suggest that in Britain inner-area landlords have been penalised by property value depreciation vis-à-vis the general price level (indeed there is some limited evidence to the contrary!) However, and particularly in the period 1965–74 when it was relatively uncontrolled, there is evidence to suggest that small-scale landlords were making investments in local furnished rental properties to acquire capital gains on housing.

A detailed study of the City of Glasgow (Maclennan 1977c; Maclennan 1978) indicated that there were a large number of new entrant, small-scale, local landlords (with property or professional backgrounds) entering the sector by purchasing moderate quality properties with price appreciation prospects. An analysis of capital value appreciation of these properties indicated that annual appreciation rates (pre-tax) of between 10 and 25 per cent (with an average of 19 per cent) were made in the period 1971–4. For such investors in the sector, where capital gain dominates replacement concerns, it is perhaps theoretically appropriate that rent assessment committees should allow relatively low (equity related) rather than high (bond related) rates of return. But how could committees make such a distinction *ex ante*? The consequence of these considerations is that particular types of landlord (capital gain oriented) may continue to let properties profitably even at very low rents or, as has been reported post the 1974 Act, be prepared to hold vacant, but appreciating (in value) stocks of property.

However it may be misleading to assess capital returns independently of the landlord's ability to dispose of assets and this requires a consideration of legislation related to tenant security of tenure.

Problems of security of tenure
Almost all legislation for rent control makes provision to increase the security of tenure of existing tenants, so that landlords cannot respond to controls by immediately evicting tenants and disposing of their rental assets. But few economists have formally analysed the economic effects of this transfer of property rights and an understanding of the effects of security of tenure are critical to an evaluation of British rental sector experience in the 1970s. Extending security of tenure to tenants may affect landlords in two ways. First, and this would be important for locally resident landlords, they would be legally incapable of evicting tenants whom they discovered, for reasons of preference or prejudice, to be 'unsuitable' tenants. That is, there would be a potential loss of psychic income. Second, and more important for the capital gain oriented landlords, the investor would no longer be free to choose when to dispose of his assets. Thus, the introduction of security of tenure for tenants may leave monetary returns unaffected but it increases the risk or uncertainty attached to earning these returns. Rational individuals, *ceteris paribus*, prefer, for a given rate of return, less risky to more risky alternatives. This issue has been analysed formally elsewhere (Maclennan 1977c), but it is sufficient to note that rent controls not only generally reduce existing rents but also increase owner risk when security of tenure provisions exist.

Taking the above considerations into account it is clear that a general prediction about the effects of rent controls cannot be made from a simple competitive model. Instead, it is important to know the structure and competitiveness of the market involved, the nature and objectives of landlords, the principles and the administration of rent and security of tenure controls and, of course, the general housing and economic context into which controls are introduced. Supply reductions are not the inevitable outcome of rent controls but they are likely occurrences where rents are set below market levels, where fixed rents are unadjusted in a period of general inflation and where increased security of tenure accompanies rent control. Where controls are flexible with respect to inflation or where deflation or stable prices pertain, or where variable maintenance and service provision can be reduced or where 'exceptions' and 'subsections' are legislatively created, then controls may have a minimal effect on the supply of number of properties.

Tenant and market adjustment

Economic analysis of rent controls, both in Britain and overseas, generally has little to say about the effects of controls on tenants and market adjustments (Walker 1977). The latter omission may be valid if security of tenure and slow tenant turnover ensure that the same population of landlords, houses and households persist without movement into the long term. In such circumstances it can be argued that tenants benefit with a redistribution from landlord to tenant (assuming no quality adjustments). In addition it may be argued that there are some misallocative effects with households urged to over-consume housing or, obversely, generate under-occupancy rates (Olsen 1972).

But such an analysis may seriously overestimate benefits to tenants if they wish to move or if there is transience or turnover in the sector. In such instances, if the market rent would exceed the controlled rent, not only will supply be reduced as prices are controlled but, and importantly, controlled rents will stimulate demand for private lets thus increasing excess demand for private lets. But if price adjustments to excess demand are not permitted, via rent controls, then how does an increasing potential rental population become housed in a declining stock? What are the allocative mechanisms involved and are they costly? The housing search adjustment model outlined in Chapter 3 has important implications in this regard. A combination of chance, access to information and the ability to execute a search strategy have been established as being an important influence in explaining the incidence of rent controls (see Maclennan 1979a, b, 1980b). Such effects reduce the net benefits to moving and new entrant renters of controls and they lead to a potentially regressive incidence of search costs.

Of course a cost-benefit analysis of rent controls would have to consider an even wider and longer term set of effects of controls. Would crowding and excess demand effects spread into other sectors, would the physical quality of core area tenements decline and induce a downward cycle of maintenance levels, would this reduce property values and in turn induce a decline in the property tax base or would the effects spread into the labour market and reduce spatial mobility in highly mobile occupations or for labour market entrants? How do landlords utilise disinvested capital? Unfortunately in the British context, and in most other countries, it is quite impossible to provide such an evaluation of rent controls. Indeed, in the next section it is apparent that it is often difficult to identify the broadly defined supply effects of rent controls let alone subsequent tenant search costs and wider market adjustments.

Rent controls in Britain – empirical evidence

The empirical evidence presented here falls into two categories. First the broad long-term changes in the private rental sector are reviewed in relation to the existence of controls. This is the level of empirical generalisation which dominates the discussion of rental sector policies in Britain. Second, and to provide a more precise and detailed account of rent policy changes in Britain, microeconomic studies of the effects of the 1974 Rent Act in Britain are reviewed.

Broad historical patterns

The absolute and relative decline of the private rental sector in Britain has been alluded to above. Taking the sector as an aggregate for Great Britain the share of total households in private rental housing fell from 89 per cent in 1914, through 61 per cent in 1947, to 25 per cent in 1964 and 16 per cent in 1975. Present estimates are of the order of 13 per cent. The Green Paper of 1977, citing figures for England and Wales only, indicated that the stock of private lets had fallen from 7.1 m. dwellings in 1914 to 2.8 m. in 1977. Of this decline 37 per cent was due to demolitions and 63 per cent due to sales to the owner-occupied sector.

These figures indicate that although absolute and relative decline has continued the rate has not been constant. Nor is it easy to associate periods of more or less rapid decline with, respectively, more or less strict rent controls. It would be misleading to suggest that massive or short-run reductions followed the 1915 Act or its post-First World War confirmation. Indeed the Green Paper (Housing Policy, Technical Volume 2, 1977) indicates that in the period between the two wars 26 per cent of new stock was built for private renting. But the limitation of controls to pre-1919 housing and the profitability of controlled rents during periods of falling wages, prices and building costs staved any rapid reduction. Of course security of tenure for existing tenants implies that any reaction in the form of disinvestment would be lagged and the length of average lag increases with average tenancy duration. Robinson (1979) correctly suggests that the interwar period should be subdivided into the period prior to 1933 when rent controls did not limit supply, and the period after 1933 when controlled rents probably lay substantially below market rents (by 20 to 30%). This position was probably exacerbated by inflation in the period 1939 to 1957 despite some ameliorative effects of the 1954 Act.

Ironically, the period of decontrol from 1957 to 1965 and the subsequent phase of rent assessment have both been marked by quite rapid reductions in the scale of the sector. An examination of the numbers of dwellings, presented in the Green Paper (plus subsequent data), indicated that an absolute decline of 2.2 m. dwellings occurred from 1915 to 1960 (45 years) and a similar reduction occurred from 1960 to 1979, despite a temporary expansion (from 1965 to 1974) in furnished lettings. Since 1965 it is difficult to assess how market rents stand in relation to controlled rents and, of course, security of tenure provision has strengthened. Robinson (1979) has also presented evidence on quality changes which are in accord with theoretical expectation — i.e. quality has reduced over time. The Green Paper was correct to suggest of rent controls that 'The effect of these legislative changes is difficult to assess' and the Review of the Rent Acts was bereft of any evidence of the effects of rent controls in the UK. This is, in itself, a damning indictment of the fashion in which British governments, of all complexions, have intervened in the housing system — policies have not been adequately researched prior to formulation nor monitored post implementation.

Several commentators have drawn attention to the difficulties of interpreting the effects of rent controlling legislation in the UK (Berry 1974; Eversley 1975).

Eversley indicated that there does not appear to be a close connection between the intensity of sector decline and changes in rent controls and he suggests that there are structural causes for the decline, which go beyond official policies.

Berry has outlined in more detail several hypotheses which could explain the sector's decline. It could be attributed to:

1. Constraints on landlords imposed by the state and public authorities, including rent control, housing, public health, fire standards, *etc.*
2. A lack of appropriate financial institutions to finance rental developments, probably caused by investors' uncertainty re future policy for the sector.
3. Competition from owner-occupation financed by the building societies. A positive income elasticity of demand for home-ownership, low and subsidised mortgage interest rates and capital gain expectations provide a plausible rationale for increased home-ownership. Using Eversley's statistics, it is possible to argue that in the UK the private rental sector demise has been offset by home-ownership rather than municipal expansion, particularly in the 1970s (see Ch. 7).
4. The system of taxing landlords' property income (discussed below).
5. The relative attractiveness of non-housing investment opportunities. Eversley notes that in the period of expansion of the private rented sector a gross return of 3 per cent was considered sufficient even after allowing for maintenance and management. In the late nineteenth century period rates of return on stocks were commonly in the range of 3–6 per cent whereas more recently 15 per cent is common. Eversley adds a sixth reason:
6. The replacement of large families by smaller higher income units (particularly with two earners) increases the possibility of house purchase.

Surprisingly neither author has stressed the role of inner-city redevelopment policy. In most of the major cities of the UK there has been a clear process of inner-city, private, rented housing being demolished and replaced by municipal (frequently peripheral) housing. Table 8.5 indicates, in a particular case, these effects quite clearly (Kemp 1979). The figures relate to the Partick East ward in Glasgow, an area of late nineteenth and early twentieth century tenements initially constructed for private renting. This Table indicates not only the decline of private rented sector throughout the period but also confirms, since 1974, an accelerating rate of decline. In this example there was a substantial flow of rental properties into owner-occupation until 1974 but, and reflecting the 1974 Housing Act, housing association purchases for rehabilitation have become more important.

Both the broad historical analysis of rent controls and specific examples cited above amount to no more than a casual empirical analysis of a time series of stock or quality changes loosely related to legislative changes with an unknown strength and no formal specification of the intensity or operational lags of policy. However, some more detailed assessment of the 1974 Act has been undertaken and the results are now presented.

Some economic effects of the 1974 Rent Act

The 1974 Rent Act
Following their return to power in 1974 the Labour government

Table 8.5 Destination of dwellings leaving the privately rented sector 1964-9; 1969-74; 1974-8

	Loss due to						
	O/O	H.A.	L.A.	ΔUse	D	C	Total
Numbers							
1964-9	427	–	70*	12	1	11	521
1969-74	311	4	24	34	141	114	628
1974-8	183	336	26	27	20	–	592

P.R.S. dwellings: 1964 – 2,855   * 48 were demolished
                   1969 – 2,334
                   1974 – 1,706
                   1978 – 1,114

Key: P.R.S. = privately rented sector; O/O = sales due to owner-occupation; H.A. = sales to Housing Associations; L.A. = sales to local authority; D = demolitions; and C = loss due to conversions to a larger (privately rented) dwelling unit; ΔUse = change of use (from residential to other sector)
Source: Kemp, P. 1979, The changing ownership structure of the privately rented sector, *Unpublished M. Phil. Thesis*, Department of Town and Regional Planning, University of Glasgow.

implemented the recommendations of the minority report to the Francis Committee which had previously sat to consider the workings of the Rent Acts (Francis Report 1971). The minority report, which was based on a small sample of tenants and landlords in London, argued that the rent registration and full security of tenure provisions should be extended to the previously relatively uncontrolled 'Furnished' sector. This recommendation was embodied in the provisions of the 1974 Act although exemptions were extended to several classes of landlord, for instance those providing 'board' or those letting their property through an institute of higher education. A new legal class of landlord — 'resident landlord' — was defined and exempted from the provisions of the Act.

The process by which the Act was introduced was also noteworthy in that although the Act was passed in August a strike at HMSO prevented publication of the Act until November. This delay, combined with the inherent complexity of the Act which had apparently been produced by a process of 'textual amendment' of earlier Acts (Farrand 1975) required the Housing Minister to make a clarifying statement in Parliament in December 1974. Thus the content of the Act and its 'announcement' process could have been expected to have the following effects:

(a) A relatively short-run reduction in property vacancies and stocks for letting would be facilitated by the transient nature of the tenantry.

(b) A series of 'announcement' effects including anticipatory orders for repossession and a post-implementation but temporary withdrawal of property from letting as landlords learned the new provisions of the Act and took appropriate measures to evade their impact.

(c) There would be a shift of landlords' letting preferences, which could be effected due to overall excess demand, towards inherently transient tenants — e.g. overseas visitors, students, *etc.*

There is considerable 'perceived' evidence to sustain these hypotheses. However, such studies were usually highly localised, were required to utilise less than perfect data and seldom utilised a formal economic methodology. A study of rented property adverts and repossession records for several boroughs in Inner London (Reynolds 1976) indicated that

i. in the year following the Act advertised vacancies were 25 per cent below the pre-1974 level (i.e. the 1972 and 1973 figures) and that protected tenancies were in fact 33 per cent less. The advertised vacancy rate made a small recovery in 1975–6, but even at this time adverts were reduced by 20 per cent;

ii. there was some evidence of an increase in repossession orders in the period prior to the Act;

227

iii. newspaper adverts indicated a switch in advertised letting preferences towards now unprotected tenants or tenancies.

A more detailed analysis on the now unprotected sector in London,
i.e. resident landlords (Paley 1978; Whitehead 1977) has indicated that
the unprotected sector was 'in a normal state of turnover'. They established that the sector was dominated by small adult households without
families who had a rapid turnover rate and that landlords, in general,
were relatively satisfied with the rate of return received. Whitehead
expressed some legitimate concerns with the new uncontrolled sector.
First, the high turnover rate made landlords rapidly able to adjust to
any change in legal or economic circumstances. Second, a large
proportion (84%) of tenants had agreed rent levels privately with the
landlord. Third, there had been increasing 'tenant-type' selection by
landlords. Finally there were still in the sector, unprotected by law and
relatively unsubsidised by government, a large number of low income
and elderly households living in houses with poor amenities and at
relatively high rents.

Some studies (see MacDowell 1976) have been less sanguine in their
conclusions about the supply effects of the 1974 Act. But almost all the
effects reported by Reynolds and Whitehead were observed in an
economic analysis of the effects of the 1974 Act in Glasgow. Reductions
in vacancy adverts, similar in order of magnitude to those observed by
Reynolds, were identified and stock reductions also took place. There
was a minor recovery in 1975–6 and there was a marked shift in
landlord letting preferences (Maclennan 1978; Maclennan 1980; Jones
1980) and many tenants, in the controlled sector, did not seek to register
their rents.

The Glasgow study, unlike the others, attempted to estimate the
effects of the Act on transient groups in the sector, particularly
students. The furnished rental housing market was discovered to be
primarily oriented to housing transient groups and to have a well-
defined seasonal peak of activity which was closely related to academic
term start times. A considerable amount of detailed survey work was
undertaken to establish how a growing population of transients were
rationed into a declining flow of vacancies or stock of properties. Using
the search adjustment model outlined in Chapter 3, the results presented in Table 8.6 were derived. These figures suggest that an
increasing number of transients were rationed out of the market, that
travel times increased, that sharing rates of properties increased, that
retention rates of properties over vacations increased, that less
preferred rental alternatives were selected and that search costs were
substantial – particularly for those groups abandoning summer employment to expand available housing search time (Maclennan 1979a,
1980b). For students, it was estimated that such frictional costs in
1974/75 were of the order of £90, almost equivalent to average rental

Table 8.6 Rent Act effects on tenants

(a) size of living and searching groups for furnished flats (students)

	Average living group size	*Average search group size*
1968–9	1.5	1.23
1972–3	1.81	1.33
1973–4	1.93	1.42
1974–5	3.24*	2.09*
1975–6	3.19*	2.15*

* Significantly greater than pre 1974 level at 0.05
Source: Gush 2, Gush 3.

(b) Average travel time university to rented accommodation (all types)

	Travel time for one way journey accommodation to university (min.)
1968–9*	14.6
1971–2	15.0
1972–3	15.6
1973–4	15.8
1974–5	18.64*
1975–6	19.2*

* Significantly greater than pre 1974 level at 0.05

(c) Sectoral imbalance[1,2]

	Imbalance[3]	
	1973	*1975*
Home	0	0
Hall or student house	− 21.2	− 17.5
Lodgings	+ 8.4	+ 12.7
Bedsit	+ 14	+ 25
Furnished flat	− 3.3	− 12.5
Unfurnished flat	+ 2.2	+ 2.6

1. Second year students are chosen as there is a distinct cycle of preferred sector types throughout the student housing career.
2. The 1973/5 figures relate solely to students in the rented sector.
3. Imbalance is defined as the percentage of students in a sector minus the percentage desiring to be in it.

payments for a term. Non-student transients were affected insofar as search costs increased and movement activity became increasingly restricted to periods outside the seasonal peak. That is, sub-optimal housing consumption became prolonged. Thus, although rents were nominally controlled, rents plus entry costs rose markedly for a group who did not require long-term security of tenure. In addition, in the absence of a rental-price rationing mechanism, properties were not acquired randomly, but the probability of acquiring a preferred outcome was systematically related to initial expectations about the temporal and spatial structure of the local rental market (Maclennan 1979a) and the information networks and channels available to households (Maclennan 1979b). Long distance and low income entrants to the system were particularly disadvantaged.

In the period since 1974 the unfurnished rental sector has continued to decline and selling landlords find a ready market for properties because of expanding owner-occupation and continued Housing Association expansion. But there have been no recent, detailed studies of unfurnished letting. As a result, and because the disappearing unfurnished stock is relatively closely substituted for by public rental housing, the final section discusses policy alternatives specifically in relation to the furnished/resident landlord sector.

Policies for the furnished rental sector

The Green Paper of 1977 stressed the necessity of considering household tastes or preferences in formulating policy and it also emphasised the importance of containing public expenditure on housing policy (viewpoints held even more strongly by the present government). Perhaps because of these considerations, and a then imminent Review of the Rent Acts, the Paper's treatment of the privately rented sector was brief. The major policy proposal was a subsequently disregarded suggestion that there should be an attempt to attract institutional investment funds into the sector. Following the Rent Act Review there were no changes in rental sector policy until the proposals on the 1980 Housing Act were implemented. The Act suggests the introduction of a series of short-term tenancies, which would be agreed between landlord and tenant, and which would restrict severely security of tenure. Some concern has been expressed, however, that although such action may prevent further decline it is not likely to attract new or reattract previous landlords into the sector (Pearce 1980). But in the longer term there may be other policy alternatives and some of the options are now outlined.

The research above indicates that there are (at least) three identifiable groups of households residing in the furnished rental sector. First there are low income households with families generally occupying low amenity property in inner-city areas. In general they have not chosen to live within the privately rented sector without first having been rejected by or evicted from the public sector. Second there are young married couples, quite often with moderately high incomes who are aspiring to be owner-occupiers. Finally there is the quantitatively most important group of young, single and multiple person households who are characteristically transient, are attracted by the informal life style and who place great emphasis on having access to work and recreational/leisure facilities.

Policies for the sector, as contained in the 1974 Rent Act, were apparently designed to shelter low income families, with respect to rent levels and security of tenure. However, the Act, as indicated above, has reduced the supply of properties and resulted in increased problems for transient households. A clearer discussion of constructive policies for the sector emerges if one considers which groups would most benefit from the existence of private furnished renting and why households are in the sector. It seems ironic that a group such as low income families who are widely recognised to be in housing 'need' on almost any interpretation of this nebulous term should be left to fend for themselves in a housing sector with excess demand and be controlled by legislation which, in the long term, may actually relatively disadvantage them within the sector. This low income group of families probably require all the benefits of care which the local housing and social work departments can provide for them. The future of this housing group should surely lie within the protection and care of the public sector. In this context, the Homeless Persons Act may now have reduced the number of low income households forced into private furnished lets.

Similarly, if a careful policy of expanding owner-occupation is implemented then it is possible that the size of the 'aspiring owner-occupier' group may also diminish. In this way the existence of a private furnished rental sector does not seem to be a necessity for any group other than for the third and major group in the sector. That is, young transients.

In the following discussion, therefore, the alternatives to private renting for young transients or short stay transients are evaluated. Several types of strategy are examined.

(a) Rental sector replacement strategies.
(b) Minor amendments to the Fair Rent system.
(c) A radical attempt to relate Fair Rents to competitive market rents or rates of profit.

The *laissez faire* alternative is not considered again as it ignores the problems of scarcity rents in the medium term and, perhaps occasionally, monopoly power.

Private rental sector replacement strategies

Municipalisation
Although the concept is now in official disfavour, calls for the munici-

palisation or public ownership of the private rental stock have been commonplace in socialist literature in the postwar period. Indeed, it is possible that an active municipalisation programme had been presumed to exist prior to the implementation of the 1974 Act by the major advocates of the Act.

The arguments for a municipal takeover of the existing stock have been summarised by Murie *et al.* (1976) who contend that such a policy could provide a more effective means of controlling multiple occupancy and overcrowding, introduce 'needs' related allocative systems where none presently exists and could provide systematic opportunities for the improvement of older housing, particularly in housing action areas. These supposed advantages are worthy of some comment.

Increased control over the sector and occupancy standards. Most local authorities currently have controls over occupational densities which are difficult to implement because individuals, landlords and tenants alike, choose to ignore them. But it can be argued (Maclennan and McVean 1978) that selected occupancy standards may exceed the occupancy requirements of young persons living in informal groups. Unless the local authority was prepared to implement less rigorous standards in the 'young transient' portion of the housing stock then fewer residential spaces at higher per capita rents may be an undesired outcome of municipalisation.

Municipal ownership of the stock would automatically ensure that the fair rent system and tenancy rights (extended and strengthened for the public sector by the Housing Act) were automatically extended to all existing tenants. This contrasts with the rather piecemeal effective cover of the Rent Acts where registration is voluntary. It is pertinent to note, that in a period of rental supply contraction by private landlords, municipalisation would at least preserve the stock of older inner-city houses to rent. The extent to which this would prevent an exacerbation of the present problems of transient groups largely depends upon the criteria subsequently utilised for allocating the stock.

Allocation systems. It was suggested above that, at present, the allocation of furnished lets takes place by a subtle combination of rents, search and queuing costs which tends to favour young persons with higher levels of incomes and experience in particular local housing market. It is not clear on what criteria local authorities would allocate municipalised stock. If the stock was treated as being available to all council tenants in the area then it is likely that existing transients would suffer losses, in that they would be less likely to be allocated spaces in inner city properties in areas with informal living arrangements and with relatively attractive leisure facilities. On the other hand the local authority could adopt allocation criteria to cater for transients in existing areas of furnished provision. If some entry procedure could be devised which avoided waiting lists or extensive prying into household living arrangements then municipalisation may not disadvantage young transients.

Financial implications.   In the above case the benefits of municipalisation would be seen by some parties to stem from the removal of private landlords and an extension of the 'fair rent' system. The costs, on the other hand, both in real and exchequer terms may be massive. There is no reason to believe that local officials could operate and maintain the system more efficiently than landlords and criteria for expanding or contracting the sector, over the long term, would have to be developed. Public expenditure would rise, not only to purchase the properties involved but also in the longer period fair rents may not cover operating, maintenance and interest costs (assuming the system is operated as in the rest of the public sector). Public ownership via local authorities does not seem, therefore, to be a viable, or indeed desirable, proposition at the present time.

Maintenance and improvement.   It is widely argued that many landlords fail to maintain their properties and this contributes to urban decay, particularly in inner-city areas. Given that there is no reason to believe that landlords are against improvement *per se*, failure to improve probably lies not in the power of landlords which arises from excess demand or market structure monopoly, but in the manner in which the Rent Acts are operated and in the system of landlords' taxation. Improvement would generally require landlords to substantially raise rents which, if the property is not already registered, is liable to trigger tenants into rent registration and therefore have the tenancy made subject to the rent and security of tenure provisions of the Rent Acts.

Municipalisation would certainly remove the problem of individual and collective uncertainty regarding and surrounding improvements and also overcome the problem of uncertain rates of return. However, it seems pertinent to question, particularly with so many poorly maintained areas and poor quality or vacant properties already in the public sector in the UK, whether or not the supply of improved properties would rise in these inner areas. There may be better strategies for funding improvement in older areas.

The issue of 'municipalisation' is, therefore, not really sensibly discussed in general terms but before proposals can be evaluated it is crucial to know the allocation, entry and pricing strategies which the local authorities would utilise in relation to newly purchased stock of previously private lets.

Expanding housing associations

Since 1974, a large proportion of rental houses have been sold to Housing Associations. There is little doubt that the products of housing association activity, particularly in the major areas of renovation, have made an impressive, if uneven, impact on the physical and community structure of the inner-city areas. At the present time houses owned by associations are renovated at substantial exchequer cost and relet on fair rent criteria. The 'voluntary' housing movement has been mooted by many as a method of replacement of private lets. But how would this shift be financed with present resource constraints? Three sources of additional finance raise possibilities for expansion.

(a) Association rents are currently set at levels of fair rents. It may be possible, if the distributional consequences were acceptable, to raise such rents. In 1980, many housing association tenants were paying less for a renovated family house than students paid for a single, sparsely furnished bedsit. Self-generation of income could lead to a marked expansion of activities, and the pricing policy of associations may merit some closer attention. Such changes are perhaps unlikely, particularly in the short term. Alternatively a proportion of association property could be sold post-rehabilitation and the 1980 Housing Act now, for the first time, gives associations rights to sell.

(b) Central government could expand grants and subsidies to the sector. Again, this is unlikely as at the present time there are real cuts in the budget of the Housing Corporation.

(c) A special fund to attract private capital (from institutional investors and building societies in particular) into the sector should be considered. The 1977 Green Paper suggested such an agency for the private rental sector but, if the general 'improvement' arguments are in favour of associations, it would seem sensible to direct or encourage funds towards the Housing Corporation which could then be channelled into rehabilitation. However, if the fair rent criterion is to continue to operate as at the present time, then institutions are likely to receive a more adequate real rate of return in other investment sectors. (British Rail, for instance, would prefer pictures of antique houses to antique houses.) It would appear reasonable to draw the conclusion that in the short to medium term (say before 1985 at the earliest): It seems very unlikely that housing associations can expand their activities sufficiently to compensate for a further decline in other forms of private rental' (Murie *et al.* 1976; 263).

Even if the financial preconditions for expansion were satisfied then some question marks remain over the ability of associations to cater for the special needs of young transients. Until recently it would appear that associations have operated by purchasing low value owner-occupied flats and, more commonly, long-term unfurnished lets. In such areas, households are likely to comprise elderly persons with low incomes, often with only one or two persons or very new households. However, if associations begin to have a substantial impact on areas with a significant proportion of traditionally short-term tenancies then the result could be a reduction in the turnover rate. For example, tenants whose initial aspirations were directed toward obtaining a local authority tenancy may decide to remain in their present dwelling as tenants of the association. But rather crudely, it could be argued that the voluntary housing movement has supported and developed through a desire to maintain and improve the physical stock and that while it may be escaping the 'prisoners' dilemma' it is not examining the present and future characteristics of the 'prisoners' themselves.

Another issue which requires consideration revolves around the creation of some form of letting scheme by housing associations which would reduce problems of transient entry. Whilst it can be argued that replacing price rationing (which would exist in an uncontrolled private rental sector) with time related queuing might be advantageous in creating a more orderly allocative system and reducing search costs, the allocation criteria for housing associations are, as in the case of local authority housing, based on the concept of need. Thus, the question arises as to what constitutes 'need' and what happens to those falling outside the prescribed 'needs' group? Moreover, in local area based associations, the housing requirements of minority groups may not receive adequate attention. Housing associations, with their focus on inner areas, their voluntary component, their attention to local detail and requirements, and, importantly, with a favourable perception of their activities, may in the long term house transient groups and reduce the need for a private furnished sector.

But in the meantime policies to reorganise the furnished rental sector rather than replace it are the realistic alternative for policy.

Minor modifications to the existing system

Under the 1974 Act, it was possible for landlords to let their furnished rental housing via recognised local or educational institutions and hence be exempted from the powers of the Act. But should such a system be expanded? (Centre for Environmental Studies 1978). Such schemes, where they are operated, could protect, and even enhance the housing possibilities of particular groups of transients. But the formation of such schemes depends on institutional responses and they add to the difficulties of transients, particularly those outside the higher education sector. The 1980 Housing Bill, as noted above, contains provisions to exempt shorthold tenancies from security of tenure provisions on an individual-contractual basis and does not, therefore, affect particular subsets within the transient group. However much this measure may prevent further furnished sales, expansion in the sector is now unlikely as owner occupation and housing associations are progressively displacing private landlords. (Since the 1974 Act, it has been estimated that a further 400,000 rental properties have been sold in the UK.) The shorthold tenancy scheme, to attract back private landlords, may not be sufficient even if it is necessary. To compete with the other tenure sectors effectively a new pricing system for regulated or registered tenancies may be required.

Major modifications of the fair rent system

It is obvious that there is much room for improvement in the current system of rent assessment and it is possible that with an informed staff, explicit procedures and operational rules rent controls need not mean the end of the private rented sector.

The following list of suggestions indicates measures which could improve operation of the private rental market.

1. All private lets should be covered by registration and the Rent Acts.
2. Landlords, or companies, should be issued with a licence to let which would not be transferable. The licence would be withdrawn if landlords were found to violate the service provision, rent or improvement clauses of their individual lets or be found guilty of harassment or illegal practices.
3. When properties were registered or licensed the Rent Assessment Committee would discuss with the landlord the level of services to be provided and improvements to be enacted and these would be allowed for in assessing rents.
4. Rents for individual properties would be assessed by a professional staff of valuers and cost accountants, who would be employed by the rent service and whose salaries and costs would be paid for by a licence fee. The introduction of a detailed consideration of costs would allow marginal rents to rise, but the system may not wish to penalise infra-marginal landlords.
5. Rents would be related to capital values with no scarcity factors to distort inter-sectoral tenure choices or to prevent long-run adjustment.
6. A fair real rate of return on capital would be allowed, possibly indexed to allowed returns on nationalised industries, and with rents linked to a chosen general price index. Or alternatively they could be linked to returns on equities since housing asset values are likely to appreciate.
7. Security of tenure provisions would be related to the type of licence held by landlords. Long-term letting landlords would be allowed a

small premium (say 1%) on rents and rates of return. There could be limits to the number of occasions on which short-term licences could be renewed for a particular landlord and tenant.

8. Capital appreciation on housing assets would be excluded from the assessment of letting returns, as such rises, in part, also reflect the rising replacement cost of landlords' capital. Disinvesting landlords would, of course, be subject to capital gains tax as at the present time.

9. A rental sector inspection service should be introduced to investigate properties to ensure that the terms of licences are being observed. This service could also investigate tenant and landlord grievances.

If these proposals were adopted a rationally planned private sector of furnished rental could be sustained and indeed expanded. A professionally orientated and informed set of assessment councils, supplemented by an effective policing system, could then proceed to operate the rental sector with fairness and precision.

Conclusion

This chapter has stressed the allocative damages of the existing system of rent controls. Critics may raise the point that existing controls redistribute income or wealth from landlord to tenant in a generally desirable fashion and that controls may be defended on such grounds. Notwithstanding these reservations, the distribution of income and wealth is probably more appropriately altered by taxation and subsidy measures which are independent of the housing system. It is possible to hold such a view even if one disapproves of an economic system which allows landlords to accumulate or inherit vast wealth, and experience has shown in the UK that such a distribution will not be substantively or efficiently altered by *ad hoc* distortions of the housing system. Small and pervasive distortions have greatly contorted the body of social and economic policy in the UK as governments struggle to avoid facing major issues such as the distribution of income or the system of housing subsidies. Most commentators agree that the private rental system should not continue in its present form, but few probably expect a radical and positive policy to actually be implemented. Neither the Green Paper of 1977 nor the Review of the Rent Acts, nor the 1980 Housing Act have led to major long-term revisions as such changes really require a fundamental shift in the way in which governments run housing policy in the UK.

9 Public housing in Britain – an economic analysis

Research and public housing

In the previous chapters of this volume there has been a concern to relate policies for housing to economic models and to existing empirical research. The material presented has been used to question the economic assumptions underlying existing policies. But a similar approach to public housing in Britain is difficult to sustain as there has been almost no applied economic analysis of the operation and effects of public housing systems. In general, analysis of public housing systems in Britain has been undertaken by researchers with a social, administrative or planning concern in mind. This mode of research, which has been historically fruitful, has concentrated on examining the development and characteristics of local authority housing stock, the assessment of housing 'need' and the administrative procedures for matching households and houses (Niner 1975; Murie, Niner and Watson 1976). Such concerns are still critical issues for local authorities but it is now increasingly recognised that economic analysis can contribute strongly to both the strategic design and management of public housing systems.

In the past economists have focused comment, largely based on deductive rather than empirical analysis, on the system of housing finance and on the pricing systems of local authorities. Unsurprisingly, in the present context of governmental anxiety over the level and quality of public housing expenditure, these economic issues are still important. But there are now new supplementary concerns. The cumulative effects of selective entry to and movement within public housing, especially in large cities, have impressed upon local authorities that housing choice processes, in which economic considerations are critical, still impact on public housing. Although price signals are not the principal rationing device within the public sector there are other rationing devices, such as searching and queuing which households may choose to pursue. The problem of individual choice still pertains within public housing. Further, and partly as a result of the development of Housing Plans and Housing Investment Programmes (HIPs), local authorities are now beginning to have to consider local interactions between public and private housing systems. However, and with few exceptions, the processes of choice and mobility within public housing, public-private interactions and the distributional incidence of public housing subsidy have not been investigated in detail. This chapter is therefore exploratory and the information presented is, by force of circumstances, only partial in coverage.

At the same time it is hoped that the chapter is not merely a repetition of previous syntheses of the economics of public housing in Britain. The chapter tries to accomplish four major objectives:

1. To describe the development of public housing in Britain and the justifications for its existence along with the evolving system of public housing finance.
2. To examine pricing, allocation and investment criteria within local authorities.
3. To assess the present reality of public housing provision in Britain.
4. To outline major policy developments likely to occur within the next decade.

Public housing in Britain

The most cursory examination of tenure structure or net new sectoral housing investment reveals the considerable significance of public housing in Britain since the 1950s (see Tables 4.1 and 7.1). Expenditure commitments for policy (Table 6.2) also establish the significance of public housing. Not only is the proportion of public housing in Britain relatively high when international averages are compared, but the proportional significance of the sector varies over regions and cities. For instance, the older industrial, depressed regions of the North and Scotland exceed 40 per cent of housing in public ownership. Further, within these regions large and small cities alike may approach a proportion of 60 per cent of housing in the public sector. And, within large cities such as Glasgow, where 58 per cent of households live in public housing, public sector estates may extend spatially to encompass populations of 40–50,000 people. Thus, within several metropolitan areas in Britain public housing is the dominant form of tenure, particularly in core urban areas, and thus an analysis of housing and urban policy in Britain has public housing as a major concern (Maclennan 1980).

In the British context there are several forms of public production and ownership of housing. But ownership of housing by government departments, say for health or military service purposes, is not considered hère nor, and these are more important omissions, are the activities of the Northern Ireland Housing Executive and the Scottish Special Housing Association examined here. Rather, the central concern of this chapter is public housing provided by local government authorities. That is, municipal or council housing.

In the British context the principal form of public housing is council housing. This housing, unlike North American public housing, embraces a variety of styles, qualities and locations. It is let at non-market rents, allocation is carried out by a series of non-price administrative procedures and it is constructed by public and private contractors and financed by long-term borrowing (usually sixty years). Repayment of interest and principal and maintenance and management expenditures are financed by rental payments from tenant to local authority, by rate fund contributions from local taxpayers and by a series of more or less housing specific grants from central to local governments. Although different at the mean from the owner-occupied and private rental sectors, age, income and social class distribution strongly overlap those of other tenure sectors.

To facilitate an economic understanding of the present public housing system in Britain it is convenient to subdivide the analysis into two principle sections. First, we consider the development of central government policies for public housing and the financing mechanisms chosen to transfer resources from the central exchequer to local housing expenditures. Second, we examine the utilisation of these transferred resources, local resources and local government property rights to produce public housing.

The origins of public housing

As in the case of private rental housing policy (Ch. 8), central government policy for public housing in Britain largely emerged as the result of social, economic and political pressures pertaining at the end of the First World War. Prior to 1914, and indeed as early as the 1860s, local governments had provided public housing in a few major industrial cities (Merrett 1979). For instance, in Glasgow and Liverpool, the rapid growth of population in a low mobility intra-urban economy had generated exceptionally high residential densities and overcrowding of low income households in privately rented housing. The resultant public provision has been justified on a variety of grounds. These have included altruism on the part of wealthier taxpayers, a desire to defuse situations of potential civil disorder or a concern to reduce the negative visual and health externalities which originated in such areas and then spread throughout the city area. From the available evidence it is not, in this case, probably possible to discriminate between Marxian or

Paretian liberal explanations of such intervention.

A more widespread and systematic concern for the housing conditions of low income households, that is 'the working classes', grew in the early decades of the twentieth century. In Scotland, the Royal Commission on Housing of 1917 (Royal Commission 1917) reported that they believed that more than one third of the population was unable to afford to rent what the Commission considered to be a minimum standard of housing. In addition the Commission expressed the belief that, at that time, public assistance to such households should be delivered through below market rents in publicly provided houses. They believed that public provision was essential because of the collapsed state of the private building sector and, again reflecting the conditions of the time, they preferred price distortions to income supports because they maintained that an adequate administrative system did not exist centrally to redistribute income even if there was a political volition to do so. A similar scenario, (see Merrett 1979), developed in the rest of Britain during the First World War. The experience of wartime led to increased rents in undermaintained properties and increased concentrations of poorly housed urban populations. The campaign of 'Homes for Heroes' raised expectations regarding short-term and extensive government action to alleviate housing difficulties and, at least in part, the threat of civil disorder, and encouraged government to make a commitment to public housing along the lines suggested by the Scottish Commission. Before proceeding to a brief description of public housing finance legislation it is important to recall the economic aspects of central government's decision to subsidise public housing and the problems associated with the transfer of exchequer resources from central to local governments.

State subsidies to and ownership of housing

In the economic analysis of public housing (Robinson 1979; Stafford 1978; Lansley 1979) the issue of public housing subsidy is conceptualised as being a direct payment or price subsidy from central or local government to the individual. The theoretical exposition may be presented as follows. The argument for subsidising housing by state provision of below market rent housing may be justified, or indeed attacked, in a series of steps. First, the existence of visual, health or income distribution externalities may, as indicated in Fig. 6.2 and on p 158, mean that society's demand curve for housing lies above the market demand curve. Second, having targeted some minimum desired level of housing consumption per capita, increased consumption of housing may be achieved by raising incomes (via income redistribution) and thus indirectly raising housing consumption. Alternatively redistribution and housing consumption goals are pursued by distorting

241

housing service prices (Fig. 6.3). Price distortions to achieve acceptable housing consumption can be defended where redistribution is sanctioned specifically to remove housing externalities or where the income elasticity of demand for housing on the part of those currently consuming substandard housing is thought to be low.

But further arguments are required to justify state ownership of housing for rent distortions, although requiring government intervention, do not make the case either for public production or ownership of housing. Government, as it does in the owner-occupied sector, could subsidise housing choices made in a private rental market. Public ownership of housing could be justified, at least in principle by the introduction of two further considerations into the above analysis. These arguments concern the costs of administering the subsidy system and the costs of expanding the stock of minimum quality housing.

These cost considerations, which imply that the supply curve for minimum quality housing has a different position and elasticity for public and private sectors, have been used as major justifications for expansionary phases in public housing in Britain. For instance, both after the First and the Second World War, governments in the UK did not believe that the private construction sector had the organisational capacity, financial stability or technology to provide the desired level of housing completions to remove housing shortages rapidly. Similarly, in relation to slum clearance and urban redevelopment the state has generally decided that the acquisition of land and property, clearance programmes and rehousing arrangements could not be planned and executed by the private construction industry. Rapid and stable expansion of the supply of adequate housing has historically been perceived (by Conservative and Labour governments alike) to require state involvement in the production process.

Continued public ownership following housing production may have been justified in relation to the relatively high administrative costs of directly providing subsidy prior to the Second World War. In the postwar period continued public ownership, which is now under severe scrutiny, was generally defended on the grounds of the need to maintain and manage local authority housing when housing shortages were still critical and where special housing 'needs' were becoming more important. The empirical evidence to justify these remarks regarding the relative position of the supply curves for publicly and privately produced housing does not, of course, exist in the UK. But it is wrong to perceive public housing development as a purely ideological approach to housing provision. Indeed it is probably correct to argue that in its origins and major phases of development, public housing was more of a pragmatic approach to severe housing shortages in relation to governmental conceptions of 'need'. As such, the expansion of public housing has been an important instrument of both Labour and Conservative housing policies.

The issues of the effectiveness of the subsidy policy and the continued ownership of public housing are discussed in subsequent sections. Here it is intended to indicate that the standard conceptualisation of public housing subsidy existing as a simple rent distortion to consumers is misleadingly oversimplified, because central government does not directly transfer subsidy to consumers in public housing in the UK. Rather, central government makes a series of grants to local authorities to assist in subsidising housing revenue accounts and it is of importance to understand the amount and form of such transfers from central to local governments.

The public housing finance system

The institutional framework

It has earlier been stressed that local governments are the main agents responsible for public housing in Britain. But in providing public housing local authorities are pursuing central as well as local government housing objectives. Thus central government, particularly where the goals of different levels of government do not coincide, is concerned to monitor and control the quality, level and cost of local authority housing output. In order to effectuate such control and to pursue its own housing objectives central government has used a variety of devices.

The overall design of the housing subsidy system for the publicly owned sector reflects a variety of central government judgements. For instance, housing provision is generally delegated to urban or district authorities rather than broader regions. Central government has also determined the broad accounting framework for public housing. The designated housing authorities are required to keep separate housing accounts called Housing Revenue Accounts. The Housing Revenue Account for England and Wales is indicated in Table 9.1 for the period 1975–79. The accounts are maintained on a historic cost basis as opposed to utilising economic or replacement cost criteria and central government decides what are allowable expenditures or incomes within the housing account. Central government has, except between 1972 and 1974 and since 1981, required authorities not to make a profit or surplus on the Housing Revenue Account. This broad operational framework does influence local authority behaviour and it may induce a variety of undesirable effects which are discussed in the subsequent section. More critical, at least in the short term, are central government decisions regarding the level of housing subsidy, the mix of housing output and the way in which housing expenditures are to be financed.

Table 9.1 Local authority Housing Revenue Account: 1974/5 to 1978/9 Year ended 31 March: England and Wales

	£ m.					Percentage of all expenditure/income				
	1974/5	1975/6	1976/7	1977/8	1978/9	1974/5	1975/6	1976/7	1977/8	1978/9
Expenditure										
Supervision and management	187	254	302	349	404	12	13	13	13	13
Repairs	265	340	395	479	590	16	17	17	18	19
Debt charges	1,105	1,315	1,577	1,663	1,942	68	66	66	63	64
Revenue contribution to capital outlay	14	52	22	33	39	1	3	1	1	1
Other expenditure	50	52	60*	65*	66	3	3	2	2	2
Residual – mainly change in end year balance	−1	11	24	67	11	–	1	1	3	–
All expenditure	**1,620**	**1,986**	**2,380**	**2,657**	**3,052**	**100**	**100**	**100**	**100**	**100**
Income										
Rents:										
Dwellings excluding amenities (rebated)	714	839	966	1,129	1,216	44	42	41	42	40
Amenities	12	17	15	23	29	3	3	2	3	2
Other properties	36	36	39	46	45					
Exchequer subsidy	486	798†	1,047†	1,141†	1,320†	30	40†	44†	43†	43
Rate fund contribution	329‡	232	227	242	308	20	12	9	9	10
Other income	43	64	86	94	134	3	3	4	4	4
All income	**1,620**	**1,986**	**2,380**	**2,657**	**3,052**	**100**	**100**	**100**	**100**	**100**

* In order to maintain comparability with previous years capital expenditure (including capital salaries and overheads charged to revenue) is included in 'other expenditure'.

† Includes £166 m. rent rebate subsidy in 1975/6, £212 m. in 1976/7, £248 m. in 1977/8 and £266 m. in 1978/9 (representing 8%, 9%, 9% and 8% of total income respectively). This subsidy was shown as part of the rate fund contribution in 1974/5. Section 3 of the Housing Rents and Subsidies Act 1975 required that from 1975/6 onwards the subsidy should be credited directly to the Housing Revenue Account.

‡ Includes £153 m. in 1974/5 (representing 9% of total income) met by rent rebate subsidy.

Source: *Housing and construction statistics* 1979.

Central government concerns

In selecting the level of housing finance and the forms of subsidy or grant to local authorities, central government has a broad range of considerations in mind. First, central government, which is usually assumed to have principal sovereignty in issues related to income distribution, will have some view on what is socially just and on the equity aspects of existing housing 'needs' and outcomes. But within central government, unlike local authorities where housing finance is segmented deliberately away from other expenditure programmes, housing priorities have to be set against other public expenditure programmes and overall economic objectives and performance. Such considerations may influence capital expenditure or other operational rules. For instance, in the 1960s the 'stop-go' performance of the economy was directly reflected in a policy cycle for new housing starts in the public sector, (Table 4.1). More recently, in the 1970s a series of *ad hoc* measures by government were used to restrain the extent to which public sector rent rises financed rising costs as it was feared that rent rises would compromise or de-stabilise voluntary wage restraint or threaten existing incomes policies. (See Postscript.)

Thus, in selecting the level of public housing support central government has to consider general taxpayer/citizen interests. Further, and again particularly in the 1970s, government has taken account of implications of housing support levels not only for public housing tenants but also for ratepayers who (at least in some areas) still make a substantial if declining contribution to local housing finance (Table 9.2). In addition, central government also gives consideration to inter-urban or inter-regional differences in housing 'needs', housing costs and local taxable resources although much less formally than in the case of the Rate Support Grant to support general local government finance. Although the introduction of Housing Plans in Scotland (since 1978) and Housing Investment Programmes in England and Wales (in 1979) have provided the basis to make a more formal assessment of local needs, resources and costs, inter-area equalisation within housing subsidy schemes has been historically accomplished on an *ad hoc* basis. Available evidence on area differences in housing need, housing costs and local financial resources suggests that such variations are important (Smith 1978) but are largely ignored in HS6 calculation.

As a result of this geographically variable relationship between required housing investment and local fiscal or domestic resources there is a strong case for the centralised control of finance for public housing aside from the additionally convincing macro-control concerns. Areas of poor housing, frequently in older core cities, appear to have a relatively low elasticity in their local tax bases and are dependent primarily on property tax revenues. The local tax burden to finance adequate housing provision in such areas would probably be sufficiently high, because of higher investment requirements and lower tax base values, to induce fiscal mobility.

Local government advantages

Whilst the financing of public housing subsidy has largely, but not exclusively, remained with central government the allocation of grants and the management of existing public stock has remained with local authorities. Thus, since it has a view on housing requirements and housing needs which does not necessarily coincide with local authority preferences, central government has to select the form as well as the level of grant-in-aid to local authorities. In addition central government may introduce other checks on the level, mix and efficiency of local authority output and management.

The above paragraphs have examined the reasons why central government should exercise sovereignty over public housing. Indirectly this raises the question, why are local authorities involved at all? This question can be answered positively, and directly, with reference to local/spatial public choice theory (Tiebout 1956). Central government may wish to decentralise and devolve control over some aspects of public housing for the following reasons:

1. The costs of administering and planning local authority housing are thought to be lower than for central government. This view was adopted in the 1920s and has remained relatively unchallenged since.
2. Whilst central government objectives are broadly defined, local authorities have more insight and information in transforming them into housing stock. That is, local managers are more X-efficient.
3. Government subsidy is not sufficient, in any time period, to remove shortages of acceptable, subsidised accommodation. Local governments are more allocatively efficient, by being locally democratically responsive in assessing priorities for policy and in selecting strategies for using scarce resources.
4. At least part of housing grant may be viewed as 'block-grant' to allow local authorities to pursue their own housing strategies.
5. Housing provision is crucially related, both in its planning and development, to other functions undertaken by local authorities in areas of environmental, social and land-use planning. Housing planning has to be integrated with these other functions. According to some authors (Hepworth, Grey, Odling-Smee 1979) there is also a case for integrating financing as well as planning.
6. The contribution of local tax revenues to housing revenue accounts, which was previously more significant than now, required at least joint local/central action on public housing.

These advantages of devolving public housing to local governments have to be offset, although to a small degree, against difficulties of co-ordinating central versus local interests. For instance, central government, as illustrated in the Cullingworth Report (1969) has tended to accord higher housing 'needs' priorities to mobile households, single persons and minority groups than emerge within local democracies. This issue is pursued further below.

Alternative forms of grant-in-aid

All these considerations enter into the selection of a structure for the housing finance system. Having devolved considerable powers to local authorities, central government then selects the form of grant and methods of control. At one extreme local authorities would undoubtedly prefer no controls, freedom to set local authority rents and rate contributions, and have an 'open-ended' block-grant system. If central control concerns and preferences were dominant, subsidy would be close-ended, output specific and the rate of subsidy subjected to short-term review. Grants would be increasingly discretionary and a higher level of inter-area resource equalisation would be pursued. The British system of grant-in-aid to local authorities for public housing has been a mixture of central and local preferences regarding the form of subsidy and this mixture has changed over time. The degree of control has fluctuated between central and local governments but, despite a popular view to the contrary, the last decade has seen a progressive shift of power and control over public housing back towards central government. At this juncture it is pertinent to illustrate the conceptual arguments presented above with a brief review of public housing grants in Britain since 1919.

The development of policy

The details of major changes in the system of grant-in-aid to local authorities for public housing are set out below. Events until 1970 can be briefly described in relation to two periods, 1919–39 and 1945–70.

1919–39
Central government policy for public housing in Britain was first enshrined in the Addison Act of 1919 and, despite considerable social and economic development since that period, many of the present-day operational rules for public housing in Britain remain fundamentally rooted in earlier legislation. Of course, the efficiency of such procedures in present circumstances is now questionable. The Addison Act was unusual in two respects. First, subsidy levels, for the provision of 'working-class' housing were open-ended. Subsidy was a deficit grant to finance provision not covered by rental payments. Second, the Act,

and here its only parallel is the 1972 Housing Finance Act, required lcoal authorities to set rents at levels comparable to those of quality private rented housing. As a result, inter-sectoral rent levels were not distorted and the average rent of public housing was almost double private rental levels throughout the 1920s (because of the higher quality of public housing). Subsidy was required as local authorities were required not to allow rent levels to exceed, on average, 30 per cent of family incomes. The open-ended nature of the potential claim on government resources was not a serious drain on exchequer resources as many local authorities were slow to initiate public housing programmes and, setting a pattern for future events, the Act was soon superseded.

The Chamberlin Act (1922) and the Wheatley Act (1923), then introduced close-ended subsidies, the latter more generous than the former, which guaranteed a fixed sum per house built over a stated period – in the Wheatley case £9 per year for 40 years. Since each new Act generally applied only to new investment in public housing and allowed previous long-term commitments to continue the pattern of subsidies received by local authorities had become complex even in the first decade of public housing. In the early 1930s, with increasing economic difficulties, government first reduced, then curtailed general subsidies on new public housing investment and tied housing aid to rehousing associated with slum clearance and later, in 1935, added a new concern for alleviating overcrowding.

As a result of these two decades of intervention, more than 25 per cent of new houses built in Britain in the interwar period were constructed for or by local authorities. Thus, in 1939, with more than one million houses already in public housing, 10 per cent of the national housing stock was provided by local governments.

1945–70

The set of subsidies and the overall design of the subsidy system which evolved in the 1930s was inherited by postwar governments, who at least into the 1960s, were more concerned with raising levels of housing output then reforming the subsidy system. This commitment to the expansion of public housing in the period to 1956 was pursued by both Labour and Conservative parties and reflected conditions in the postwar economy.

The conditions prevailing then (Merrett 1979) were dominated by a situation of acute housing shortage and a run-down private construction sector. In wartime one million dwellings had been destroyed and population had grown by more than a million. Even if rent controls (Ch. 8), had not stifled private adjustment to this shortage, the building industry in 1946 was only one third of its prewar size and, until 1953, there was an acute shortage of building materials. In the 1946 Act, Bevan introduced a provision to allow four public housing starts for each private start. The inter-party agreement on this strategy was reflected by the subsequent Macmillan Act (1952) which had a specific target of providing 300,000 public houses each year. Although subsidies on previously constructed dwellings remained as before, postwar subsidies had a different form and were relatively higher. For instance, under the 1952 Act regime, the interest and construction costs for a project were estimated and the contribution to financing projects from rate fund and central government contributions were set so that average rents would not exceed more than 10 per cent of the average wage. This rent/wage relationship was estimated nationally and not for each dwelling.

The postwar consensus on the development of public housing was terminated with the 1956 Housing Act. In this Conservative Act, the role of local authorities as residual rather than central providers of housing was stressed and 'general needs' subsidies were severely reduced and slum clearance given priority. At least some commentators (Duclaud-Williams 1979) consider that these subsidy reductions, combined with the abortive attempt to stimulate private rental housing, largely contributed to observed increasing housing shortages and 'homelessness' which emerged in the early 1960s. Partly as a response to these difficulties the 1961 Act, attributable to Sir Keith Joseph, was introduced. To deal with the outcomes of the unplanned and intendedly rapid privatisation of the housing sector embedded in the 1956 Act, the 1961 Act re-introduced 'general needs' subsidies. From an economic standpoint the 1961 Act was an interesting and rational development of the housing subsidy system which, unlike previous legislation, attempted to target exchequer resources to the areas of greatest 'need', and related them to local authority 'ability-to-pay'. For each local authority, the costs of public housing provision were set against notional housing income. This income was defined, somewhat crudely, as being twice the value of the rateable value of local authority housing. If this notional income exceeded costs of provision no subsidy was provided, but if costs exceeded income then the rate of subsidy rose with the size of deficit (Housing Policy, Technical Volume 3, 1977). The subsidies, a fixed nominal sum per dwelling, were to be payable over sixty years.

The Labour government returned in 1964 did not, until the 1967 Act, revise the provisions of the 1961 Act. But by 1967 the rate of inflation, then low by present standards, had undermined the 1961 system and reduced the real value of public housing subsidies by 20 per cent. The subsidies were fixed in nominal terms, wage and cost inflation increased costs and revaluation of local authority housing raised notional income. The major innovation of the 1967 Act was to attempt to 'inflation-proof' subsidies on new public housing investment. This was to be accomplished by relating subsidy to interest costs. That is, subsidy for a new dwelling — and of course the panoply of existing subsidies on existing investment continued — was the difference between interest paid and a nominal interest rate of 4 per cent. At the same time, with this potentially expensive subsidy local authorities became subject to an increasing series of controls on the cost and form of output. Local authorities throughout the postwar period were always required to seek central government approval to borrow for capital projects and in this way governments controlled total local authority housing expenditure. In the late 1960s this macroeconomic control was reinforced by central government controls over public housing costs and output mix. The cost yardstick was introduced in 1967 to monitor local developments and the Parker Morris standards were introduced to ensure that local authorities provided a minimum standard of housing which met central government preferences (in England and Wales).

Thus in the period 1945–70, although central government consensus on the role of local public housing broke down, in the period 1956–70 there was a continued growth in public housing with macroeconomic fluctuations rather than ideological shifts being responsible for variations in housing output. Similarly the system of housing subsidy evolved as the result of economic events rather than political differences. Insofar as party ideologies differed they were reflected more clearly in actions towards the private rental market rather than the public sector. But such conclusions would not apply to the most recent and complex decade of public housing finance.

Post–1970

Since 1970 there have been three major changes in the system of financing public housing. These changes have all reflected attempts to adapt the financing system to very rapid rates of inflation and, in somewhat less systematic fashion, have mirrored central government attempts to dampen local rents and rate rises which have threatened to stimulate inflationary wage bargaining. But the two major changes of 1972 and 1975, and the differences in interpretation of the 1977 financing system proposed in the Green Paper have reflected major ideological differences between Conservative and Labour Governments.

The Housing Finance Act of 1972 represents the only major attempt to reform the financing and pricing of public housing in Britain in the postwar period. The theoretical basis for policy at that time represented a shift towards a preference for market allocation systems (or at least price signalling) with subsidies primarily related to income levels rather than rent distortions. Central government then proposed that the rents of council houses should be set on an individual basis (akin to the Addison Act) and that the 'reasonable' rents charged should reflect comparable values, 'fair rents', in the private sector. Although such rents may generally have implied rent rises for most tenants, who were paying rents largely determined by historic cost structures, in some areas reductions could have occurred. The rent setting procedures chosen (Ch. 8), were intended to reduce public/private sector rent distortions. Individuals were now to be subsidised by a nationally financed system of rent rebates (allowances) which rationalised previously locally funded schemes of a similar nature.

As a result of charging 'reasonable' rather than historic cost-related rents, and with the abandonment of the no profit rule in the housing revenue accounting procedure, many local authorities were expected to generate surpluses from rental income which were to be reallocated to central government to finance the rent rebate scheme. Although the rent rebate scheme has survived subsequent government changes, (Table 6.2), the Housing Finance Act remains a remarkably clear example of how apparently rationally based (from the Paretian standpoint) policies cannot survive political pressures. Three such pressures were important. First, the change in the structure of subsidies from price distortions to income supports implied a complex pattern of gainers and losers within public housing. Thus many tenants, perhaps because the new income rebate scheme was not sufficiently well financed or structured, regarded any policy which raised their rents as being detrimental. Second, local authorities were hostile to the Act as it effectively removed their sovereignty over rent fixing and surplus generating authorities resisted the planned transfer of rental surpluses to central government. Similarly, deficit generating areas were suspicious that the proposed system would reduce the 'equalising' advantages of past subsidy systems. Finally, the deteriorating national economic performance, in conjunction with high rates of price inflation and cost-of-living related wage bargaining resulted in a suspension or phasing of planned public sector rent increases. The intentions for long-run 'allocative' efficiency in the public rental sector were quickly sacrificed for short-term macroeconomic concerns.

From the economic standpoint the central principles of the 1972 Act were, however, at least allocatively efficient. But it may be that too much reform was attempted too quickly. In addition, whilst the proposed system was likely to be allocatively more efficient between and within rental sectors, there were some drawbacks. Not only was the pricing system selected inadequate but the 'distributional' shifts to areas or individuals did not generate more 'gainers' than 'losers'. It is interesting to note that on returning to office in 1979 the Conservative government have not explicitly reshaped the basis of the system along the lines of the 1972 Act. Since 1980 reductions in HSG with local authority rent raising and restructuring may have achieved a similar effect.

The Labour government, returned in 1974, were directly committed

251

to repealing the 1972 Act and they introduced the 1975 Housing Subsidies Act. Although this measure was intendedly temporary it was still operational in 1980 in England and Wales although it was reformed in Scotland in 1979. The 1975 Act was designed to restore rent-setting powers to local authorities and to restore the 'no profit' rule for the Housing Revenue Account. In addition, since it proposed a mix of predetermined and deficit subsidies, it was hoped that the Act would stimulate public sector house building. The predetermined, or 'producer', subsidies were intended to stimulate investment, whereas the deficit subsidies were aimed at reducing the consequences of unanticipated short-term inflation and to allay the effects of loan charges on debt which were then rising as interest rates adjusted upwards with the inflation rate (Webster 1978; Harrison and Smith 1978).

The predetermined subsidies contained four main elements. First, a basic grant of 33 per cent of interest costs on existing debt was introduced to ensure, at the local authority level, apparently equal 'subsidy' rates to public housing and owner-occupation. Supplementary financing was available to alleviate the costs of short-term rises in interest rates. The other elements were a general subsidy to new investment, covering 66 per cent of the interest costs on new capital projects, and special high cost subsidies. The deficit subsidy was estimated by comparing, in broadly similar fashion to the 1961 Act, the notional rental income of an authority with the actual income received. Central government retained the right to vary, on a year by year basis (or even across different local authorities) what was allowable income and expenditure for deficit purposes and to vary deficit subsidy rates. Thus the 1975 system reflected a mix of predetermined subsidies, which are thought to encourage local economy of resource use and to ease the housing planning process by guaranteeing subsidy rates, and deficit grants which, on the other hand, allow central government to reduce rates of rent and local property tax contributions to Housing Revenue Accounts. As a result, the 1975 Act largely committed central government to finance the incremental costs of public housing. Thus, in a period of rising real interest rates and rising real building costs, central government commitments to public housing expenditure rose markedly despite the existence of cash limit controls on programmes (Table 9.2). Thus the 1975 Act, as interpreted by its sponsoring government, moved central government commitment to public housing in the direction opposite to that intended in the 1972 Act.

The growing central government commitment to funding the public housing programme and the problems of rapid inflation generated a new proposed subsidy system in the 1977 Green Paper (Webster 1978; Harrison and Smith 1978). The 1977 proposals suggested that government should move to a deficit subsidy system which would increase central government's short-term discretionary control over the level and pattern of public housing grants. The suggestions contained in the Green Paper are clear lineal descendants of the 1975 deficit components. The no profit rule was retained and this suggestion was really quite inappropriate in the present economic context. Inflation may generate both unexpected profits and losses and a planning rule which *a priori* precludes surpluses arising in a given period biases decision taking towards the generation of deficits. The basic subsidy floor of 33 per cent, was retained and the remainder of subsidy was to be deficit grant. Deficit grant, as under the 1975 Act, was to be related (at a rate to be annually decided by central government) to the difference between notional income and real expenditure. The details of the assessment of notional income are reported elsewhere (Webster 1978) but two important features of the calculation of allowable expenditure and income are noted here. First, allowable expenditures were to be assessed in relation to Housing Investment Programmes which were to be prepared in detail by local authorities and submitted to central government for funding and approval. HIPs and Housing Plans in Scotland, where the above system has been operational since 1978/79, requires considerable informational and planning inputs from local authorities and, at the same time, increases central government scrutiny of and discretion over local authority housing expenditures. Further, in assessing deficit grant, the Housing Policy suggested that local authority rental contributions should increase at a rate equivalent to the average rate of money wage increases. Interestingly, where the HPR system was operationalised, in Scotland public sector rents rose by 29 per cent in 1978–9.

The deficit financing system proposed in the Housing Policy Review, whilst it may have strengthened central government control over local public housing in a period when macroeconomic concerns have become pressing, would have done little to improve the distributional or allocative efficiency of the system of public housing grants. Not only would the system have made public housing policy more susceptible to short-run changes in central government policy but it would not have alleviated, by retaining the no profit rule, the problems of financing planning in periods of inflation. Equitable treatment between local authorities would have been at the discretion of central government and financial flows and assessments of costs and revenues were still to be largely related to historic costs and financing. Further, the system of grant-in-aid, despite the scrutiny implicit in HIPs would not ensure either the efficient expenditure of grants within local authorities nor the generation of distributionally fair solutions. These issues of pricing within local areas are discussed in the next section. Before considering them it is pertinent to consider the Housing Support Grant proposals contained in the 1980 Housing Act.

In most regards the housing subsidy system proposed in the 1980 Act follows the deficit financing principles suggested in the Housing Policy Review. But it is impossible, at this stage, to predict the long-term impact on the form and level of central government support for public housing. For the Act represents a further strengthening of central government discretion over public housing finance. Continuing the existing conceptual and accounting framework it is proposed that the level of housing grant will be determined by the use of the accounting identity

$$HS = BA + HCD - LCD$$ (as long as the term $(BA + HCD - LCD)$ exceeds zero).

In 1981/2 the Base Amount, BA, is to be set equivalent to the basic subsidy under the 1975 Act. That is, at 33 per cent of loan charges. The housing cost differential, HCD, is the difference between current reckonable expenditure and reckonable expenditure in the previous year. Similarly, the local contribution differential, is the difference between current reckonable rental income and reckonable income in the previous year. The Act leaves the definition of reckonable income and expenditure to the Secretary of State who is empowered to vary allowed income and expenditure, for subsidy purposes, across different areas or time periods. In addition, the Act states that the Secretary of State will determine reckonable expenditures and incomes after consultation with local authorities and subject to the approval of the Treasury.

Given present economic circumstances and the overall tone of government policy in the foreseeable future, two forms of conflict are likely to politicise and destabilise the level of housing grant. First, unlike the Housing Policy Review proposal, the present Bill makes no commitment to raise rental income in line with money incomes. Rather, rents will be raised according to 'expected movements in incomes, costs and prices'. It is unlikely, however, that rents will rise less than money wage rates. As a result conflict between rent payers and government is likely. Second, reckonable income and expenditure can be varied across areas at the discretion of central government. Thus conflicts between areas, as occurs in determining the formulas to generate Rate Support Grant, may well emerge over the allocation of Housing Support Grant. Thus the Bill increases financial and allocative control over local authorities by central government and, simultaneously, transfers property rights traditionally held by local authorities to individual tenants. For instance, and most importantly, the right to buy local authority houses. There has therefore been a substantial transfer of sovereignty over public housing away from local authorities which has not, at least up to the present, generated the same hostile reaction as surrounded the 1972 Act. Instead dissent has focussed on the real level of cuts in intended support (see Postscript).

The pricing and investment policies of public housing authorities

In choosing to provide public housing through a system of direct local authority provision with non-market rents, British governments have explicitly abandoned the more or less useful price signals which a market system generates. These price signals not only allocate consumers across the existing housing stock but they also generate information which can direct housing investment to particular locations, house types, etc. If the earlier chapters of this volume are accurate in their analysis of the housing market, such signals may be imperfect. In addition the willingness to use such signals for housing planning also indicates an ethical prediliction for consumer sovereignty. Thus in selecting a non-market system for the provision of public housing, governments may choose to pursue non-Paretian welfare functions. But they are then required to develop alternative criteria for pricing existing stock and selecting investment strategies. That is, a set of planning rules and devices requires to be devised.

Investment in public housing

The pricing of local authority housing is considered below and here investment guidelines for public housing are discussed. Throughout the postwar period there has been a strong consensus in government policy, and in the writings of housing policy analysts, that public housing allocation and investment policies should be based on the concept of 'housing need'. Housing need and needs assessment have come to be viewed as the touchstone for planning and managing public housing. But now, and particularly amongst economists, there is growing concern over the adequacy of the 'housing needs' concept and its operational significance.

The concept of housing need
One of the early and major proponents of 'housing needs' outlines the concept as follows

> The 'need' for housing, as with the 'need' for health services, or roads, or recreational facilities, is dependent upon the awareness, recognition and definition of 'problems': these in turn are dependent upon the standards of 'adequacy' adopted and the factors which are accepted as being relevant to them. All these constantly change: as one 'problem' is met, another emerges. A 'need' is a socially accepted aspiration, and the faster that one is met the faster do new aspirations arise (Cullingworth 1979: 31).

This notion of what the concept of 'need' implies is conventionally accepted although, at least in the short term, 'need' may be more correctly construed as a socially preferred strategy rather than as an aspiration. Thus applying the 'needs' principle to public housing requires that policy priorities are ethically ordered in the planning process, the prevalence of 'need' in the local housing system assessed and 'needs' provision is made insofar as resources are available.

The concept of local housing need can be illustrated diagrammatically (Fig. 9.1) (Harrison and Paris 1978). In this instance *CC* is a marginal cost curve for housing provision and *DD, GG* and *LL* are respectively the housing demand curves of individuals, central government and local governments respectively. The horizontal axis refers to the quality level of housing services for a given house. Under a market system of provision individuals will consume S_m units of housing service at a rent R_m. But central government takes the view that, because of environmental or distributional externalities, a minimum consumption standard is required or 'needed' and S_G units of housing service should be provided. The cost of providing this unit S_G is C_G and the rent for the tenant is not specified until the subsidy/rental burden is fixed. The subsequent rent, say R_G, may in fact lie above the free market rent R_m. Similarly the local authority may wish to implement an even higher standard of provision, that is S_L, central government may introduce preferential grants for type S_G or, under the present planning system, only approve projects containing houses of the standard S_G, for

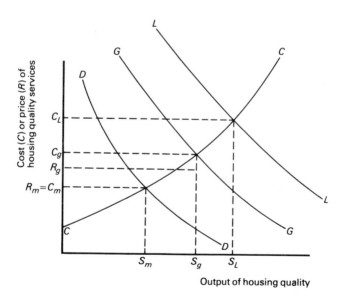

Fig. 9.1 Housing need.

Source: adapted from Harrison and Paris 1975: 29

instance houses of Parker Morris standard. Similarly where S_L exceeds S_G grant-in-aid may be restricted. In addition the housing cost yardstick is an attempt by central government to ensure that the marginal cost curve, CC, reflects efficient resource use in housing production.

Problems in using the 'needs' concept

Although the concept of need appears to be straightforward there are considerable operational and conceptual difficulties. First, many local authorities start with the assumption that housing consumption levels which they view as being inadequate reflect the constraints rather than the preferences of households (Maclennan and MacVean 1978). Or, and more probably, they omit from their definition of standard or 'need' some attributes of housing which individuals view as being important. Thus, housing need is not a summation of individual preferences or aspirations for housing but is an externally and ethically determined aggregate.

The strength of this criticism has to be muted, however, where individual voter or political preferences for housing are transmitted through a representative local democracy. But it is not at all clear that needs priorities reflect the housing policy preferences embedded in a well-defined, democratically selected social welfare function. Although housing policy issues now dominate local politics in many parts of Britain only a small proportion of voters generally vote at such elections. Moreover, over a long period of time, the scale and form of public housing developments have probably been utilised to create well-defined political constituencies. Even where the local political system generates majority based preferences the assessment of needs in this fashion may create biases deemed undesirable by higher levels of government. For instance, local authorities in the United Kingdom have been slow to assign priorities to the provision of housing for mobile non-residents or to consider housing particular groups such as single young persons. When such distortions occur Cullingworth suggests (Cullingworth 1979) that the local housing decision takers, planners and politicians alike, have a social obligation to prioritise such groups and to perform an educational role for the community. And this raises, yet again, the issue of whose perceptions of 'needs' guides allocative decisions – citizens, elected officials or housing technocrats? If the latter have a major role in designing, locating and prioritising public housing development then the local government provision process has become essentially undemocratic. As a result there is a case, depending on ethical persuasion, either to increase central government control over resource or to privatise public housing.

Even where housing priorities are acceptably determined, the assessment of the expenditure levels required to satisfy 'need' is complex and requires detailed information on the existing pattern of provision in an area. But generally such extensive information does not exist and, as a result, need has tended to be assessed in relation to overall shortages of particular physically defined types of dwelling. That is, 'need' is articulated as constituting a requirement of x houses of size y and type z. Relatively scant attention is paid either to household circumstances or to the other attributes of housing which generate satisfaction. For instance, locational and neighbourhood requirements of households have been given scant attention in public housing planning. These omissions are important because, traditionally in the UK, housing planning has been divorced from local employment considerations or broader programmes of environmental improvement strategies.

In the past, particularly in the 1950s, the concern with housing shortages and the basic physical standards of housing may have been consistent with the dominant problems and income levels then prevalent. But, as absolute local shortages have declined and as incomes have increased, tenant concern with locational and neighbourhood attributes of housing have become significant. Local authorities have been slow to respond to such tenant demands and it may be that individual demand curves for these services, at least in the poorer quality parts of the public sector, have grown more rapidly than politically perceived 'needs'. Conceivably, in such areas, public authorities may be reducing rather than increasing housing consumption (broadly defined) from its market level. The inclusion of a broader conception of housing demand or aspiration in an externally determined needs assessment requires considerably more information and conceptual skills than are currently used in needs assessment and there must be some doubt as to whether local housing plans can contain the relevant information (at least given the present system of pricing public housing). When a complex set of housing preferences or demands exist then a price system may contain fewer imperfections and yield more information for planning than a system designed along present lines.

The pragmatic difficulties of accurately assessing housing 'need' are not, however, the sole source of discontent with the concept. A series of conceptual difficulties of the needs concept have been identified in other areas of public provision and they are equally applicable in the public housing context (Williams 1974, 1978). These are:

1. The assessment of housing need tends to set problems in a very specific and narrow context. For instance, in the public housing context, the provision of public housing to meet slum clearance needs tended to be perceived as the solution to the problems of 'slums' whereas a whole series of complementary non-housing investment was also required.

2. The identification of needs tends to direct policy effort towards a limited range of lexicographically ordered or absolute priorities. For instance, instead of tackling a single objective comprehensively a

trade-off between different mixes of policy may be required. But, as Williams notes, 'needs' strategies are generally antithetical to resource or policy trade-offs.

3. As a result of (2), the general 'needs' approach is not suitable for assessing individual investment priorities when more than one objective or conception of 'needs' exists.

4. When resources for policy are not available to finance 'needs' provision there is an inherent tendency to revise needs or aspirations downwards. As Needleman has noted:

> The choice of minimum socially acceptable standards is not completely independent of the incomes and prices prevailing in the country concerned, while the same demographic factors that largely determine housing needs also strongly influence the effective demand for dwelling units. (Needleman 1965: 18).

And, of course the emergent difficulty as locational and environmental 'needs' are assessed below desired tenant consumption levels have been indicated above.

Whilst this section has strongly criticised the notion of need and suggested some of its operational difficulties there are relatively few positive recommendations which emerge for local authorities. In essence they amount to ensuring that local housing policy objectives are well articulated, that they are defined across the variety of housing attributes which tenants attach importance to, that the different objectives of policy are traded-off against each other, that complementary investments are forthcoming from other local services, and that housing plans and programmes are assessed against detailed empirical information in the local housing system. In particular, although price signals are non-existent in the public sector, non-price indicators of economic responses to public housing provision do exist – namely, transfer requests, vacancy rates, entry preferences and departure rates. Through processes of choice and movement, at least in the long term, tenants express intra-public sector preferences and inter-public/private preferences. The present state of the public sector in many large cities in Britain can only lead to the conclusion that public housing investment has not assessed needs effectively in all instances and that major resource mis-allocations can occur.

The allocation and pricing of local authority housing

Previous sections have examined how central government transfers grant-in-aid from central to local governments and discussed the criteria for local authority investment in public housing. But the transformation of grant-in-aid into effective public housing subsidies is determined not only by investment policy but also by allocation and pricing policy. At this stage it is hoped to clarify the reasons for labelling the conventional economic analysis for public housing subsidies on housing choice as being naïve. First, the subsidised housing provided by the public sector is not available to all households. Second, even those individuals deemed eligible for public housing are only offered a restricted number and range of the house types available within the public sector. Third, within the public housing sector the relationship between actual rents and the market value of houses varies as the pricing system is not related directly or consistently to market values.

Allocation rules

The allocation rules adopted by local authorities reflect an attempt to ensure that those households deemed to be in housing 'need' receive public housing priorities. On joining the local authority housing list individuals are awarded 'points' in relation to a variety of socio-economic characteristics and the condition of their existing accommodation (Niner 1975). These administratively determined scores, which may vary across local authorities for a given individual then influence the speed with which a public housing offer is made and the quality of accommodation offered. Apart from broad considerations, for instance preferring not to allocate disabled persons or households with families to high flats, local authorities reputedly to not make discriminatory allocations of poorer quality housing or poorer quality areas to low income households. In principle, and subject to the constraints of the rental system chosen, the local authority strive to directly break down the relationship of low income and poor housing. And of course, especially in the larger cities, a diverse range of income groups do inhabit public housing. In Britain there is a very considerable overlap of the income distribution of council tenants and owner-occupiers (see Fig. 7.5). However, there is now increasing concern over the apparently growing concentrations of low income households, especially with large families in poorer quality public housing. Some limited empirical evidence (Niner 1975; English and Norman 1974) indicates that the effective 'gate keepers' of public housing, that is housing management professionals, can frustrate political commitments to social and economic admixture by matching houses and households according to their own preferences and prejudices. But since housing allocation policies explicitly exist to prevent such spatial concentrations appearing it is pertinent to consider whether such patterns may emerge from the economic choices which consumers make within public housing. This requires, first, a more detailed understanding of pricing policy in public housing.

Local authority rent structures

The rents charged for local authority houses, on an individual or scheme basis, are not directly related either to market values or to replacement costs. Instead rents charged primarily reflect local authority accounting procedures and the historic costs of provision. Rents are set via a two stage process:

1. The overall rental contribution to the Housing Revenue Account is determined.
2. Administratively determined rent structures are devised, then applied to existing houses and households to raise the revenues required.

The overall rent contribution. In the Housing Revenue Account, (Table 9.1), major items are for interest and capital repayments on historically incurred debt for housing provision and, although less important, for maintenance and management costs. All houses contributing to the account are aggregated together and clearly, with the inflationary pattern of building cost and general price appreciation, older houses have a lower historic cost and debt burden. Thus, *ceteris paribus*, the older a local authority's housing stock the lower the burden of debt and redemption payments required. On the revenue side of the account, central government grants and rate fund contributions required do not necessarily vary with age of stock or its historic cost. Thus, when a 'no profit' accounting rule is operational, the rental revenue required to balance the housing revenue account will, *ceteris paribus*, be lower the older the housing stock in the local authority's portfolio. In this way, the capital gain incurred in the public housing sector accrues to the tenant, on the average, in the form of reduced rental payments (Hepworth, Grey and Odling-Smee 1979).

The rent structure. Most local authorities then raise the required rental from public housing not by directly relating rents to the historic cost of a given house but according to a locally decided rent structure which is broadly related to the quality and size of houses. In Glasgow, for instance, there are eight grades of public housing. But these initially oversimplified rent structures, at least when compared with the continuous range of private rents and prices, reflect authority and not individual views on the value of housing quality/services provided. The rents set in many local authorities bear a broad relationship to rateable values. However, rateable values are, of course, also assessed valuations which, moreover, are only intermittently revised. For instance, unlike the private market, local authority rents in an area are unlikely to be varied if the transport system to a scheme is improved or if there is a neighbourhood improvement scheme or if there is a marked rise or fall in local vacancy rates.

This combination of rent pooling, historic cost pricing in aggregate and administered rent structures for individual schemes means that it is difficult to generate economic conclusions from Housing Revenue

Accounts or to make general statements about the relationship between observed rents and market rents. By implication this frustrates the development of conclusions about the overall level of housing subsidy and its distribution within a public housing sector.

Rents and subsidies

The negative conclusion of the preceding paragraph may be illustrated by re-conceptualising the economic nature of the public housing subsidy offer to tenants. Assume that initially local authority rent offers will always, for a house of a given quality, lie below market rents. That is, grant-in-aid is effectively transformed into tenant subsidy. The prospective tenant is now assumed to be offered a limited series of local authority houses, A_1, A_2, A_3 which all have different effective subsidy rates. The tenant is assumed to be free to choose any of the offered houses or to remain at m, the private market alternative. In this instance, as is indicated in Fig. 9.2, the individual will maximise welfare by choosing option A_2. The offer A_2, in this instance, implies neither the highest rate of subsidy nor the largest quantity of housing offered to the tenant. If the tenant had only been offered housing in the vicinity of the point A_1 would have still implied a choice of public housing but a reduction in housing services below the level consumed in the market at m.

Subsidy received by an individual, with the exception of limited rent

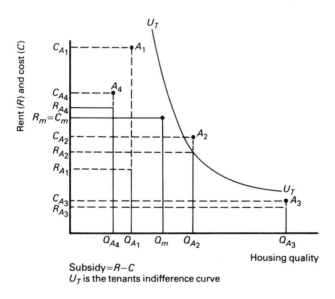

Subsidy = $R - C$
U_T is the tenants indifference curve

Fig. 9.2   The nature of public housing subsidies.

rebates (Table 6.2), is not generally income or housing quantity related, but is a specific subsidy tied to a given house or scheme. Thus, it readily becomes apparent why movement within and between local public housing authorities may become frustrated. For instance, over time, a household may wish to transfer to a larger house and consume more housing services but it may emerge that only very low rates of subsidy effectively accrue on such larger properties and the relative price structure precludes movement. Similarly, as families mature and leave the adult nucleus the price structure may discourage the parent tenants from moving to a smaller house. The house specific subsidy, combined with allocation rules discriminating against non-residents, may also discourage mobility over local authority boundaries and there is some evidence, even in periods of globally high unemployment, that the regional variation in pricing and allocation rules has a dampening effect on labour mobility (Robertson 1979; Mackay 1977; McCormack 1979).

When the above assumptions are relaxed some further economic problems of public housing may be illustrated. First, in receiving the offers A_1 to A_3 it has been assumed that only subsidy rates and quantity of housing services offered varies. But this partial analysis is misleading. For instance, each of the offers may have labour market implications. The offers A_1 to A_3 may occur at different locations relative to workplace and this may imply increased travel time for the household. In the labour market context this may increase direct costs of travel and reduce working hours. An interesting attempt to assess some of the labour market impacts of the move into public housing has produced some tentative empirical results. In the city of Glasgow, Engleman (1977) established, that moves into council housing raised travel to work costs and positively affected job quit rates. Thus the set of choices A_1, A_2, A_3 shifts both income and housing possibilities.

It is also possible, and locally empirically justifiable to relax the assumption that, for a given property, grant-in-aid is turned into effective subsidy. That is, for some houses or schemes, the local authority, since it is a monopoly landlord, may set rents of houses above the likely market level of these houses. Individuals may be offered houses represented in Fig. 9.2 by the point A_4. The rational short-term economic strategy for the individual would be to reject offer A_4 and, in the absence of other public sector offers, select the market solution m. Such a move may be curtailed, however, if there is an inadequate supply of available alternative private rental or owned housing or if a period of residence at A_4 is a necessary strategy to secure long-term public offers such as A_2. It is important to stress that this is not a theoretical point but that abandonment of public housing, with emergent high vacancy rates in locationally peripheral public housing schemes, a particularly severe problem, has become an important problem in several major British cities (Donnison 1979b). However, as discussed in the subsequent section, local authorities have not tackled such difficulties via changing the pricing system.

There are strong grounds therefore for the belief that the pricing of local authority housing is both allocatively and distributionally inefficient. A recent critique of local authority pricing has made the following telling points which can serve as a summary of the previous discussion (Hepworth, Grey and Odling-Smee 1979). They maintain:

1. That the pooled rental system allows local authorities to disguise the existence of over-costly or badly designed schemes.
2. The rental pricing system does not generate long-term replacement funds.
3. As illustrated above, the pricing system is allocatively inefficient.
4. Comparisons of the distribution of subsidy within the public sector and between public and private sectors become impossible.
5. The need for local authorities to be explicit regarding rates of capital gain on public housing is removed.

The authors then propose a pricing system, backed by a revised accounting framework, which would relate public housing prices to market determined capital value with the present income rebates scheme being strengthened. In this way the public housing system would be allocatively efficient, both in pricing and investment, and horizontal and vertical equity concerns could be rationally pursued. It is, however, difficult to envisage in the short term how such capital values would be accurately assessed, unless a comprehensive council sales policy provided comparable values, but area vacancy and mobility rates could help formulate suitable prices. Leaving aside such difficulties, the scheme is in many respects similar to the 1972 Act proposals. At the present time it is not apparent that all local governments intend to pursue new rental strategies for public housing.

Present problems and priorities in public housing

Because of the grant-in-aid and pricing strategies discussed in the previous sections public housing in Britain has increased in scale throughout the postwar period, although its relative significance is now declining as, at least in statistical terms, owner-occupation and housing associations replace private rental housing. Short-term macroeconomic considerations apart, the role of public housing in Britain is now open to sustained critical debate. This debate is not merely sustained by the currently fashionable ideological commitment of central government to market systems of provision, but is primarily generated by a more pragmatic concern that public provision has been generally unresponsive to economic and social changes since the Second World War.

The perception of the role of public housing has been revised for a number of reasons. Four main explanations may be advanced.

1. It is now argued (see Housing Policy, 1977) that past housing and population developments have produced an approximate overall balance of houses and households in the United Kingdom. Thus past housing shortage has been replaced by balance or surplus (though overall shortages may reappear in the 1980s) and at a local or regional level surplus, deficit, overall balance or combined surplus and deficit (reflecting local structural imbalances) may still pertain. Thus local authority housing is faced with the task of trying to satisfy more detailed objectives regarding housing preferences of tenants. As mentioned above, there is some scepticism as to whether public housing planners can perform this task efficiently.

2. Throughout the postwar period economic trends, particularly real income growth, high rates of inflation and low interest rates on savings have, in conjunction with owner-occupied subsidy schemes, increased the demand for owner-occupation. With rising real private house prices and rising vacancy rates in public housing there are at least *prima facie* grounds for re-allocating housing stock from public to private sectors.

3. The allocative and distributional inefficiencies discussed above have become increasingly apparent.

4. The allocative and distributional inefficiencies inherent in the financing and pricing system have been exacerbated by maturation of and differentiation within the public sector. Public sector housing is not of a uniformly high physical or environmental quality. Not only have different standards and styles of housing been developed in a diversity of locations but the stock now covers a sixty year age range of properties. In addition differential entry and mobility patterns of different income or socioeconomic groups within public housing have now apparently produced a broad housing quality to socioeconomic status relationship within public housing. Thus, just as the idealised conception of a market was criticised in the previous chapters, it is essential to stress the realities of public housing and their divergence from the socialist ideal. At the present time three particular problems face local authorities. First, they have to deal with the problems of more precisely meeting tenant preferences. For instance, applied research in Newcastle and London (Bird 1976) and in Glasgow (Glasgow District Council 1979) has indicated that, respectively, 25 per cent and 45 per cent of tenants are currently seeking transfers. In the Glasgow context the bulk of transfer requests (which, at present rates of change, would not be accomplished in this century) are for inter-scheme moves and there is a well-defined pattern of council estates where the requests for transfer-

in do not balance requests for transfer-out. Such patterns tend to correlate with the socioeconomic status of the areas concerned. Thus the second major operational problem is to reduce or assuage the emergent concentrations of poverty and deprivation within particular estates. Third, and reflecting an interaction of the previous concerns, local authorities are now faced with the problem of property abandonment (Taylor 1979; Donnison 1979a). Again in the context of Glasgow, where the problem is most serious, urban population decline has not resulted in abandonment of older core area private properties but public vacancy rates have risen most rapidly and are highest in peripheral public housing. Throughout the rest of the United Kingdom difficult to let houses have been identified on particular estates, but in Glasgow more than 15,000 public sector houses now lie vacant and vacancy rates are expected to rise.

Strategies for public housing

At least in the major, older urban centres in Britain it is now arguable that there is a growing organisational and managerial crisis. It is arguable that the likely difficulties for public housing in the next decade are not primarily financial. For, if levels of new building are to be severely curtailed and as long as interest rates do not rise rapidly above present levels, then the historic cost accounting procedures will, *ceteris paribus*, imply a falling real average cost per house per year.

This argument, however, must not be overstressed. However, falling real incomes, high mortgage rates and rising unemployment which now pertain in the macroeconomy and which are likely to persist until the present government recognises that the theoretical monetarist short run may extend beyond politically acceptable durations of mass unemployment, are likely to sustain an increased 'need' for council housing. In addition the falling average historic cost argument would not apply where major modernisation, rehabilitation or replacement expenditures are required within a local authority. And financial difficulties will be encountered where past and present management practices result in houses with outstanding loan debt being abandoned or where central government policy results in the enforced selling of council houses which currently, via the pooled rent system, make a net contribution to the Housing Revenue Account. But here organisational and management difficulties are emphasised.

Since there currently appears to be no commitment to revising pricing and subsidy strategies within local authorities, the organisational problems outlined above can be tackled by at least three broad strategies:
1. Local authorities could pursue more effective management and monitoring techniques.

2. Modernisation and improvement strategies could be devised for poor quality public housing areas.
3. Local authorities may sell the housing stock.
These strategies are now considered briefly.

Improving management and monitoring techniques

In the major phases of postwar public housing development sophisticated management and monitoring of public housing have not generally been perceived to be a necessity. Policy was primarily concerned with alleviating overall housing shortages. The waiting list size and the numbers of starts and completions of houses were the major operational concerns. Moreover, investment strategies were pursued on a criterion which was not concerned with long-term benefits of a diverse kind but was rather focused on the question 'is public housing an improvement on what exists?' Inevitably, given pre-existing conditions of slum housing, this question was answered positively.

But now a second, economically more rational, question can be asked. With existing resource commitments to public housing, can public housing systems be improved? Maturation of and differentiation within public housing, combined with the evolving preferences and demands of tenants now require local authorities to be primarily concerned with allocating existing stock rather than planning new developments. Thus the detailed planning and management of public housing within local authorities have become important in the 1970s. Not only have local authorities begun to examine 'needs assessment' in detail but they have increasingly striven to monitor processes operating in the public sector. For instance, area or house type preferences, entry patterns, transfer patterns, vacancy rate monitoring have been undertaken in many local authorities. The introduction of HIPs and Housing Plans have contributed to the acceleration of local authority management and planning and it would be undesirable for the present government to enact their threat to discontinue such plans. The introduction of computer data storage and analysis systems have all facilitated this strategic planning task. At the same time increased speed of data handling has improved managerial efficiency and could speed up the process of matching entrant and transfer request households to vacant houses. It is, however, unfortunate that improved management and planning techniques within public housing have postdated the emergence of major structural problems within the sector. The existing difficulties will not be directly solved by these new techniques.

Local authorities have also displayed an increasing sensitivity to the diversity of tenant preferences and this is reflected in a number of ways. Consider for example the city of Glasgow. Three major strands have emerged in an attempt to operate public housing more effectively.

Attempting to assess tenant preferences

Although preference and attitude surveys have severe limitations (Ch. 2), the local authority is now, for the first time, attempting to systematically analyse the area preferences of tenants and entrants. In addition, in house modernisation schemes past practice has been to impose selected specifications on tenants, including detailed colour schemes. In addition individual tenants' improvements were always removed and replaced. This authoritarian approach to 'property tailoring' has always been a considerable source of discontent to tenants (see BMRB 1977). A new tenants' improvement grant scheme has effectively given tenants a block-grant to meet broadly required specifications in the ways which they prefer and at the same time programme costs have been reduced.

Decentralising management

Historically in Glasgow the major managerial functions of public housing such as allocation, transfer, rent arrears collection, repairs and maintenance have been executed centrally. Now parts of these functions are being decentralised to area offices. Not only will this reduce the repeated travel costs, particularly for peripheral area residents, but locally orientated management may be able to respond in a rapid and integrated fashion to local problems and opportunities. It is not yet possible to assess the efficiency of this change but its very existence reflects a new managerial style and an imaginative attempt to manage public housing in a previously conservative local authority with a massive socialist commitment to public housing.

Devolving choices from management to tenants

A more radical, and currently less extensive, shift in local management practices has been to devolve limited controls to area based tenant co-operatives. In such instances, local management has allowed tenant co-operatives discretion over an effective block-grant for repairs, maintenance and environmental improvements and to influence letting policy. The intention of such co-operatives is not only to improve allocative efficiency but to generate a greater commitment on the part of tenants to their housing and neighbourhood. But again the long-term problems of such developments have not been fully assessed. For instance, how does the co-operative deal with non-co-operative or antisocial tenants within the co-operative's area? Or, if the co-operatives becomes extensive how will the local authority co-ordinate maintenance, block-grant, letting and transfer policies across a large public sector? Until present experiments with co-operatives run their full course a detailed assessment is not possible.

Although changes in management style and structure may both increase allocative efficiency within the public sector and reduce expenditure requirements on maintenance and modernisation, they are not improvements which deal with existing structural problems alluded to above. For instance, regarding low income and difficult to let estates, preference assessment merely confirms their existence, decentralised management has neither the resources nor powers to deal with the areas concerned and it is probably in such areas that tenant co-operatives will be most difficult to establish.

Changing the existing public sector stock

In any housing system, public or private, incomes, tastes, preferences and numbers and types of household are constantly changing – sometimes unpredictably. At the same time, and at a much slower and more constant rate housing stock physically depreciates. Thus, in the public sector, local authorities have to devise strategies to maintain and improve the quality of existing housing stock and/or adapt to its relative decline.

At the present time many local authorities are faced with structural inadequacies of existing stock. There are 'difficult to let' or abandoned neighbourhoods, there is a growing mismatch of houses and household size and this is reflected in a shortage of smaller dwellings and there is an apparent reluctance to living in high rise dwellings. In a market pricing system two adjustments to these kinds of structural imbalance would be forthcoming. First, rents would rise in desired house types and locations and fall in undesired house types and locations. Providers of housing services could then react to these relative price changes in selecting investment strategies. Second, individuals would be induced to improve or convert the existing housing stock in line with their housing preferences, although such individual improvements are less likely to occur for external environmental aspects of housing, see p. 107.

Tenants have been, historically, discouraged from improving public housing and the rehabilitation of existing stock has been left to the discretion of local authorities. At the present, public sector repairs and maintenance expenditures are growing rapidly (Table 9.2), and if 'difficult to let' estates are to be improved then further increases may be required. It is possible that, in the long term, tenants' co-operatives could develop a public sector rehabilitation strategy similar to those of community orientated housing associations. But there is the danger, at least in central cities with a declining population, that modernising public housing in areas of abandonment will compete with private sector rehabilitation schemes for exchequer resources, skilled manpower and even tenants. Thus, in taking the decision to modernise poor quality public housing the local authority must be convinced that such schemes are justified by the size of waiting list, population trends and expenditures on rehabilitation in other sectors. Otherwise the abandon-

Table 9.2 Sales of local authority dwelling

	England and Wales only			
	Number of dwellings	Capital value of disposals £ thousand	Initial payments received £ thousand	Average discount on sales by English authorities %
1970	6,816	n.a.	n.a.	n.a.
1971	17,214	n.a.	n.a.	n.a.
1972	45,878	n.a.	n.a.	n.a.
1973	34,334	n.a.	n.a.	n.a.
1974	4,657	n.a.	n.a.	n.a.
1975	2,723	n.a.	n.a.	n.a.
1976	5,793	n.a.	n.a.	n.a.
1977	13,020	93,700	25,500	16
1978	30,045	248,350	80,400	18
1979	42,735	394,900	108,750	27

Source: *Housing and construction statistics* 1975, 1979.

ment and vacancy problem may merely be shifted to the public estates which are perceived to constitute lowest quality housing.

Thus, in regenerating abandoned properties or difficult to let estates within the public sector, local authorities could supplement improved physical structures with new managerial approaches. Given such conditions it is the tenants who will, in the near future, determine housing and neighbourhood quality in the area.

Alternative strategies for low quality public housing

Where the size of the effective public sector waiting list is limited, or where there is public housing surplus, three strategies can be pursued to deal with poor quality, vacant housing. First, and this re-emphasises the limitations of the needs concept, public sector entry conditions may be revised. For instance, in many local authority areas short let tenancies for young single persons and students are now advocated as a means of raising rental income and reducing policing costs for such dwellings. Second, where such letting schemes are unlikely to succeed or if there is an apparent excess demand for lower value owner-occupied housing, then local authorities may choose to sell or 'homestead' such dwellings. The latter strategy, which has been widely discussed in the United States but which had only dealt with less than 3,000 families prior to 1979, consists of authorities selling poor quality properties and attaching conditions regarding subsequent self-improvement activity by the household. Such activities are now existing or being considered in all the major British cities with difficult to let housing.

Homesteading is a much less drastic solution to the large-scale vacancy problem than the third strategy, which would imply partial or total demolition of estates. If the waiting list is small and private sector excess demand would be deficient for previously vacant housing after physical improvement (if the houses are locationally or environmentally obsolescent, for instance) then the local authority must assess the relative costs of demolishing houses or allowing them to stand vacant. If the houses are demolished, demolition and site clearance costs have to be added to the costs of financing interest and principal loan debt which remain after demolition. Thus, this solution imposes severe financial penalties on residual rate, rent and taxpayers. But if the houses remain vacant they will generate social costs in the form of visual and social externalities as they may begin to generate abandonment in contiguous but presently inhabited public stock. In addition, policing and management costs will remain. The financial deficits generated by demolition are particularly high in modern properties. Thus, the demolition of the Piggeries in Liverpool (built in the late 1960s) and the Darnley demolition in Glasgow (built in the mid-1970s) indicate how acute the financial effects of public sector mis-investment in housing may be.

However, demolition of public housing stock in Britain is likely to contribute negligibly to the relative decline of the sector. Council house sales, apart from homesteading schemes, are a more likely substantive source of reduction in the scale of the public sector.

Selling council houses

The sale of public sector housing stock has been alluded to at several points in this book. It is an issue which bears upon not only the disposal of unlettable houses but it is centrally related to the future development of the owner-occupied sector and to the long-term scale and character of public housing in Britain. The disposal of public sector housing not originally built for sale is not a new phenomenon in Britain (Table 9.2). Sales have fluctuated with governmental changes. Labour governments, until after 1977, have tended to severely curtail disposals. Throughout the 1970s the issue has aroused a great deal of ideological ire but little useful information or analysis. Indeed, it is only since the Green Paper in 1977 that debate has become informed as local governments and policy analysts have switched concern from the general question 'should council houses be sold?' In fact neither central nor local governments have had sufficient information to evaluate general policies for council sales. Instead, and more pragmatically, there was the beginnings of an attempt to answer more specific questions such as 'which houses should be sold', 'to whom' and 'at what price?'

The debate on selling council houses since the mid-1970s had begun

271

to illuminate the issue constructively when the present government undertook a very substantial change in policy. In the past the sale of council houses had been at the discretion of local authorities, subject to ministerial approval, and limited discounts were offered to purchasing tenants. The legislation, introduced in the 1980 Acts (The Housing Act 1980, and The Tenants' Rights (Scotland) Act 1980) have now, with few exceptions, transferred power over potential sales to individuals by giving them the legal right to purchase council housing. In addition the legislation allows government to provide a discount of up to 50 per cent on purchase price depending on the tenant's length of residence in the dwelling and also provides guarantees to ensure that mortgage finance will be forthcoming. This legislation, which is yet another badly designed intervention in the housing system, finesses, by its statutory nature, the issues of which houses should be sold, to whom and at what price. But it may still be valid to raise such questions in a more negative fashion which leads to a critique of present policy.

The arguments for selling council houses

In this chapter, the wider political interests in advocating or opposing council sales are not discussed. Clearly socialists with an aversion to private ownership of property will oppose sales on ideological grounds whilst the present government have made a commitment to sales which seems, on examining the evidence, to represent a commitment to subsidising the creation of a property-owning democracy. However, here the naïve assumption is made that council sales policy can, or indeed, should, be assessed in relation to tenants' and owners' preferences and constraints.

If the latter approach is made to formulating a policy for selling council houses then it will become apparent that sales policy will have to reflect local housing conditions thus rendering the present statutory approach highly inappropriate. For optimum tenure structures may vary across cities and regions. In assessing what or how much council stock to sell and the means of selling, three particular questions are critical.

1. Does selling council houses reflect tenant preferences and does selling council housing increase the stability and efficiency of the local housing system?
2. Since selling publicly owned housing stock changes the subsidy regime pertaining to the transferred stock what are the exchequer or financial implications of sales?
3. Does the selling of council housing stock compromise the ability of local or central government to achieve its stated objectives for the public housing sector?

The housing market effects of selling council houses

At any point in time there is an established relationship of price levels and population movements within housing submarkets (Ch. 2), and between public and private housing. Thus selling council houses may change the relationships for supply submarkets and also shift patterns of movement from public to private sectors. In the short term it can be argued that sales to existing tenants may reduce price pressures therein. But this argument should not be overemphasised for empirical evidence suggests that a large proportion of council house purchasers would not otherwise have moved into private housing. Leaving aside the question of discounts, sales in such cases do not, in the short term, reduce market pressures although they do allow an expression of tenure preference on the part of previous tenants. The flow of tenants from public to owner-occupied housing largely consists of newly formed households with local authority parental addresses or of continuing households who have moved into private housing not merely to express tenure preferences but to leave poor quality public sector environments and locations. These flows are unlikely to alter in the short term. Over the longer period, if previously public housing becomes integrated into the wider private housing market when initial purchasers move on then the market pressure arguments may have some validity.

Of course the housing market impacts, subject to the above comments, depend critically upon which houses are sold. If, as has been the experience in major English cities, high quality public housing with a low vacancy rate is sold then there will be limited housing market effects. In Fig. 9.3 there are n public houses and x tenants unwilling to buy houses. Then $n - x$ houses and households will move into the owner-occupied sector. In the private housing market supply and demand will shift compensatingly and leave prices unaffected. Assuming no public housing shortage and that $n - x$ households were determined to become owner-occupiers then the sale of $n - x$ houses prevents inflation in the private market and vacant stock in the public sector. But, as noted above $n - x$ households would be unlikely to wish to purchase in the private housing market particularly without an entry subsidy of equivalent size to the council sale discount.

A clearer case for selling houses can be made when, in Fig. 9.4, n represents public stock, x represents inhabited public stock and $n - x$ thus represents other than frictionally vacant public housing. Again, if it is assumed that there is no shortage of public housing, then the abandoned public stock could be transferred into the private sector. In this instance there could be an outward shift to the supply function $S_T S_T$ but no initial shift in $D_T D_T$. As a result private house prices, or more probably the rate of house price appreciation, would be reduced.

273

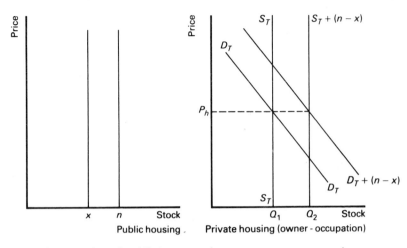

Fig. 9.3 Transfers of public houses and tenants to owner-occupation

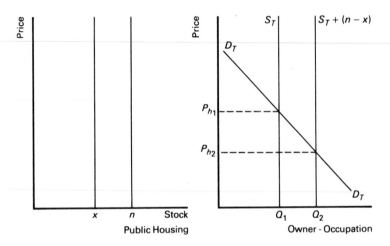

Fig. 9.4 Transferring vacant public housing to owner-occupation

However, a less optimistic view of the effects of sales can occur when selling generates an effective increase in the population of an area. This case is most apparent in rural areas with a private housing market for second or retirement homes. If the local resident population remains fixed in size over time, then sales redistribute households across tenure sectors. But, when council houses are resold, then newcomers to an area may have sufficient resources to displace local residents onto the waiting list or into overcrowded private rental housing. The rise in private sector prices may eventually stimulate new private housing

274

supply but perhaps raising new private supplies rather than council sales should have been the initial focus of policy. Where excess demand for private housing exists from non-local populations in an area then long-term displacement effects could be serious. It is awareness of the mixed effects of selling council houses and the variety of local housing conditions which has resulted in local authorities reacting strongly against current legislation. If the policy had reaffirmed the right of councils to sell or had allowed councils to fix quotas on stock sales of particular house types or locations then some long-term housing system problems could have been minimised.

Throughout the 1970s, as indicated in Chapter 5, there have been periods of surplus and shortage in the availability of mortgages. As long as there is a macroeconomic policy with rising or fluctuating interest rates shortages of building society funds for lending will occur. Both 1979 and 1980 have been periods of mortgage shortage. This raises the concern, particularly in the short-run phase of large-scale council sales of how sales are to be financed. If financing, either by building society or local authority loans diverts loans from the existing stock of funds then there may be a danger of collapsing existing markets – particularly in the inner city. However, during 1981 loanable funds have been plentiful.

Financial effects

In implementing policies to sell council houses both the present government and its Labour predecessor appear to have laid great stress upon the exchequer implications of selling council houses. The mixed results and limited methodologies of the two recent financial assessments of council sales are discussed below. But here it must be stressed that these financial arguments have been overemphasised in selecting the direction of policy and too little attention has been paid to the real costs and benefits of sales in relation to private market owners and continuing public sector tenants.

Central government assessments of the financial effects of selling council houses have been used to justify the modest sales policy of 1977–79 (DOE 1978) and the policy embodied in the Housing Act (Housing Act 1980). The contents of the former document were not made widely available to the public, apart from newspaper leaks, and here reliance is placed upon a perceptive assessment made by Kilroy (1980).

The evaluation of the financial effects of selling council houses is based upon the analysis of major financial flows which governments perceive will change upon selling a house. In selling the house the local authority forgoes rental payments, removes its management and maintenance expenditures and it no longer has a commitment to make rent rebates for the tenant but it is required to repay existing principal and interest debt incurred in constructing the house. In addition, rate fund

275

contribution and public housing subsidy for the house are not required. After the sale of the house, central government is required to subsidise mortgage interest payments through tax relief and of course the purchase discount has to be funded. Following sale, payment is made through mortgage repayments which are fixed in nominal terms. These financial concerns are common to both assessments.

In order to quantify the likely size of flows government is then required to make assumptions about the future course of rent payments, house prices, interest rates and improvement expenditures. Further critical assumptions must be made about how often the former council property is resold. This assumption is important as it determines the flow of mortgage interest relief. First, because for a given period mortgage interest decreases as a proportion of payment overtime. Thus, even at a fixed house price, rapid reselling will raise interest relief payments. Second, reselling inevitably, in periods of inflation, raises the nominal value of the property sold.

A second important assumption relates to the characteristics of the house sold and the duration of residence of tenant prior to purchase. The latter consideration influences the size of discount offered whilst the former has a variety of effects. If higher value houses with low maintenance and repair costs are sold, then repair and maintenance savings are decreased but future mortgage interest relief increased. On the other hand if low quality or abandoned property with presently near zero rental yield, a low market price and high maintenance and policing costs was sold then sales may be more likely to generate surpluses (but not necessarily). The assumptions made in the two major financial assessments are, following Kilroy, indicated in Table 9.3 along with the range of outcomes of these exercises.

The assessment in 1980 biases the results towards a surplus by assuming the sale of average rather than high value public housing but the higher rate of inflation and interest rate assumed are likely to raise deficits. The critical reason for the divergence of results between the two papers for the fifty year evaluation, according to Kilroy, are that the 1978 paper allows public sector improvement expenditures to be offset against higher end period values of housing stock. The 1980 paper includes the improvement expenditure item but, illegitimately in accounting terms, excludes end period benefits from improvement.

The critical assessment of the financial evaluations provided by Kilroy is broadly correct given the assumptions of the analyses. But the assumptions of both papers are somewhat unrealistic and are not clearly based on past experience. For instance, the assumptions regarding interest rates, house price rises, earnings, and the general rate of inflation are all set below average values for the period 1974−9. The assumptions probably underestimate quite substantially, as a result, future mortgage relief magnitudes. In addition the assumption that the

Table 9.3 Assessing the financial effects of selling council houses

	Assumptions (%)			
	New paper		Old paper	
	(Nominal)	*Real*	*(Nominal)*	*Real*
Inflation	(9%)		(7%)	
Interest and discount	(12%)	3%	(10%	3%
Earnings growth	(11%)	2%	(9%)	2%
Rent increases	In line with earnings		in line with earnings	
Range of sales outcome (+ = *Gain* − = *Loss*)	+ £2,185 to	− £3,635	− £5,530 to	− £4,500

Source: *Roof*, January 1980.

mortgage incurred with initial price minus sales discount is likely to last fourteen (1978) or twenty-five years (1980) is quite unrealistic. The average family in the UK moves at least once every seven years.

The official analyses, as presented by Kilroy, also suffer from potentially important omissions. Public housing maintenance and repair costs may be reduced but, on transfer to the private sector will these houses never be subject to improvement or repair grants? On the other hand, will the exchequer not benefit from stamp duty on resales of former council stock and if former council houses enter the asset structures of owners who then die will inheritance tax revenues not increase? Or what of the incomes and profits taxes to be levied on the selling and conveyancing fees of professionals involved with formerly council housing?

Thus the financial assessment of selling council housing has produced, on the basis of a limited accounting framework and information, a variety of tentative assessments none of which conclusively support the massive commitment to sales embodied in the 1980 Housing Act and all of which, the 1980 document excepted, suggest the emergence of exchequer losses after 1990.

Effects on existing tenants
It is difficult to conceive of any benefits for continuing tenants from the sale of council housing except for houses which are vacant. Otherwise the quality of housing sold influences only the extent to which continuing tenants are potential losers from sales. Such potential losses are long term rather than short term in nature.

If sales of council houses continue to be of high quality public houses in better than average public estates then sales will jeopardise the long-term quality of public housing careers for those households who are currently in poorer quality dwellings. In the short term this effect will be negligible as tenants sufficiently committed to purchasing a public house will be unlikely to move whether or not the house is sold. In the longer term, however, cumulative reselling instead of public reallocation may reduce the probability of upward movement within the public sector for existing tenants. A critical question in this regard, however, is who purchases resold council houses? At one extreme, as in the case of rural holiday homes cited above, resold houses are reallocated to satisfy excess demands from non-local residents. At the other extreme, houses may become part of the cheaper owned housing stock and be purchased by individuals moving out of lower quality public stock. In such instances the existing set of housing system linkages would be undisturbed by tenure changes. But, as is likely, where excess demand for owned housing operates outwith the public sector, then reselling will alter movement linkages. In particular, in the next five years new household formation is likely to generate price pressures on lower value owned stock which will now include resold council houses.

These arguments assume that local authorities will be constrained not to build or buy replacement stock for old houses. If there is, on the other hand, an expectation of such replacement then why are council houses being sold whilst the private building industry is collapsed and unsubsidised? As a result sales are likely to reduce the size of the public housing stock and they will reduce average quality of residual public housing stock which will probably be inhabited by lower income public sector tenants as well as by tenants with an aversion to owning. The long-term size of the sector will be further influenced by the path of public sector rents and the more rapidly they rise the more likely purchase decisions will be triggered although exchequer financial advantages of sales will be reduced.

Conclusion

If the council sales policy of the present government is effective in its objectives then the nature of public housing in Britain will change, if gradually, to comprise a sector of lower quality housing for lower income tenants. This will heighten rather than lessen the structural problems within public housing. But, in the long run, such as tendency may already be inevitable if, as is suggested by empirical evidence, the demand for owner-occupation and income growth are positively correlated. In either case, a more constructive challenge to public housing is to examine how public and private sectors may be re-integrated in spatial and subsidy terms. Large concentrations of low quality public housing are not the inevitable outcome of a privatisation of housing if government pursues constructive public housing policy. Government could pursue at least three constructive strands for policy. Council sales and purchases, combined with rehabilitation, could be directed towards achieving a local scale admixture of public and private housing. Rent structures and price structures could be rationally linked and a *substantial* redistribution of tied housing aid, akin to housing vouchers, should be directed towards lower income households in both private and public sectors. Finally, for the groups who will not respond to income related subsidies, two strategies can be adopted. A pure market oriented approach would abandon such groups to their chosen fate even if choices were uninformed or anti-social or had severe costs on affected families. A caring society, which still wished to rely on market price mechanisms for general allocations, could still choose to house such groups at minimal rents on houses distributed throughout the housing system. Disregard for the latter group reflects not market failure but societal failure to make particular distributional judgements.

Postscript

Synoptic textbooks of this kind are inevitably made redundant by the flow of new evidence, theories and policies. New developments since the initial draft of this work, require that a short summary of recent trends is provided as a postscript. There has been a gentle, if insistent, tide of new theoretical ideas. In particular, neighbourhood level analysis of economic phenomena (Ch. 1) has grown in importance and there is increasing theoretical concern regarding the role of the housing sector in the macroeconomy. Both these themes are important but cannot be developed here. In the British policy context there has been a veritable surge of policy change, for not only have the provisions of the 1980 Housing Act been important, but there has also been a marked change in the thrust of and resource commitment to housing policy in Britain. Reflecting its overall economic and social philosophy, the government is now radically reducing public housing expenditure, even if it has little in the way of purposive privatisation policy. Indeed, commentators correctly claim that macroeconomic policy from 1979 to 1981 has discouraged rather than encouraged the 'privatisation' of British housing. Since the overall tone of this volume has been in favour of greater, but careful, use of housing policies implemented through market systems this critical conclusion requires some elaboration. Recent policy developments can be clarified by outlining recent public cuts and then indicating private sector reactions to them.

Public expenditure commitments to policy

The 1980 Housing Act, by introducing the Housing Support Grant (HSG) system for Great Britain, has conferred on government the necessary powers to exert close and discretionary control over current expenditure on housing policy (Ch. 9). The public expenditure plans for the UK to 1983/84 indicate that government intends to reduce markedly both current and capital expenditure on housing in the public sector. Indeed housing expenditure is likely to be the public expenditure heading most reduced, both absolutely and proportionately. As a result, *de facto*, there is likely to be a further shift in the pattern of governmental control over housing.

When the periods 1975–79 and 1979–81 are compared, in constant prices, then there is a marked shift in the direction and structure of housing expenditures. Regarding capital expenditure, there was a real decline in annual expenditures over the period 1975–79, and housing investment by the public sector formed a declining share of public capital formation. This is unsurprising in a period of general economic difficulty, restrictions on public spending and an apparently growing surplus of dwellings over households. Nevertheless within this declining total, rehabilitation expenditures and housing modernisation all grew rapidly, reflecting the policy changes of the early 1970s. But capital spending has fallen even more rapidly in the period 1979 to 1981. Current expenditure on housing, however, rose throughout the 1970s and public sector subsidies, both direct (income related) and indirect (via the Housing Revenue Account pooling system), also rose. From 1979 to 1981 overall current expenditure was intended to fall with a modest reduction in indirect subsidies partially offset by an expansion in income-related expenditures. These expenditure cuts have, despite the great deal of political debate surrounding them, not yet produced a radically different expenditure scenario from that prevailing since 1977. But the planned cuts, to be rapidly implemented, are non-marginal. Real expenditure on all housing policy expenditures in the UK is intended to fall at the rates indicated below:

% Reduction in each year
1979–80/80–81	– 12.5
1980–81/81–82	– 18.3
1981–82/82–83	– 15.4
1982–83/83–84	– 14.2

The geographic pattern of reductions is to be uneven – with 50 per cent reductions in England and Wales, 30 per cent in Scotland and 15 per cent in Northern Ireland. Details of the planned pattern of cuts are not yet available. However, the already reduced local authority total of capital and current expenditure on housing in 1980/81 was £3,607 million. But, by mid-1982, it is planned that the combined rate fund and central government contribution to local authorities will fall below the real value of central government's own contribution in 1975/76, housing capital expenditure will be at less than one-third of the 1974/75 level and the real budget of the Housing Corporation will lie below its 1976/77 level. Thus, from 1981 onwards the cuts are to be significant and sustained.

It must be stressed that cuts in public expenditure are neither a necessary cause of housing sector gloom nor overall economic optimism. Indeed, it could be argued that the allocative and distributional inefficiencies of existing policy expenditure are such that net addition to social welfare could be achieved in the context of reductions in public expenditure. For not only could public sector efficiency be raised but local and housing authorities could, in fulfilling their comprehensive housing role, usefully interact with the private sector. But such an interface has two prerequisites. First, this requires careful and imaginative housing planning and policy formulation within housing authorities. It is not at all clear that even a crudely conceived housing policy exists presently in many local or housing authorities in the UK. So far only a limited number of authorities on the mainland and the Northern Ireland Housing Executive have demonstrated the capacity to formulate major initiatives in conjunction with the private sector (that is, building societies and construction firms).

A second prerequisite is that government creates a general economic environment conducive to private sector development of housing. The present administration has singularly failed in this regard and is, further, in danger of raising 'tax-expenditures' on housing so far that there will be no beneficial effect on net government debt. However, the macro- and microeconomic effects of the cuts will largely depend upon the specific pattern of expenditure reductions made and the ability of the private sector to channel housing investment efficiently. Let us then consider the likely pattern of reductions and their effects.

Reducing public capital expenditure

From this year (1981) there will be no fixed headings for Housing Investment Plan capital expenditures. Thus the reducing total expenditure for the housing sector may be allocated in a number of ways. It has been suggested that new public housing construction will be reduced to a maximal UK rate of 30–40,000 houses per annum. At the same time, capital account expenditure on modernisation and improvement and for home loans will be further reduced. The major implications of local authority capital expenditure cuts are therefore likely to be that:

1. The public sector housing stock will at most grow slowly and, at least, fall in scale if sales policies are successful.
2. The capital investment required to renovate depreciated public housing and to repair and maintain it at a suitable standard is not likely to be forthcoming. Local authorities have already begun to face this reality. In a number of cities such as Belfast, Liverpool and Glasgow,

new forms of tenant improvement grants, better management of previously vandalised dwellings and successful 'homesteading' schemes have all improved the efficiency of public housing spending.

3. In many inner city areas the improvement grant and home loan activities of local authorities have been, in conjunction with housing associations, critical influences in arresting decline and stimulating confidence in inner areas. In the Scottish cities, at least, public support of this kind for the private sector has been instrumental in attracting private improvement and new building in central cities. And many of these developments are now at a critical stage where sudden reductions in expenditure may prove irreversible. It can only be hoped that, in the reducing resource context of the 1980s, local authorities will not withdraw their rehabilitating and repair functions, developed in the 1970s, in order to concentrate on their traditional new building concerns.

A continuing local authority resource commitment to the repair and improvement of older housing is also essential as the budget of the Housing Corporation is not likely to expand in real terms. And this will have complex repercussions on housing association rehabilitation. The situation varies across the UK regions but consider the Scottish experience by way of example. Until 1980 there was no binding financial constraint on Scottish rehabilitation, rather programme growth was only limited by the capability to plan and programme projects. Some associations, nearly all of which were territorial and located in the inner city, grew rapidly and early whilst others shared a more gradual and lagged pattern of development. But the Housing Corporation in Scotland now faces several new problems. Acquisitions for improvement have run well ahead of rehabilitations and even without further purchase schemes will take five years to improve already acquired stock. Thus a state agency will have become, for quite a sustained period of time, a large-scale landlord of slum properties. In addition, locally based associations have begun to seek a more 'explicit' and 'fairer' allocation of the rehabilitation budget which now effectively constrains improvement. Therefore, central-local relations within the Housing Corporation are now an issue of concern. And at a different level of organisation, hard pressed local authorities may come to covet the protected budgets of the Housing Corporation and press for its demise and the incorporation of released funds into HIP's expenditure entitlements.

To cope with internal and external pressures the Housing Corporation can make several adjustments. Rehabilitation standards may fall and there may now be greater attempts to channel private capital into rehabilitation either by encouraging owners to improve or by exercising the right to sell rehabilitated properties as long as central government allows an internal recycling of capital realised in this way. Indeed there is a great deal of evidence to suggest that if, instead of a crude policy of cuts in this sector, there was some positive policy to raise private involvement then public expenditure commitments could be reduced without prejudicing inner city areas currently being rejuvenated. Once again, mainland authorities would do well to examine the accomplishments of the Northern Ireland Housing Executive in this difficult field of policy.

Reducing current public expenditures

Although precise figures have not yet been indicated it is clear that the present intention of government is to reduce Housing Support Grant to minimal levels by 1983/84. Assuming no massive sales of council housing in that period this must imply falling real HSG per house. The nature of Housing Revenue Account cost structures is such that it is very difficult to reduce cost levels. Interest rate payments are out of the present authorities' control and it is difficult to reduce management and maintenance costs. Since rises in per house rate fund contribution will be resisted or centrally controlled, as currently occurs in Scotland, then the HRA can only be balanced by marked rises in rent per house. Since HSG was introduced in Scotland rents have risen by over 20 and 30 per cent in successive years and 40 per cent rises are quite likely in 1982/83 assuming an overall inflation rate of 10 per cent. Of course, since subsidy is best measured as the gap between administered and market rents, this may still imply the existence of a considerable rate of public sector subsidy and approval or disapproval of such rises is a normative issue. The overall effects of the rise in a given local authority will depend upon local circumstances and adjustments. For instance, local authorities may restructure their rent systems – a move long overdue in many housing authorities – so that rents rise more rapidly on good rather than poor quality dwellings. And of course, negating any overall public expenditure effects, rent increases for lower income groups may be offset by rebate systems or by supplementary benefit payments. Rises in local authority rents of this magnitude are likely, particularly in better quality council property, to stimulate demands for the right to buy. Thus the public expenditure savings of reduced HSG in this way may be largely offset by new tax expenditures arising in the owned sector and by sales discounts leading to a failure to reduce outstanding council debt on dwellings. All we can say with any precision in this field is that government has yet to provide us with a convincing logical and rational estimate of the expenditure and public debt implications of council house sales. A further difficulty of raising all rents is that housing already difficult to let may become impossible to let and, as a result, incorrect rent levels and rent structures will raise vacancy levels, with ongoing debt commitments and no rent income, in the public sector whilst raising private sector demand and tax expenditure commitments.

Private sector responses

The reduction in the role of and resources for the local authority housing sector would not necessarily be problematic if housing resources could be efficiently transferred to the private sector. And even falling levels of new private investment need not presage housing shortages if the demand for housing is static or falling. In the long term the demand for housing depends critically upon growth in household formation and household numbers and upon real income growth, in addition to price and interest rate considerations. Demographic and social trends indicate that the number of households will rise to the end of the 1980s (see estimate below), and there will be a particular growth in demand from new households and older smaller households. Thus, in fairly crude terms, unless there is a major surge in housing investment in the private sector there are likely to be marked signs of housing shortage more akin to the 1950s than the 1970s. Further, in the 1980s, there is likely to be continuing growth in demand for owner occupation as middle incomes grow modestly – although, and ironically, government policy to control the macroeconomy may now be discouraging such growth. For high inflation rates and low interest rates have encouraged ownership in the 1970s. Their reduction may make renting more attractive.

There are few encouraging signs to suggest that positive measures are being introduced to encourage privatisation in British housing. For instance the construction sector has been ravaged by macroeconomic policy and government's unwillingness to stabilise or directly subsidise the level of new private construction. Official statistics indicate that the sector has now reached prewar levels of collapse and it is unlikely that rapid recovery, primarily due to materials supply problems, will take place before 1983 at the earliest. And although mortgage interest relief and other favourable tax expenditures will continue there have been no proposals to improve financing, surveying and bidding arrangements in the market – that is, traditional areas of imperfect competition will persist in the housing market.

The implications of these housing sector trends are that housing shortages will re-emerge in all sectors. The Association of Metropolitan Authorities have recently suggested the following scale of shortages is likely:

Household dwelling balance 1971–86 (England and Wales: thousands at mid year)

	1971	1976	1981	1986
Total dwellings	17,024	18,086	19,054	19,715
Total households	16,750	17,574	18,331	19,132
Crude surplus	+ 274	+ 512	+ 703	+ 583
Less				
Second homes	150	150	175	200
Vacant (not previously occupied)	100	100	100	100
Vacancy reserve (excluding those not previously occupied) as per cent of the stock	3.2%	3.8%	3.6%	3.6%
Adjusted balance	− 512	− 425	− 238	− 427

Further, in the private-owned sector these shortages could be reflected in a real house price boom (particularly by 1983) unless real national income falls markedly. Of course, such price rises will further increase tax expenditure on mortgage interest relief at the same time as HSG is considerably reduced and this must raise issues of inter-tenure subsidy equity. Public sector waiting lists will grow. Ultimately, the areas and groups which inevitably suffer in periods of housing shortage — such as inner city areas and the low paid — will be the major losers.

The housing sector has in the past absorbed in a relatively inefficient and distributionally questionable fashion a great deal of national resources. But the path to a fairer and more efficient use of housing policy resources does not lie in constructing negative controls on public investment and in denying private sector subsidies. In the longer term that is only likely to lead to massive public redirection of resources following governmental change. The transition to a private housing market, which I believe could work effectively in most market situations, requires a gradual, planned and fair shift of resources. Central government in Britain does not appear to have any positive or constructive policy for the private sector; it merely has a negative view on public provision, and the shift in sovereignty and resources away from local government means that local government can do little to assuage the adverse effects of present policy unless they actively pursue a policy of joint initiatives with the private sector.

References

Alonso, W. 1964, *Location and Land Use*. Harvard University Press, Cambridge, Massachusetts.

Atkinson, A.B. and King, M.A. 1980, Housing policy, taxation and reform, *Midland Bank Review*: 7–15.

Ball, M. 1973, Recent work on the determinants of relative house prices, *Urban Studies*, **10**: 213–33.

Ball, M.J. and Kirwan, R.M. 1977, Urban housing demand: some evidence from cross-sectional data, *Applied Economics*, **9**: 343–66.

Becker, G. 1965, A theory of the allocation of time, *Economic Journal*, **75**: 493–517.

Benston, C.J. 1979, *Mortgage Redlining Research: a review and critical analysis*. Mimeo, University of Rochester.

Berry, F. 1974, *Housing: The Great British Failure*. Knight, London.

Berry, B.J.L. and Horton, F.E. 1970. *Geographic Perspectives and Urban Systems*. Prentice-Hall, Englewood Cliffs.

Bird, H. 1976, Residential mobility and preference patterns in the public sector of the housing market, *Transactions Institute of British Geographers*, N.S. **1**: 20–33.

Boddy, M. 1976, Polictical economy of housing: mortgage financed owner occupation in Britain, *Transactions, Institute of British Geographers*, N.S. **1**.

Boddy, M. 1980, *The Building Societies*. MacMillan Press, London.

Bourne, L.S. 1976, Monitoring change and evaluating the impact of planning policy on urban structure, *Plan Canada*, **16**; 5–14.

Bourne, L.S. and Hitchcock, J.R. (eds) 1978, *Urban Housing Markets: recent directions in research and policy*. Univ. of Toronto Press, Toronto.

Bowden, E. 1978, *Econometrics of Disequilibrium*. North-Holland, Amsterdam.

Bradbury, K., Engle, R. Owen, I. and Rothenberg, J. 1977, Simultaneous estimation of the supply and demand for housing location in a multizoned metropolitan area, in Ingram, G.K. (ed.), *Residential Location and Urban Housing Markets*. National Bureau of Economic Research, New York: 51–86.

British Marketing Research Bureau 1977, *Housing Consumer Survey*. NEDO, London.

Building Societies Association (BSA) 1978, *The Housing Policy Review and the Role of Building Societies*. BSA, London.

BSA 1980, *A Compendium of Building Society Statistics*. Building Societies Association.

Byatt, I.C.R., Holmans, A. and Laidler, D.W. 1973, Income and the demand for housing: some evidence for Great Britain, in Parkin, M. (ed.), *Essays in Modern Economics*. Longman, London.

Carliner, G. 1973, Income elasticity of housing demand, *Review of Economics and Statistics*, **55**: 528–32.

Carr, J.L. 1954, Rent control and housing policy, *The Economic Journal,* **64**: 25–38.

Carter, C.F. 1958, The building industry, in Burn, D. (ed.), *The Structure of British Industry*. Cambridge University Press, Cambridge: 47–75.

Catalano, A. and Massey, D.B. 1978, *Capital and Land*. E. Arnold, London.

Centre for Environmental Studies 1978, A Discussion of Proposals for a Landlords Registration Scheme. Mimeo.

Charles, S. 1977, *Housing Economics*. Macmillan, London.

Clark, W.A.V. 1965, Markov chain analysis in geography: an application to the movement of rental housing areas, *Annals of the Association of American Geographers*, **55**: 351–9.

Clark, W.A.V. 1980, *Housing Search Models: An Overview*. Paper presented at the Housing Market Search Seminar, University of California at Los Angeles (UCLA), May 1980.

Clark, W.A.V. and Smith, T.R. 1980, *The Supply of Housing Market Information*. Paper presented at the Housing Market Search Seminar, UCLA, May 1980.

Clayton, G.C. *et al.* 1975, The Portfolio of Debt Behaviour of British Building Societies. Series 16A. Société Universitaire Européenne de Recherches Financières.

Coase, R.H. 1937, *The nature of the firm, Economica*, **4**: 386–405.

Committee to Review the Functioning of Financial Institutions (Wilson Report) 1980, Cmnd. 7937. HMSO, London.

Cooper, M. H. and Stafford, D.C. 1975, A note on the economic implication of fair rents, *Social and Economic Administration*, **9**: 26–9.

Craven, E. 1970, Private residential development in Kent, in Pahl R.E. (ed.), *Whose City*. Longman, London: 165–84.

Cullingworth, J.B. 1963, *Housing in Transition*. Heinemann, London.

Cullingworth Report 1969, *Council Housing Purposes, Procedures and Priorities*. Ministry of Housing and Local Government, HMSO, London.

Cullingworth, J.B. 1979, *Essays on Housing Policy: the British scene*. Allen and Unwin, London.

David, M. 1962, *Family Composition and Consumption*. North-Holland, Amsterdam.

Davidson, N.M. 1970, The pattern of employment densities in Glasgow, *Urban Studies*, **7**: 69–75.

Davies, G.W. 1978, Theoretical approaches to filtering in the urban housing market, in Bourne, L.S. and Hitchcock, J.R. (eds.), op. cit.: 139–63.

Dawson, D.A., Jones, C.A., Maclennan, D. and Wood, G.A. 1980, The cheaper end of the owner occupied housing market in Glasgow, *Glasgow Housing Market Study*. Glasgow University (Mimeo).

De Leeuw, F. 1971, The demand for housing: a review of cross-section evidence, *Review of Economics and Statistics*, **53**: 1–10.

De Leeuw, F. and Ekanem, N. 1971, The supply of rental housing, *American Economic Review*, **61**: 806–17.

DOE 1978, *The Financial Aspects of Sales of Council Houses.*

Diamond, D. 1978, *The Analysis of Residential Land Prices,* cited in MacDonald, J.F. *op.cit.*

Diamond, D.B. 1980, Income and residential location, *Urban Studies,* **17**: 1–12.

Dildine, L. and Massey, F. 1974, Dynamic model of private incentives to housing maintenance, *Southern Economic Journal,* **40**: 631–9.

Doling, J.F. 1977, The use of content analysis in identifying the determinants of house prices, *Urban Studies,* **15**: 89–90.

Donnison, D. 1979(a), Empty council houses, *Housing Review,* **28**: 131–3.

Donnison, D. 1979(b), Housing the poorest people, *Housing Review,* **28**: 67–70.

Duclaud-Williams, 1978, *The Politics of Housing in Britain and France.* Heinemann, London.

Duffy, M. 1970, A model of U.K. private investment in dwellings, *Discussion Paper* 18, Econometric Forecasting Unit, London Graduate School of Business Studies.

Edel, M. 1972, Filtering in a private housing market, in Edel, M. and Rothenberg, J. (eds.), *Readings in Urban Economics*, Macmillan, New York.

Elliott, B. and McCrone, D. 1975, Landlords in Edinburgh: Some preliminary findings, *Sociological Review,* **23**: 539–62.

Engleman, S. 1977, The move into council housing: the effect on quit rates, *Urban Studies,* **14**: 161–8.

English, J. and Norman, P. 1974, One hundred years of slum clearance in England and Wales – policies and programmes 1868–1970, *Discussion Paper* 4, *Social Research*, University of Glasgow.

Evans, A. 1973, *The Economics of Residential Location.* MacMillan, London.

Evans, M.K. 1969, *Macroeconomic Activity.* Harper and Row, New York.

Eversley, D. 1975, Landlords slow goodbye, *New Society,* **31**: 119–21.

Fair, R. 1974, Monthly housing starts, in Ricks, B. (ed.), *National Housing Models.* D.C. Heath, Lexington.

Fair, R. C. and Jaffee, D. M. 1972, Methods of estimation for markets in disequilibrium, *Econometrica*, May.

Farrand, J.T. 1975, *The Rent Act 1974.* Sweet & Maxwell, London.

Firey, W. 1947, *Land Use in Central Boston.* Harvard University Press, Boston.

Fisher, E.M. and Winnick, L. 1951, A reformulation of the filtering concept, in Menton, R.K. (ed.), *Social Policy and Social Research in Housing.* Association Press, New York.

Ford, J. 1975, The role of the building society manager in the urban stratification system: autonomy versus constraint, *Urban Studies,* 12.

Foster, J. 1974, The demand for building society shares and deposits 1961–71, *Discussion Papers in Economics,* 9. Department of Social and Economic Research, University of Glasgow.

Frankena, M. 1975, Alternative models of rent control, *Urban Studies*; **12**: 303–8.

Freeman, M.R. 1979, The hedonic price approach to measuring demand for neighbourhood characteristics, in Segal, D. (ed.) *op.cit.*

Ghosh, D. 1974, *The Economics of Building Societies.* Saxon House, London.

Glasgow District Council 1979, Housing Management Department. *Annual Report*.

Goldberg, M. 1978, Developer behaviour and urban growth, in Bourne, L.S. and Hitchcock, J.R. (eds) *op. cit.*: 181–227.

Grebler, L. 1952, *Housing Market Behaviour in a Declining Area*. Columbia University Press, New York.

Grigsby, W. 1963, *Housing Markets and Public Policy*. University of Pennsylvania Press, Philadelphia.

Grigsby, W. 1978, Response to Quigley, J.M., in Bourne, L.S. and Hitchcock, J.R. (eds), *op.cit.*

Hadjimatheou, G. 1976, *Housing and Mortgage Markets*. Saxon House, London.

Hahn, F. 1973, *On the Notion of Equilibrium in Economics*. Cambridge University Press, London.

Haig, R.M. 1926, Towards an understanding of the metropolis, *Quarterly Journal of Economics*, **40**: 179–208 and 402–34.

Harris, A. 1978, Environmental Amenity: a critique of the house price approach, *Discussion Paper* 77–101, Department of Political Economy, University of Aberdeen.

Harris, A. and Edwards, R. 1978, Valuing environmental amenity: the hedonic approach. University of Aberdeen, Discussion Paper, 78–104.

Harrison, A. and Smith M. 1978, Reacting to crisis: the impact of economic fluctuations on local authority finance, *CES Review*, **4**: 40–4.

Harrison, A. and Paris, C. 1978, Housing, *CES Review*, **4**: 27–34.

Harrison, D. and Kain, J.F. 1974, Cumulative urban growth and urban density functions, *Journal of Urban Economics*, **1**: 61–98.

Harrod, R.F. 1947, *Are These Hardships Necessary*. Hart-Davis, London.

Hendry, D. and Anderson, G.J. 1976, Testing dynamic specification in small simultaneous systems: and application to a model of building society behaviour in the United Kingdom, *Econometrics Programme, Discussion Paper* A4, London School of Economics.

Hepworth, N., Grey A., and Odling-Smee, J. 1979, *Housing Costs, Rents and Subsidies*. CIPFA.

Hill, S. and Gough, J. 1980, Concentration and efficiency in the building society industry, *Discussion Paper in Economics* 1/80, University of Wales (UWIST, Cardiff).

Hillebrandt, 1974, *Economic Theory and the Construction Industry*. Macmillan, London.

HMSO, 1977 and 1979, *Report of the Chief Registrar of Friendly Societies, 1977 and 1979*. HMSO, London.

Hochman, H.M. and Rodgers, J.R. 1964, Pareto optimal redistribution, *American Economic Review*, **54**: 652–7.

Holtermann, S. 1975, Areas of urban deprivation in Great Britain. An analysis of 1971 census data, *Social Trends* 6. HMSO, London.

Housing Bill 1980, HMSO Parliamentary Press, London.

Housing Policy: A Consultative Document 1977, Cmnd. 6851, HMSO, London.

Housing Policy. Technical Volumes 1 to 3 1977, HMSO, London.

Hoyt, H. 1939, *The Structure and Growth of Residential Neighbourhoods in American Cities.* Government Printing Office, Washington, D.C.

Hurd, R.M. 1903, *Principles of City Land Values.* The Record and Guide, New York.

Ineichen, B. 1975, *A Place of Our Own.* Housing Research Foundation, London.

Ingram, G.K. (ed) 1977. *Residential Location and Urban Housing Markets,* Ballinger Publishing Company, Cambridge, Mass.

Ingram, G.K. and Oron, Y. 1977, The production of housing services from existing dwelling units, in Ingram, G.K. (ed.), *op.cit.*: 273–314.

Jones, C.A. 1978, Household movement, filtering and trading up, *Regional Studies*, **12**: 551–61.

Jones, C.A. 1979a, Housing: the element of choice, *Urban Studies*, **16**: 197–204.

Jones, C.A. 1979b, A Survey of Building Society Managers. Mimeo.

Jones, C.A. 1980, On the interpretation of vacancies in the furnished rental sector of the housing market, *Economic Journal*, **90**: 157–8.

Kain, J. and Quigley, J. 1975, *Housing Markets and Racial Discrimination.* National Bureau of Economic Research, New York.

Karn, V. 1979, Pity the poor home owners, *Roof*, **4**: 10–14.

Kemeny, J. 1978, Urban home-ownership in Sweden, *Urban Studies*, **15**: 313–20.

Kemp, P. 1979, The changing ownership structure of the privately rented sector, *Unpublished M.Phil. Thesis*, Department of Town and Regional Planning, University of Glasgow.

Kilroy, B. 1980, From roughly right to precisely wrong, *Roof*, **5**: 16–17.

King, A.J. 1976, The demand for housing, in Terleckyj, N. (ed.), *Household Production and Consumption.* National Bureau of Economic Research, New York.

Kirwan, R. and Ball, M. 1977, Accessibility and supply constraints in the urban housing market, *Urban Studies*, **14**: 11–32.

Koeneker, R. 1972, An empirical note on the elasticity of substitution between land and capital in a monocentric housing market, *Journal of Regional Science*, **12**: 299–305.

Kristof, F.S. 1965, Housing policy goals and the turnover of housing, *Journal of the American Institute of Planners*, **31**: 232–45.

Lancaster, K. 1966, A new approach to consumer theory, *Journal of Political Economy*, **74**: 132–57.

Lancester, K. and Lipsey, R.G. 1957, The general theory of the second best, *Review of Economic Studies*, **24**: 11–32.

Lansing, J.B., Clifton C.W., and Morgan J.N. 1969, *New Homes and Poor People:* A study of chains of moves. Surrey Research Centre, Ann Arbor.

Lansley, S. 1979, *Housing and Public Policy.* Croom Helm, London.

Law, D. 1977, *A model of Building Society Behaviour.* Mimeo.

Leven, C.L., Little, J.T., Nourse, H.O. and Read R.B. 1975, *The Contemporary Neighbourhood Succession Process.* Institute for Urban and Regional Studies, St. Louis.

Loasby, B.J. 1972, Hypothesis and paradigm in the theory of the firm, *Economic Journal*, **81**: 861–85.

Lomas, G. 1978, Aspects of owner occupation: a statistical note, *CES Review*, **4**: 62–7.

Lowry, I. 1960, Filtering and household standards: a conceptual analysis, *Land Economics*, **36**: 362–70.

McCormack, B. 1979, Council Housing and Labour Mobility. Centre for Environmental Studies, Urban Economics Conference 1979.

MacDonald, J.F. 1979, *Economic Analysis of an Urban Housing Market.* Academic Press, New York.

MacDowell, L. 1976, Students and the 1974 Rent Act, *Research Paper No. 3, Student Accommodation Project*, Urban and Regional Studies Unit, University of Kent at Canterbury.

Mackay, D.I. and Reid, G.L. 1972, Redundancy, unemployment and manpower policy, *Economic Journal*, **82**: 1256–72.

Mackay, D.I. 1977, *Scotland 1980*. Q. Press, Edinburgh.

Maclennan, D. 1977a, Some thoughts on the nature and purpose of house price studies, *Urban Studies*, **14**: 39–71.

Maclennan, D. 1977b, Information, space and the measurement of housing preferences and demand, *Scottish Journal of Political Economy*, **24**: 97–115.

Maclennan, D. 1977c, The 1974 Rent Act – supply effects, *Discussion Paper, No. 4*, Department of Political Economy, University of Aberdeen.

Maclennan, D. 1978, The 1974 Rent Act: some short run supply effects, *Economical Journal*, **88**: 331–40.

Maclennan, D. 1979a, Information and Adjustment in a Local Housing Market, *Applied Economics*, **11**, No. 3: 255–70.

Maclennan, D. 1979b, Housing economics: a review and introduction, *Scottish Journal of Political Economy,* **26**: 324–9.

Maclennan, D. 1979c, Information networks in a local housing market, *Scottish Journal of Political Economy,* **26**: 73–86.

Maclennan, D. 1981b, The 1974 Rent Act: impacts on tenants, *Social Administration* (forthcoming).

Maclennan, D. 1980 On the interpretation of vacancies in the furnished rental sector of the housing market: a response, *Economic Journal*, **90**: 159–60.

Maclennan, D. and Jones, C.A. 1980, The Area Lending Outcomes and Policies of Building Societies. Paper delivered at SSRC Study Group on Urban and Regional Economics, April 1980.

Maclennan, D. and MacVean, P. 1978, Policies for the furnished rental sector: a positive approach, in Maclennan, D. and Wood, G.A., *op.cit.*

MacAvinchey, I.D. and Maclennan, D. 1981. Regional House Price Inflation in Britain, 1967–76. *Urban Studies*, 18 (Forthcoming).

Maclennan, D. and Williams, N. 1980, Some problems in applying revealed preference analysis, *Environment and Planning* (forthcoming).

Maclennan, D. and Wood, G.A. 1978, *Housing research and housing policy in Scotland: a response to the Green Paper*. Aberdeen University, Aberdeen.

Maclennan, D. and Wood, G.A. 1980a, The Determinants of Entry to Owner Occupation. Mimeo.

Maclennan, D. and Wood, G.A. 1980b, The Income Elasticity of Demand for Housing: Some Fundamental Problems of Specification and Measurement. Mimeo.

Maclennan, D. and Wood, G.A. 1980c, *Housing Search and Household Con-*

sumption Adjustment. Paper presented at the Housing Market Search Seminar, UCLA, May 1980.

Mayes, D. 1979, *The Property Boom*. Robertson, Oxford.

Merrett, S. 1979, *State Housing in Britain*. Routledge and Kegan Paul, London.

Mill, J.S. 1848, *Principles of Political Economy*. People's Edition, Longmans.

Mills, E. 1972, *Studies in the Structure of the Urban Economy*. John Hopkins Press, Baltimore.

Moore, E.G. 1972, *Residential Mobility in the City*. Association of American Geographers, Resource Paper 13. Washington D.C.

Moorhouse, J.C. 1972, Optimal housing maintenance under rent control, *Southern Economic Journal* **39**: 93–106.

Murie, A. and Leather, P. 1977, Developments in housing strategies, *Journal of the Royal Town Planning Institute*, **63**: 167–9.

Murie, A., Niner, P. and Watson, C.J. 1976, *Housing Policy and the Housing System*. Allen and Unwin, London.

Muth, R. 1960, The demand for non-farm housing, in Harberger, A. (ed.), *The Demand for Durable Goods*, the University of Chicago Press, Chicago.

Muth, R. 1964, The derived demand for a productive factor and the industry supply curve, *Oxford Economic Papers*, **16**: 221–34.

Muth, R. 1969, *Cities and Housing*. University of Chicago Press, Chicago.

Muth, R. 1971, The derived demand for urban residential land, *Urban Studies*, **8**: 243–54.

Muth, R. 1976, A vintage model of housing production, in Papageorgiou, G. (ed.), *Mathematical Land Use Theory*. D.C. Heath, Lexington, Massachusetts.

Nath, S.K. 1969, *A Reappraisal of Welfare Economics*. Routledge and Kegan Paul, London.

National Economic Development Office, 1977, *Construction in the Early 1980's*. HMSO, London.

Nationwide, 1977, 1980. Nationwide Building Society, *Occasional Bulletins*.

Needleman, L. 1965, *The Economics of Housing*. Staples Press, London.

Nelson, R. 1972, Housing facilities site advantages and rent, *Journal of Regional Science*, **12**: 249–59.

Nevitt, A.A. 1970, The nature of rent controlling legislation in the U.K., *University Working Paper* No. 8, Centre for Environmental Studies.

Niner, P. 1975, Local authority housing policy and practice – a case study approach, *Occasional Paper* 31, Centre for Urban and Regional Studies, University of Birmingham.

O'Dea, D. 1977, *Cyclical Indicators for the Postwar British Economy*. Cambridge University Press, Cambridge.

Odling-Smee, J. 1975, *The Demand for Housing*. Centre for Environmental Studies, Papers from the Urban Economics Conference.

OECD 1979, The Financing and Management of Urban Public Services. Environment Directorate Discussion Document.

O'Herlihy, C.St. and Spencer, J.G. 1972, Building societies behaviour 1955–70, *National Institute Economic Review* **61**.

Olsen, E.O. 1969, A competitive theory of the housing market, *American Economic Review*, **59**: 612–22.

Olsen, E.O. 1972, An econometric analysis of rent control, *Journal of Political Economy*, **80**: 1081–100.

Onibokun, A.G. 1973, Environmental issues in housing habitability, *Environment and Planning*, **5**: 461–76.

Ozanne, L. and Struyk, R.J. 1978, The price elasticity of supply of housing services, in Bourne, L.S. and Hitchcock, J.R. (eds), *op. cit.*: 109–38.

Paish, W. 1950, The economics of rent restriction, *Lloyds Bank Review*, **16**: 1–17.

Paley, R. 1978, *Attitudes to Letting in 1976: a Survey of the Privately Rented Sector*. HMSO, London.

Park, R.E. (ed.) 1925, *The City*. University of Chicago Press, Chicago.

Pawley, M. 1978, *Home Ownership*. Architectural Press, London.

Pearce, B. 1980, Prospects for shorthold tenure, *Housing Review*, **29**: 23–5.

Pennance, F.G. and Gray, H. 1968, *Choice in Housing*. Institute of Economic Affairs, London.

Pesaran and Deaton, A. 1978, Testing non-nested non-linear regression models, *Econometrica*, **46**: 677–94.

Phelps, E.S. *et. al.* (ed.) 1970, *Microeconomic Foundations of Employment and Inflation Theory*. Norton, New York.

Phillips, R.H.S. 1973, The regional structure of the construction industry in Britain, *Regional Studies*, **7**: 287–300.

Pissarides, C.A. 1976, *Labour Market Adjustment*. Cambridge University Press, London.

Polinsky, A.M. 1977, The demand for housing: a study in specification and grouping, *Econometrica*, 45; 447–61.

Porter, J. and Davies, C. 1976, The Timing of the Residential Development Decision. Mimeo.

Quigley, J.M. 1977, Comment on Bradbury *et. al.*, in Ingram, G.V. (ed.), *op. cit.*: 87–92.

Quigley, J.M. 1978, Housing markets and housing demand: analytic approaches, in Bourne L.S. and Hitchcock, J.R. (eds), *Urban Housing Markets*. University of Toronto Press, Toronto.

Quigley, J.M. and Weinberg, D.H. 1977, Intra-metropolitan residential mobility: a review and synthesis, *International Regional Science Review*, **2**: 41–66.

Ratcliff, R.U. 1949, *Urban Land Economics*. McGraw-Hill, New York.

Rees, A.E. 1966, Information networks in labour markets, *American Economic Review, Papers and Proceedings*, **56**: 560–6.

Reid, M. 1962, *Housing and Income*. University of Chicago Press, Chicago.

Report of the Royal Commission on Housing in Scotland 1971, Cmnd. 8731, HMSO, London.

Report of the Committee on the Rent Acts 1971. (Francis Report), Cmnd. 4609, HMSO, London.

Report of the Royal Commission on Legal Services in Scotland 1980, Cmnd. 7846. HMSO, Edinburgh.

Reynolds, L. 1976, *The 1974 Rent Act*. Middlesex Polytechnic. Mimeo.

G.B. Richardson, 1959, *Information and Investment*. Oxford University Press.

Richardson, H.W., Vipond, J. and Furbey, R. 1975, *Housing and Urban Spatial Structure*. Saxon House, Farnborough.

Richardson, H.W. (1977), *The New Urban Economics.* Pion, London.

Riley, M. 1974, A Model of Building Society Behaviour. HM Treasury. Mimeo.

Robertson, G. 1979. Housing Tenure and Labour Mobility in Scotland. Economics and Statistics Unit, Scottish Office, Edinburgh.

Robinson, R. 1979, *Housing Economics and Public Policy.* Macmillan, London.

Robson, B.T. 1969, *Urban Analysis.* Cambridge University Press, Cambridge.

Romanos, M.C. 1976, *Residential Spatial Structure.* D.C. Heath, Lexington, Massachusetts.

Rosen, S. 1974, Hedonic prices and implicit markets, *Journal of Political Economy,* **82**: 34–55.

Rothenberg, J. 1967, *Economic Evaluation of Urban Renewal.* Brookings Institute, Washington D.C.

Rothenberg, J. 1977, Comment on Ingram and Oron, in Ingram, G.K. (ed.), *op.cit.*: 315–21.

Rothenberg, J. 1979, Heterogeneity and Durability of Housing: Centre for Environmental Studies, Urban Economics Conference.

Rowley, C.K. and Peacock, A.T. 1975, *Welfare Economics: A Liberal Restatement.* Robertson, London.

Rydell, P.C. 1976, Measuring the supply response to housing allowances, *Papers of the Regional Science Association,* **37**: 31–57.

Scottish Development Department 1976, *Social Area Analysis of 1961–1971 Censuses.* Mimeo.

Scottish Development Department 1977, *The Review of the Rent Acts: A Consultation Paper.* SDD, Edinburgh.

Scottish Housing: A Consultative Document 1977, Cmnd. 6852. HMSO, Edinburgh.

Schifferes, S. 1980, Housing Bill 1980, the beginning of the end for council housing, *Roof,* **5**: 10–13.

Schnare, A. and Struyk, R. 1976, Segmentation in urban housing markets, *Journal of Urban Economics,* **3**: 146–66.

Schumpeter, J.F. 1954, *The History of Economic Analysis,* Oxford University Press, New York.

Segal, D. (ed.) 1979, *The Economics of Neighbourhood.* Academic Press, New York.

Sirmans, C., Kau, J. and Lee, C. 1980, The elasticity of Substitution in urban housing production: A VES approach, *Journal of Urban Economics,* **7**.

Smith, M. 1978, Alternative approaches: unit cost versus deficit system, *CES Review* **2**: 68–77.

Smith, W.F. 1963, Forecasting neighbourhood change, *Land Economics,* **39**: 292–7.

Smith, W.F. 1970, Filtering and neighbourhood change, in Stegman, M. (ed.), *Housing and Economics.* The MIT Press, Cambridge, Massachusetts.

Stafford, D. 1978, *The Economics of Housing Policy.* Croom Helm, London.

Stegman, M. (ed.) 1970. *Housing and Economics,* The MIT Press, Cambridge, Massachusetts.

Stegman, M.A. and Sumka, H.J. 1978, Income elasticities of demand for rental housing in small cities, *Urban Studies,* **15**: 51–61.

Steuart, Sir J. (1769), *Principles of Political Economy*. Scottish Economic Society, 1966.

Stigler, C.J. 1961, The economics of information, *Journal of Political Economy, 69*: 213–25.

Straszheim, M. 1975, *An Econometric Analysis of the Urban Housing Market*. National Bureau of Economic Research, New York.

Strathclyde Regional Council, 1978, Working Papers on Housing Policy, Glasgow.

Struyk, R. 1976, *Home-Ownership: The Economic Determinants*. Lexington, London.

Sweeney, J.L. 1974, Quality, commodity hierarchies and housing markets, *Econometrica, 42*: 147–67.

Taylor, P.T. 1979, 'Difficult-to-let', 'Difficulty-to-live-in'. Centre for Urban and Regional Development, Newcastle. Mimeo.

Tenants Rights Act, 1980. *The Tenants Rights etc (Scotland) Act*, 1980. HMSO. London.

Tiebout: C. 1956, A pure theory of local expenditure, *Journal of Political Economy; 64*: 416–24.

Timms, D. 1971, *The Urban Mosaic*. Cambridge University Press, Cambridge.

Vipond, J. and Walker B.F. 1972, The determinants of housing expenditure, *Oxford Bulletin of Economics and Statistics, 34*: 169–87.

Von Boventer, E. 1978, Bandwagon effects and product cycles in urban dynamics, *Urban Studies, 15*: 261–72.

Von Thunen, J.H. 1875, *Der Isolierte Staat*. Hamburg.

Walker, M. 1977, *Rent Control: A Popular Paradox*. The Fraser Institute, Vancouver.

Watson, C.J. 1973, Household movement in West Central Scotland, *Occasional Paper* No. 26, Centre for Urban and Regional Studies, The University of Birmingham.

Webster, D. 1978, How one subsidy system works: The 1975 Act system, *CES Review,2*: 78–87.

Weintraub, E.R. 1979, *Microfoundations*, Cambridge University Press.

Welham, P. 1978, The Fiscal Advantages of Owner Occupation. Mimeo.

White, H.C. 1971, Multipliers, vacancy chains and filtering in housing, *Journal of the American Institute of Planners, 32*: 88–94.

White, L. 1977, How good are two-point estimates of urban density gradients, *Journal of Urban Economics, 4*: 292–309.

Whitehead, C.M. 1974, *The U.K. Housing Market*. Saxon House, Farnborough.

Whitehead, C.M. 1977, Neutrality between tenures: a critique of the HPR comparisons, *CES Review, 2*: 33–6.

Whitehead, C.M. 1979, The role of the resident landlord, *CES Review, 5*: 16–18.

Whitehead, C.M. and Odling-Smee, J.C. 1975, Long run equilibrium in urban housing – a note, *Urban Studies, 12*: 315–18.

Wilkinson, R. 1973, The income elasticity of demand for housing, *Oxford Economic Papers, 25*: 361–77.

Wilkinson, R. and Archer, C. 1977, Uncertainty, Prices and the Supply of Housing. Mimeo.

Williams, A. 1974, Need as a demand concept, in Culyer M.A.J. (ed.), *Economic Policies and Social Goals*. Martin Robinson, London.

Williams, A. 1978, Measuring the quality of life for the elderly, in Wingo, L. and Evans, A., *Public Economics and the Quality of Life*. CES, London.

Williams, P. 1976, The Role of Institutions in the Inner London Housing Market. *Transactions Institute of British Geographers*, N.S. **1**.

Index

COLLEGE
CANCELLED
LIBRARY